INTRODUCTION TO RUSSIAN REALISM

PUSHKIN

Introduction

GOGOL   DOSTOEVSKY

to Russian

TOLSTOY   CHEKHOV

Realism

SHOLOKHOV

□◆□◆□◆□◆□◆□◆□◆□

by ERNEST J. SIMMONS

INDIANA UNIVERSITY PRESS
BLOOMINGTON

THE PATTEN FOUNDATION

Mr. Will Patten of Indianapolis (A.B., Indiana University, 1893) made, in 1931, a gift for the establishment of the Patten Foundation at his Alma Mater. Under the terms of this gift, which became available upon the death of Mr. Patten (May 3, 1936), there is to be chosen each year a Visiting Professor who is to be in residence several weeks during the year. The purpose of this prescription is to provide an opportunity for members and friends of the University to enjoy the privilege and advantage of personal acquaintance with the Visiting Professor. The Visiting Professor for the Patten Foundation in 1964 was ERNEST J. SIMMONS.

PREFACE

In the preface of his recent brilliant book, from which I have learned much: *The Gates of Horn: A Study of Five French Realists*, Professor Harry Levin mentions in passing that he spent more than fifteen years of intermittent effort on this extensive work. One may safely conjecture that a similar comprehensive investigation of Russian realism would require about as much time and industry. I hasten to add, however, that I have had no such aim in mind in the present brief study. It is a somewhat augmented version of the Patten Foundation Lectures which I was invited to deliver at Indiana University in February and March of 1964. Within this framework the effort can claim to be merely an introduction to a vast and profoundly challenging subject, in which I have stressed not so much the problem of the definition of realism, so adequately handled by Professor Levin, but rather the place—in terms of developing Russian realism—of certain literary works in the minds of their authors and in the literary, social, and political movements of the age. My only hope is that this short introduction to the subject will persuade some younger and more able scholar to attempt an exhaustive study of Russian realism.

The form of the work has been necessarily dictated by the lectures. Though there may seem to be some arbitrariness in the selection of the six authors used as examples, they were chosen because it seemed to me that each had an important contribution to make to the forward progress of Russian realism. But I frankly admit that another student of the subject, faced with the same task, might alter the selection with good reason.

I have taken the liberty of omitting the usual ample apparatus of footnotes and bibliography which appeared to be out of place in a study of such limited scope. Further, I hope I may be forgiven the use I have made of books and articles I have published on some of these authors, for I have depended on them for occasional factual data and also for translations I had previously made of Russian memoirs, diaries, letters, etc. However, footnotes are given for translations other than my own. I should like to thank the following publishers for permission to quote from works under their copyright: University of California Press, for excerpts from *Eugene Onegin*; Oxford University Press, for excerpts from the *Tolstoy Centenary Edition*; Alfred A. Knopf, for excerpts from *The Overcoat and Other Stories*, Ilya Ehrenburg's *Chekhov, Stendhal, and Other Essays*, and *The Silent Don*. I have also drawn upon my book, *Dostoevsky: The Making of a Novelist* (New York, 1940), for a critical approach, which I have somewhat elaborated in the present study, in the interpretation of his fiction.

Some of the research and much of the writing of this book were done at The Center for Advanced Studies, Wesleyan University. I am deeply grateful to the Center's Administration for its material aid and the ideal facilities it provides for living and working, to the thoughtfulness and assistance of its able staff, and to the constant encouragement of its distinguished scholars and artists in the creation of things of the mind and spirit.

CONTENTS

INTRODUCTION TO RUSSIAN REALISM

I · PUSHKIN

The Poet as Novelist

IT IS NOT MY PURPOSE here to formulate a conclusive definition of realism in the course of a comprehensive examination of Russian fiction. My objective is a much more modest one—to explore and analyze the inception and development of certain aspects of realism in significant works of six major Russian authors.

Frankly I distrust efforts to define realism with the finality which scientists define physical laws of nature. A literary critic ought to be guided by the humility of common sense when confronted by a problem so complicated by human imponderables of life and art. In any event, he ought not to begin, as a Madison Avenue mogul might, with the clinching assertion that the product, like a doctor's prescription, contains twelve ingredients.

If it is anything, realism in fiction is a literary artist's way of looking at life. Although this harried word, realism, which comes to us from the fine arts, is supposed to signify life as it actually is, we know perfectly well that in the art which grapples with, assimilates, and interprets reality, the subjective element plays an enormous role, to say nothing of the purely subjective

3

element in the reader, viewer, or listener reacting to the artist's reactions to reality.

With disarming frankness Maupassant, in the preface to *Pierre et Jean*, tells of the artist's subjective involvement in the realism of his fiction: "Into the characters whose hidden, unknown being we pretend to reveal, we can only partly transplant our own vision, our own knowledge of the world, our own ideas of life. . . . The writer's skill lies in not allowing the reader to recognize his ego behind the various masks which he assumes to hide it."

When Henry James described the novel as "felt life," he was at once criticizing the conventional conception of realism and emphasizing the author's personality and imagination in embodying the images of characters, situations, and scenes. In short, though the novelist must use his senses and intellect to explore reality, he observes things and persons and their activities in the external world not always objectively, but through the prism of his own impulses and emotions. In fact, he is often concerned with man not only as he is, but as he ought to be, and to this extent the novelist can be an illusionist, though we would all agree that illusion may also be a definite feature of reality.

In our own day realism in fiction has taken on still other dimensions which some critics believe are bringing about the demise of the novel as we understand it, although this judgment seems rather premature. The realistic novelist has often been critical of some of the conventions of existence, but nowadays he can be in violent conflict with reality in his effort to fashion a truthful picture of the world. And this picture can and does represent a reality which the reader has never experienced, a personal, ambiguous world of the novelist himself—a symbol of contemporary "reality." Carried a bit further, this trend has developed into the nonrealistic novel of our time.

It has been argued that realism in fiction, because it assumes an impossible point of view—one that lacks a viewer—can never correspond to the reality of life. This is being semantically absolutist to an intolerable degree, as though art did not always involve artifice. To say that a novelist does not reflect the world but creates an entirely imaginary world true to his personal vision is to place an unwarranted limitation on his function as an artist. The purely imaginary does not exist. In *L'Homme révolté* Camus correctly observes that art cannot reject reality, and with insight he adds that real literary creation "uses reality and only reality with all its warmth and its blood, its passion and its outcries. It simply adds something which transfigures reality."

It has been said that every age has its own realism, a somewhat sweeping generalization that gains nothing in convincingness if we add that so does every country. However, one does not have to be a devotee of Marxian determinism to observe a striking correlation between social change in historical time and the birth and subsequent growth of realism in fiction. It will be instructive to say something briefly about this pattern of cause and effect in Western Europe, for its impact on the beginnings of Russian realism proved to be significant.

The wealth of fiction from the ancient and medieval worlds contributed nothing to the conception of the modern novel except an interest in sheer storytelling and a passing curiosity about men and women. If the classical epic and the medieval romance, the first of which glorified a ruling military society and the second a courtly one, have left any mark on the novel today, it is an idealized reflection of social aspects that still have some relevance. After all, the military is a well-known staple of society in all ages, and even hard-bitten modernists sometimes dwindle into romance, both risqué and roseate. The tunnel of romantic escape from a reality too much with us is as irresistible now as it was in the medieval past. As for ancient myth, well we are more than partial to it in the novel today where centaurs and unicorns in modern dress only go to show that there is nothing new under the sun in life or in fiction.

Rabelais and Cervantes, spanning the expansive Renaissance transition between medieval feudalism and the first stirrings of capitalism, created something less than the form of the modern novel and something more than its traditional content. For if *Gargantua* and *Pantagruel* discovered the human body with all its coarse delights, *Don Quixote* placed a soul in it. The result was a heavy brew of realism that intoxicated the mind and exhilarated the spirit. Toward the end of his famous quest, the good Knight of the Sorrowful Countenance confessed that heaven can be conquered but not the world of men, that inaccessible goal of both heroes and antiheroes in so much modern fiction. Unlike later philosophical novels, such as those of Kafka, Thomas Mann, Sartre, and Camus, where the burden of weighty speculation tends to disintegrate the absorbing fabric of life, the philosophy of *Don Quixote*, perhaps the most philosophical novel of Western literature, is carefully sublimated in an atmosphere of riotously funny adventures. In this burlesque of outmoded romances of chivalry, the Don is a tragic hero who is compelled to realize in the end that man cannot shape reality and his own destiny in the image of his chosen ideal. Turgenev and Tolstoy regarded the work as a supremely great book. Its hero influenced the creation of that positively good man, Prince Myshkin, in *The Idiot*, and the grateful Dostoevsky declared: "In all the world there is nothing more profound and more powerful than *Don Quixote*. Further than this, it is the last and greatest word of human thought, the most bitter irony that man can express." Such praise is not accidental. The art of Cervantes in his masterpiece and that of these great Russian realists had much in common.

If a country's dominant social class tends to create the art form which will provide the fullest and most accurate expression of its behavior pattern and economic consciousness, then it would seem almost inevitable that England's rising middle class, a product of the burgeoning eighteenth-century industrial revolution, would create the novel. Its inevitability, however, might just as easily be accounted for by the widespread commercialization of printing at this time and by the development of publishing as a big business. For English novelists of the eighteenth century would perhaps have echoed Arnold Bennett's answer in the twentieth to a starry-eyed worshiper who asked what inner urge had driven him on to create his masterpiece, *Old Wives' Tale:* "I needed the money," he replied.

Certainly a merchandizing value was not far removed from Daniel Defoe's mind when he created *Robinson Crusoe,* often regarded as the first English novel and even as the very first of all novels. But material rewards have never been incompatible with man's compulsion to express himself artistically, and *Robinson Crusoe* is art of a high order. It defined the novel, however inadequately, as the art form of bourgeois society. For if Defoe was unaware that the novel's distinguishing feature, as E. M. Forster put it, was to make the secret life of man visible, he did recognize that it must deal with man's struggle against society and against nature, but a struggle waged in a real world where the balance between man and society is often lost.

Like Defoe, other great English novelists of the eighteenth century, such as Fielding in *Tom Jones* and Smollett in *Humphry Clinker,* were concerned primarily with an objective picture of society. The inner life of their characters they either evaded or did not think important. As writers in the grand epic tradition of the ancient past, action and not the analysis of its motives or of the feelings of the hero of action claimed their principal attention. The lack of this important dimension of realism, so pervasive in the novel today, was overcome by the discovery of sensibility which so markedly affected those other masterpieces of eighteenth-century fiction—Richardson's *Clarissa*, Sterne's *Tristram Shandy*, and Rousseau's *Nouvelle Héloïse*. Here the consciousness of the individual and an intense preoccupation with motives and the intimate feelings of the heart became the focus of the novelist's view of reality. In truth, Sterne went even further. For him analysis was an end in itself, and he substituted relativism for the "tapeworm of time," that temporal framework of all fiction up to this point. It was an approach anticipating in certain respects that of Proust and Joyce more than a century later. But one danger of excessive emphasis on analysis is the separation of the individual from society which ultimately marks a retreat from reality.

Despite the contributions of the eighteenth century, especially in England, to a definition of the modern novel, they had failed to bring within the compass of a single work a comprehensive picture of developing middle-class society involving, let us say, an artistic treatment that combined the epic approach of action of a Fielding with the close analysis of motive and feeling of a Richardson.

2

The English realistic novel caused a literary stir in eighteenth-century France and Germany where it influenced fiction writing. The response in Russia was considerably different. Though Russia had existed as a separate nation for several hundred years, it was still struggling to achieve national self-consciousness, a necessary condition for the development of an original literature and culture. Various political, economic, and social factors had caused the delay. Among them may be mentioned the continued existence of serfdom, which had begun to disintegrate in the West as early as the twelfth century, and the country's isolation and fear of foreigners, perhaps more a heritage of the long Tatar yoke than a fault of the insularity and xenophobia of the Church, as has sometimes been charged. Though Peter the Great, in the early years of the eighteenth century, is credited with ending this segregation by opening his famous window to the West, it must be said that it was hardly a bay window but rather one of those Russian *fortochkas*, a tiny pane of glass in a large sealed window which allows just enough fresh air into the room to keep one from suffocating in the winter. Without minimizing Peter's service in introducing Russia to many features of the most advanced civilization of the West, he plainly overlooked one of Europe's greatest glories—its literary culture. The only books that concerned him were those that could be put to practical use in his reforming zeal. Belles lettres he scornfully described as "mere tales that simply waste time." Historically speaking, perhaps he was right. Before Russia could absorb the finer aspects of European culture, a great deal of elementary preparation had to take place.

Culture is international common tender and over the centuries the coins of literary and artistic achievement of each of the major countries of Western Europe made their way from one to the other multiplying and enriching the culture of all. In addition, these countries were cultural beneficiaries of Greece and Rome and the brilliant literary and artistic efflorescence of the Renaissance. Circumstances deprived Russia of these influences throughout its formative period, and its contacts with Byzantium in no way compensated the country. An indicator of its relative backwardness is the fact that printing did not begin in Russia until 1564—the year of Shakespeare's birth!

By the time of Peter's death in 1725 Russia was nearly ready for invasion of European literature and thought. During the transition period from Catherine I to Catherine II (1725-62), a span of thirty-seven years, German and French favorites close to the throne furthered Peter's open-door policy to the West. By this time the grand tour in Europe had become a kind of social status symbol among members of the gentry. New educational institutions—the Academy of Sciences, a university at St. Petersburg and one at Moscow, and several preparatory and special schools—were staffed largely by French and German teachers. In fact, the education of the generation of writers who now inaugurated Russia's continuous literary development was more European than Russian. After being exposed to a foreign-oriented initial training in Russia, such future authors as Lomonosov, Kantemir, Tredyakovsky, and Sumarokov traveled to countries of Western Europe to finish their education.

The Russian cultural time-lag was also reflected in the foreign literary influences that dominated these early writers; they succumbed completely to the French neoclassical school without being aware that its contemporary significance was fast waning. Corneille, Molière, Racine, Boileau, and later Voltaire and the Encyclopedists were imitated, often slavishly, and the vogue of French neoclassicism lasted for years in Russian literature.

During the long reign of Catherine the Great (1762-96) which, culturally, marks the beginning of modern Russia, this Gallomania swept all before it. It has been estimated that three fourths of the books read in Russia over these years were French. Anything regarded as *comme il faut* in Paris was sure to be imitated in St. Petersburg and Moscow. Among the upper classes French virtually usurped the place of the Russian vernacular as a medium of polite communication. Years later the critic Belinsky, whose combination of ignorance and knowledge resulted somehow in remarkable judgments on literature, wryly commented on this situation: "Imagine a [Russian] society that spoke, thought, and prayed to God in French." In Fonvizin's satire of this pervasive foreign influence on social life in his well-known comedy, *The Brigadier*, the character Ivanushka, who in default of his body hoped that his soul might be French, limned the Frenchified Russian type for all time: "Everyone who has been in Paris has the right, in speaking about Russians, not to include himself in their number, for he has already become more French than Russian."

The example of Catherine herself, who had some pretension to authorship, encouraged the growth of belles lettres. Although this activity centered mostly in court circles and readers were not numerous, still the long, slow task of creating a national literature had begun in real earnest. Poetry was emphasized, most of it uninspired imitations of French verse, and dramas, largely modeled on neoclassical French plays, conformed to the unities and were devoted to themes of love and duty. Only two figures, Derzhavin in poetry and Fonvizin in comedy, rose above the dreary level of imitativeness and created works that were original and belong to the body of enduring Russian literature.

Catherine was the prime mover in promoting an interest in moral and satirical journals, many of which were published during her reign. Nothing is so calculated to convince one of the derivative nature of Russian literary efforts at this time than a close examination of these periodicals. Their origin was not only inspired by foreign models, but their contents were often made up partly or entirely of translations from English, French, and German journals. And sometimes the social abuses satirized in the few original articles had more relevance to foreign countries than to Russia.

English eighteenth-century satirical and moral journals were heavily drawn upon, especially the *Spectator*, and this wealth of material on English life, customs, manners, and culture contributed to developing a degree of Anglomania which was welcomed in some Russian quarters as a desirable offset to the devotion to everything French. Here, too, the Empress, with her admiration of English institutions—she even attempted reworkings of several of Shakespeare's plays—set something of an example. One result was the accumulation in Catherine's Russia of a rather extensive body of English literature in translation.

It is interesting to observe, however, that this Anglomania was in many respects a kind of by-product of Russia's Gallomania. For after the Edict of Nantes was revoked in 1685, thousands of French Huguenots fled to England. But they did not sever connections with the motherland and for over half a century these refugees, through numerous publications and visits to the Continent, were the means of disseminating a knowledge of English life, thought, and culture in France. Anglophiles among such men of letters as Prévost, Voltaire, Montesquieu, Rousseau, and Diderot popularized English literature in France, and an endless stream of translations of poetry, plays, and fiction flooded the country.

Russia, with its inordinate cultural dependence on France, appropriated also this French Anglomania. Since English was then little known in Russia, people read English literature in French translations which in turn were often rendered into Russian. And one of the genres that appealed most, aided no doubt by its popularity in France, was the English realistic novel.

Hitherto fiction in Russia had been limited to translations of medieval heroic romances and a few original tales of the chapbook variety. But in the reigns of Elizabeth and Catherine the French *romans d'aventure* of such authors as La Calprenède, Scudéry, and Madame La Fayette became a veritable craze. After the establishment of a translation department in the Academy of Sciences in 1767, by far the majority of books issued by the press were these French romances. Although their improbable characters and sensational adventures were sometimes denounced in Russia for poisoning the minds of youth, such romances as *Cassandre*, *Faramond*, and *Artamène* were curiously credited with awakening an intellectual interest among a people who up to this time had not come into contact with any extensive narrative literature.

The sweeping popularity of the English realistic novel in France, which contributed to undermining the vogue of the romances there, also served the same end in Russia. French and German translations of English novels, and imitations or highly original works influenced by this new form, such as Rousseau's *Nouvelle Héloïse* and Goethe's *Werther*, were translated into Russian and eagerly read. In the second half of the eighteenth century, for example, Russian translations of the following English novels appeared, in some cases in several editions: Defoe's *Robinson Crusoe;* Richardson's *Pamela, Clarissa,* and *Sir Charles Grandison;* Fielding's *Tom Jones, Joseph Andrews,* and *Jonathan Wild;* Smollett's *Roderick Random* and *Humphry Clinker,* and Sterne's *Sentimental Journey (Tristram Shandy,* though probably read earlier in French translation, did not appear in Russian until 1804-7).

Here were superb models, among them some world masterpieces of the new modern trend in fiction, which, if conditions had been ripe, might have initiated the great stream of Russian realism decades before it actually began. The age of Catherine, however, was in no sense prepared for such a development. Literature was still largely derivative for it lacked the centuries of continuous growth of the literatures of England and France. And that all-important concomitant of maturity in belles lettres —a sophisticated self-criticism—had not yet got underway. The social and economic conditions that had given rise to the realistic novel—a nascent capitalism and an emerging middle class—were not present in this semifeudal Russia with its vast, amorphous population of serfs, its landed gentry, and ruling aristocracy. Implicit in the realistic novel is the freedom to comment on and even to criticize the social and political institutions that form and condition men's lives. Yet when Nikolai Novikov attacked serfdom in his satirical journal, Catherine promptly banned all such journals. And when Nikolai Radishchev, in 1790, dared to criticize social and political abuses in his famous book, *A Voyage from St. Petersburg to Moscow*, the Empress had all copies of the work impounded and the author exiled to Siberia. Whatever liberal tendencies she may have displayed before the French Revolution, after it she would tolerate no criticisms of Russian life that reflected on her absolute power. In short, if one of the principal aesthetic problems of realism is adequate presentation of the complete human personality, this problem was quite irrelevant in Catherine's Russia where the individual as such did not exist in a political and social system that exacted blind obedience to the state from every subject.

Though the unvarnished realism of Fielding's novels was admired in eighteenth-century Russia, readers, once again bowing to French taste, preferred Richardson and his moral and moralizing heroines. The importation of English sensibility or sentimentalism, also through the medium of France, undoubtedly contributed to this preference.

Russian eulogies on Richardson, especially in introductions to translations of his novels, border on the rhapsodic, as they did in France and Germany. He was praised not as a master of realism, but as the creator of creatures of enchanting sentiment and impeccable virtue. In the 1787 version of *Pamela*, the Russian translator, after confessing that he experienced every terror of the heroine and wept over her unhappiness, declares: "All families will wish to have in their homes a Pamela who may serve as a shining example of honor and unyielding virtue." Obviously this Russian admirer would hardly have appreciated Fielding's sly notion that though Pamela regarded her virtue a pearl of precious price, she tended to place too much emphasis on the price.

In this initial period of Russian fiction it was also Richardson among the English novelists who was accorded the flattery of imitation, and in one case at least also inspired an original effort in his manner. Two years after the translation of *Pamela* a novel by P. Lvov appeared, entitled *A Russian Pamela, or the History of Mariya, a Virtuous Peasant Girl*. The author informs us in a foreword that his heroine "was as much honored in her actions as, for example, the heroine of *Pamela* written by the glorious Richardson. For this reason I have called her a 'Russian Pamela,' for there are among us such tender hearts of noble sensibility in lowly circumstances." It is the story of the love of a young member of the landed gentry for a comely peasant girl, in which the couple are kept apart for many pages by the actions of a cynical friend of the hero. In Mariya we have a sedulous imitation of Pamela. Like her English model, she is modest to a fault and is given to a specious kind of moralizing at great length. Her lover, however, resembles the faultless Grandison more than Pamela's designing Mr. B., whose traits reappear in the hero's crafty friend.

A more sophisticated and more independent effort was the short novel, *Poor Liza* (1792), by the eminent author Nikolai Karamzin. This story, which won fantastic popularity, involves the same general theme as Richardson's *Pamela*, but the peasant heroine's love affair takes a tragic turn and she commits suicide. Richardson's notions of social equality in marriage are preached in *Poor Liza*, whose heroine embodies more of the features of Clarissa than of Pamela.

Within a few years Russian readers would laugh over such tales with their exaggerated sentiments and idealized peasants who resembled the utterly unreal shepherds and shepherdesses of French neoclassical poetry. So deeply engrained was the habit of imitation that these Russian authors, with their foreign models too much in mind, failed to observe the native life around them.

It is clear that in this first phase of Russian literature the development of a realistic approach in fiction was incompatible with the spirit and practice of the times. Belles lettres had not yet become a profession. It bore an entirely official character and depended on the patronage of the court for its existence. Instead of faithfully depicting man and society as complete entities, authors were disposed to idealize Russian life and people or even to substitute for them the portrayals found in their French neoclassical models. In fiction alone some conception of the reading public's inability to overcome their devotion to foreign literature may be gathered from the fact that 463 translations of French, German, and English novels appeared during this period and only 32 by Russian authors, that is, on the average less than one a year!

3

At times the Communist Party line has compelled Soviet critics to forsake internationalism in an un-Marxian nationalistic effort to prove that Russian literary development over the centuries was uncontaminated by foreign influences. This chauvinistic "discovery" was apparently dictated by the political need to identify a continuum between pre- and postrevolutionary literature without ever running the risk of uncovering Western European skeletons in the Soviet cultural closet.

The literature of no nation fails to benefit from the cultural advances of its neighbors, and only a distorted patriotism would regard such borrowings as in any way demeaning. Belinsky, whom Soviet authorities, after much doctrinal shuffling, have accepted as a kind of early nineteenth-century precursor of the Marxian approach to literature, regarded the matter otherwise. He saw clearly that Russia's manifold borrowings from the West since the reign of Peter the Great could not essentially alter the country's emerging nationality which, he declared, was the aggregate of all the spiritual powers of the Russian people. He wisely understood that these foreign riches, which reanimated the people with the spirit of a new and fuller life, were necessary during the early stages of Russia's cultural growth.

To some extent this conviction was borne out in the reign of the enlightened Emperor Alexander I (1801-25), when vigorous discussions took place on Russia's need for an original literature of its own, and writers, who increased in number, where held in higher esteem and regarded as important factors in the body politic. Further, the French invasion of 1812, which shook the whole country, revealed unexpected sources of strength. Russia's victorious participation in the Napoleonic wars stirred up national consciousness and pride, encouraged the birth of publicity as a forerunner of public opinion, and brought the triumphant country face to face with Europe for the first time.

Neoclassical theory and practice continued down into the reign of Alexander but less inclusively so and eventually surrendered important ground to another movement, the cult of sensibility, which had begun to penetrate Russia from England, France, and Germany at the end of Catherine's reign. Though initially an outgrowth of such novels as *Clarissa, Nouvelle Héloïse, Werther*, and especially Sterne's *Sentimental Journey*, the movement was soon infused with the special qualities of feeling to be found in such English works as Thomson's *The Seasons*, Young's *Night Thoughts*, and the *Poems of Ossian*, all of which were translated into Russian and much imitated. A veritable philosophy of feeling absorbed a number of writers and acted as an antidote to the rationalism of neoclassicism.

Karamzin, the author of *Poor Liza*, became the high priest of the new sensibility, especially after his immensely popular *Letters of a Russian Traveler* (1797) where the analysis of his own feelings, his "joy of grief," and tearful sadness before the beauties of nature amounted to a revelation to the reading public. His utter subjectivism and emphasis on his own spiritual experiences, so alien to the neoclassical outlook, were influential among literary disciples in the first part of Alexander's reign. However, neither his poetry nor tales, written in the spirit of the cult of sensibility, nor those of his followers, contributed anything memorable to Russian literature. Karamzin's real service was as a historian and the creator of a literary language that was modern and supple enough to be used in a variety of genres, the lack of which hitherto had been a serious hindrance to the development of Russian prose.

As in the previous periods, original fiction was mostly neglected. The literary historian N. I. Grech, in reviewing the total output for the single year 1814, could list only two novels, and these were both translations from the German. Though Karamzin never wrote a full-length novel, some of his later short stories—he was really the first to introduce this form into Russian literature—such as *A Knight of Our Times*, reveal a degree of artistic form and skill in characterization not to be found in the sparse body of previous fiction. However, in his almost exclusive preoccupation with tearful and noble sentiments of simple hearts, he never comes to grips with reality. The only full-length novel to reflect the manners and customs of the times, perhaps more influenced by Smollett's blunt realism than by that of Fielding, is Vasily Narezhny's *A Russian Gil Blas*, the story of a wretched squire's adventures in the provinces and in the two capitals. It is a crude effort, for Narezhny lacked the imagination and art to endow reality with life, and hence the work failed to play any part in the future development of the novel.

A writer at this time who observed life closely and possessed the art to charge it with living reality was Ivan Krylov, whose nine volumes of fables appeared between 1809 and 1820. Though the verse fable was an approved and popular neoclassical genre, Krylov easily surpassed his Russian rivals in form and in the realistic, instead of prettifying, manner in which he handled his subjects. The result was a classic of Russian literature. In these fables Krylov, in a style that drew upon the speech of common folk, satirized and ridiculed the foibles, especially arrogant stupidity, of high and low. Though the limitations of the form hardly allow for realistic treatment in depth, Krylov's animals no less than his peasants come to life. And the world they live in, despite its restricted dimensions, is a very recognizable Russian world filled with healthy humor and good practical common sense. Belinsky once remarked that if the work of any Russian writer up to this point were translated into a major European language, foreign readers would have found it of no interest because they would have long ago read this kind of thing in their own literature, whereas they would have welcomed a translation of Krylov's fables as something different and quintessentially Russian. Actually these fables were a first step in the direction of that kind of realism which later became the hallmark of Russian literature. They very likely influenced the course of Pushkin's realism and also Griboyedov's famous comedy, *Woe from Wit*, whose characters were so brilliantly stamped out of the common clay of Russian existence, and they no doubt contributed to the "poetry of real life" which characterized so much of Gogol's fiction.

In truth, during Alexander's reign decades of preparation were approaching an end and literature advanced from imitativeness to originality in the wonderful flowering of verse described as Russia's "Golden Age of Poetry." Though Pushkin emerged as the leading figure of the movement, it included a sizable group of unusual poets of whom Zhukovsky, Batyushkov, and Baratynsky are the most remarkable ones. The intellectual and artistic climate was still that of Western Europe, but it was now an entirely assimilated climate reflected in verse that was European without being imitative. The verse of these poets, nearly all of whom belonged to the gentry class, was distinctly classical, especially in the purity of its form, and also, to a large extent, in its subject matter.

By 1820, however, this movement began to encounter the strident claims of European romanticism and its concomitant German idealism. Soon a critical debate ensued in the monthly reviews, which now played an important role in literature, between proponents of strict rules of French neoclassicism and those who favored romanticism with its greater freedom in form and content. Then the death of Alexander I and the Decembrist Revolt, which ushered in the reign of Nicholas I in 1825, were events that deeply affected cultural developments. The revolt ended in the suppression of many of the intellectual elite among the gentry and new plebeian writers took their place. A growing commercialism started to make inroads on literature, and one result was a decline in the popularity of poetry and a rise in the importance of prose. In the very year of revolt Alexander Bestuzhev-Marlinsky, a young poet and later an extremely popular fiction writer, asserted in a letter to Pushkin: "People no longer listen to poetry now that everyone is able to write it. The current murmur has risen to a general outcry: 'Give us prose! Prose!—Water, plain water.' " With romanticism in the saddle, it was only natural in these circumstances that its greatest representative in fiction, Sir Walter Scott, should have prompted and influenced new developments in the Russian novel.

Unlike the West, in Russia romanticism never assumed social or political dimensions, nor did it reflect individual revolt against real or imaginary evils of society. It never amounted to much more than a narrow and even ephemeral literary movement almost wholly stimulated from abroad. Though the works of certain French writers and German philosophers were eagerly read, the writings and personalities of Byron and Scott were by far the largest influence in introducing romanticism into Russia. In 1827 the able poet and critic Peter Vyazemsky declared, perhaps with some exaggeration: "In our age it seems impossible for a poet not to echo Byron or for a novelist not to reflect Walter Scott." Abundant evidence indicates that Scott became a kind of literary hero, the object of endless admiration and curiosity in the pages of Russian periodicals. From 1820 to 1830 no less than thirty-nine translations of Scott's novels were published, often running into several editions and including nearly every title in the long series. These works served to arouse the interest of Russians in their country's past and also influenced the writing of a considerable number of historical romances.

The most popular of these, and certainly the most enduring, was *Yury Miloslavsky, or the Russians in 1612* (1829) by Mikhail Zagoskin, who won the sobriquet of the "Russian Walter Scott." It was also published in England in 1834, an unusual tribute, for translations of Russian literature into English were very rare at this time. The background of the novel is the Time of Troubles when the Poles occupied Moscow. Yury falls in love with a beautiful noblewoman, and after various adventures, in which Kirsha, the stout bodyguard of the hero performs prodigies of valor, Yury wins his fair damsel. Zagoskin wrote other historical novels but none of them achieved the fame of *Yury Miloslavsky*.

Faddei Bulgarin also contributed historical romances, such as *The False Dmitri* (1830) and *Mazepa* (1834), but he won much more réclame with his picaresque novel, *Ivan Vyzhigin* (1829), in which the effectiveness of rough but genuine transcripts of Russian life is unfortunately neutralized by the author's excessive moralizing. Similarly Bestuzhev-Marlinsky, who published an historical romance, *Incursions*, as early as 1824 and followed it up with others less satisfactory, won his widest popular success with purely romantic tales of his adventures as a soldier in the Caucasus, such as *Ammalet Bek* (1832). But the author who more than Zagoskin deserved the title of "Russian Walter Scott" was Ivan Lazhechnikov who wrote a series of historical romances. One of his earliest, and in some respect the best, *The Last Novik* (1831-33), drew from Belinsky these words of praise: "It reveals in the author a considerable talent and establishes his claim to the honorable place of first Russian novelist."* This tribute is not hard to understand, for *The Last Novik*, a story centered in the epoch of Peter the Great, is peculiarly modern compared to the archaic flavor of all preceding Russian fiction. Though the hero is most unconvincing, several of the secondary characters emerge as real human beings.

None of these writers occupies a lofty place in the annals of Russian literature, but they are worth mentioning because they came at a point when the Russian reading public first evinced a need for fiction, and by and large they attempted to answer it, in the spirit of the times, with the historical romance. Realism, as the art of trying to envisage the ever-changing and tangible world, is as relevant to the past as to the present, a fact that Balzac recognized when he stated in the introduction to *The Human Comedy* that he regarded his own novels as continuations of the historical romances of Scott. He saw clearly that Scott emphasized the development of social elements instead of the external glitter of historical events. And Balzac praised him for assigning secondary roles to great historical figures in order to concentrate on the spirit and morals of an age or on the causes which lead to and explain significant events.

For the most part these early Russian writers of historical romances largely missed this concentration, perhaps because they lacked Scott's extraordinary talent and the long development of

* V. G. Belinsky, *Selected Philosophical Works* (Moscow: Foreign Languages Publishing House, 1948), p. 89.

literary culture that informed it. They were not endowed with
the magical art with which he conjured the varied atmosphere
and scenery of his events and incidents, nor did they have his exceptional power of vivifying the past on an extended scale.
Though they faithfully imitated his brilliant efforts to provide
the local color of a vanished epoch by historical research, they
were unable to transcend the trivial and the average in a quest
for the deeper essence of reality hidden beneath the surface. The
reality of atmosphere of a past age which they sought to grasp
conveyed nothing of that wonderful ancient Russianism which,
let us say, is conveyed in medieval ikons. They were not analysts
of human nature. Scott often fails in his non-Scotch characterizations, but the pulse of real life throbs in his native portrayals,
which is rarely the case with any of the characters of these early
Russian historical novelists. And though they and Scott are unconvincing in their love scenes, the Russians tend to emphasize
the love element, failing to realize that Scott regarded his novels
not as romances of love but rather as the romance of human life
and its activities. So very often, it seems, the flavor of these Russian historical novels was not that of real life but of make-believe.

4

Throughout the eighteenth century no writer had appeared
who possessed the genius to identify himself completely with
the national epos in original creative endeavors and give the kind
of direction to Russian literature that would enable it to take a
worthy place in the stream of world literature. Alexander Pushkin (1799-1837) performed this service in the early years of the
nineteenth century and richly deserves the title accorded him by
genealogically minded native critics of "the father of modern
Russian literature."

Of course, no attempt can be made here to evaluate Pushkin's extraordinary accomplishments in a variety of literary genres, although a fresh assessment that would avoid both the exaggerated praise and depreciation of nineteenth-century critics and the sprightly dullness of Soviet worshipers, who regard him as a kind of predecessor of socialist realism, is very much needed in our own day. Our concern is with Pushkin's contributions to the Russian novel and, more specifically, to the formation of its realistic traditions.

Within this limited sphere Pushkin's unusual artistic qualifications conditioned the nature of his contributions in a unique manner. Though writing in the nineteenth century, the qualities of his mind and art were formed largely by the eighteenth. That is to say, he was a classicist in his literary tastes, in his sense of form, and in his habits of thought and feeling. The special intellectual essence which we associate with the classical approach to life and art—nothing over much, a preference for the reality of things, and an intense dislike of excess and insincerity—characterized not only the manner in which he wrote, but also the themes he selected. Unlike such great writers of fiction as Balzac and Dostoevsky, who by becoming emotionally involved at times in the life they observed and in the men and women they created and to this extent distorted the realistic image of their milieu, Pushkin's artistic detachment enabled him to remain quite objective even when there could be no doubt of his social sympathies or prejudices. Irony appealed to him more than direct criticism, subtle satire more than forthright denunciation. Like Tolstoy, his breeding as a member of the gentry colored his whole outlook on life, but unlike Tolstoy, his "six-hundred-year-old ancestry" never turned him into a conscience-stricken nobleman.

Pushkin, however, did not remain serenely above the battle. In his youth he evinced political sympathies close to those of the Decembrist rebels and literary tendencies that allied him with romanticism. But he was a literary artist and not a political thinker. Disheartened by persecution during the reign of Alexander I, he hopefully made his peace with the new regime of Nicholas I. And the classical discipline of his artistic temperament soon compelled him to repudiate romanticism. Though his magnificent "Southern Verse Tales," such as *The Robber Brothers* (1821), *The Captive of the Caucasus* (1822), and *The Fountain of Bakhchisarai* (1824), were clearly inspired by Byron's "Eastern Verse Tales," Pushkin was too dedicated to technical mastery to tolerate Byron's faults of form and too rational to have any sympathy with his pessimism, disillusion, and romantic posing. In rejecting Vyazemsky's request in 1824 that he write a fifth canto to *Childe Harold* as a tribute to Byron after his death, Pushkin remarked: "You are sad about Byron, but I am quite happy in his death, as a lofty theme for poetry. Byron's genius faded from his youth. . . . There was no gradation; he suddenly ripened and matured, sang and then grew silent, and his first melodies never returned to him."

The beginning of Pushkin's transition from romanticism to realism may be discerned as early as 1824 in the exquisite dramatic narrative poem, *The Gypsies*, in which both strains are curiously mingled. The subject has romantic overtones: the sophisticated hero Aleko deserts civilization for life among the gypsies. Later, enraged by his sweetheart's betrayal of him, he kills both her and her lover. As punishment these children of nature, who believe that one cannot say to a young girl's heart: "Love only one, you must not change," oblige the murderer to leave them. It is possible that some thirty years later Leo Tolstoy had Aleko and the theme of *The Gypsies* very much in mind when he wrote his novel *The Cossacks*, in which he poses a somewhat similar conflict between the unreflecting natural life of the Cossacks and the conventional worldly existence of his hero Olenin.

In *The Gypsies* an effective concentration on descriptive details of setting and action in order to achieve verisimilitude and convey atmosphere strikes an entirely new realistic note in Russian literature. Some notion of these effects may be obtained from a literal, unrhymed rendering of a few of the opening lines, however much violence it may do to the poetic beauty of the original:

> The gypsies in a noisy crowd
> Wander over Bessarabia.
> Today they spend the night
> In tattered tents by a river bank.
> Like freedom their camp is joyous,
> And they sleep peacefully under the sky.
> Between the cart wheels,
> Half-covered by rugs,
> A fire burns; a family round it
> Prepares supper; in the open field
> Horses graze; before a tent
> A tame bear lies untied.
> All is lively in the steppe:
> Peaceful family cares,
> Preparation for the morrow's short journey,
> The singing of women, shouts of children,
> And the sounds of a portable anvil.

There is much more in this vein, all of which led Belinsky to date the beginning of Russian realism with this opening passage of *The Gypsies*.

Aleko is hardly a typical Byronic figure with the usual romantic trappings. This fact is made amply clear in the famous passage at the end of the poem where the old father of the slain girl, speaking for all the gypsies, explains to Aleko: "You for yourself desire freedom," and he bids him leave them in peace. The individual will is defeated by the will of the community. Pushkin's resolution of the tragedy is classical in intention—

Nemesis presides over the destiny of man. Not the vengeance of the gypsies overtakes Aleko, but a kind of tragic poetic justice.

It is difficult to accept the judgment of so acute a critic as Mirsky that *The Gypsies* is "the most temptingly universal imaginative work in the Russian language." Various writers have discovered in it a profound philosophical meaning. Dostoevsky, for example, in his speech at the unveiling of the Pushkin monument in Moscow in 1880, acclaimed Aleko as the primordial type of the unhappy Russian wanderer who must learn—as Aleko did from the humility of the gypsies—to humble his pride and thus achieve his freedom. Only when the intelligentsia learns this lesson, Dostoevsky concluded, will it be able to lead the people in fulfilling its manifest destiny of reconciling the proud and discordant Western world to the Russian universal message of humility.

Pushkin's classical realism eschewed overt philosophizing. The only major Russian author who resembled him in this respect was Chekhov, a fact recognized by Doctor Zhivago many years later. For Pasternak's hero prefers the modest reticence of Pushkin and Chekhov who, unlike Dostoevsky or Tolstoy, thought it pretentious and presumptuous to indulge in speculation on the ultimate purpose of mankind. To all those who attempt to discover a deep or hidden meaning in his writings, Pushkin would characteristically answer, as he in fact did in the case of Zhukovsky: "You ask what is the purpose of *The Gypsies?* What should it be? The purpose of poetry is poetry. . . ."

Pushkin had hardly finished *The Gypsies* when he took another step in the direction of realism. He had discovered Shakespeare, and with that innovating boldness which was a distinctive trait of his genius, he decided to write a historical tragedy that would end the long neoclassical tradition of Racine in the Russian theater and, hopefully, start a new trend in native drama. "Verisimilitude of situations and truth of dialogue—here is the real rule of tragedy," he wrote his friend Nikolai Raevsky in 1825. "(I haven't read Calderon or Vega), but what a man is this Shakespeare! I can't get over it. How small Byron the tragedian looks in comparison with him!"

The play, of course, is *Boris Godunov*, and though it has failings as a historical tragedy in blank verse, Shakespeare's full-blooded realism is reflected in the best of the characterizations, in the mob scenes where the dialogue so naturally suits the lowly speakers, and especially in the comic scene of the two miscreant monks in the inn at the Lithuanian border.

At that time *Boris Godunov* was a unique Russian effort to re-create the historical past in drama. In the same realistic pursuit, but now with a difference, Pushkin attempted to modernize Shakespeare. Impishly wondering what would have happened in *The Rape of Lucrece* if the lovely victim had only thought of slapping Tarquin's face at the appropriate moment, Pushkin provided an answer, in a contemporary setting, in his verse tale *Count Nulin*. The gay count mistakes the coyness of his charming hostess as an invitation to something more intimate. But when he attempts to pursue this idea the resounding slap in the face she gives him forces the count into a humiliating retreat. In short, while he was realistically treating a historical theme in *Boris Godunov*, Pushkin revealed his ability, in the delightfully narrated *Count Nulin*, to depict a slice of modern Russian life with convincing realism.

5

This natural movement in Pushkin's artistic development from neoclassical fugitive poetry, verse epistles, and Anacreontic lyrics of his novitiate, and romantic "Southern Verse Tales" of his youth, to concentration on literature of realism at the outset of maturity found its first major expression in his great master-

piece, *Eugene Onegin*. He announced the beginning of this long
narrative poem of over five thousand lines in a letter to Vyazemsky on May 9, 1823: "I'm not writing a novel, but a novel in
verse—a devil of a difference—in the manner of *Don Juan*." But
long before *Eugene Onegin* was finished eight years later,
Byron's initial influence had vanished in the slow, forward progress of perhaps the most original work Pushkin ever wrote, and
one that endeavored to present a comprehensive and realistic
picture of one whole segment of contemporary Russian life.

Pushkin did not share the confusion of that estimable Mon-
sieur Jourdain—he knew that he was writing, if not speaking,
poetry in *Eugene Onegin*. Yet he liked to regard this long poem
as a novel and actually divided it into chapters instead of cantos.
And if one cares to accept Pushkin's odd but meaningful description of *Eugene Onegin*, containing much of his finest verse, one
may regard it as the first Russian realistic novel, for it possesses
the ordinary surface features of the genre: characters, a plot
with well-marked beginning, middle, and end, and a treatment
of the precise content of life in given circumstances.

A realistic embodiment of this Russian way of life in either
poetry or prose was a challenge, for nothing quite resembling it
existed in Western Europe, although the eighteenth-century
squirearchy of Fielding's *Tom Jones* bears points of similarity.
Catherine the Great's charter of 1785, defining the privileges and
responsibilities of the nobility, gave moral impetus to the growth
of a class of middle nobility or landed gentry. They spent most
of their time on estates in the country, except for a few winter
months of intense social activity in the capitals or large provincial cities. With their special privileges and similar education and
tastes, this class over the years developed a spiritual and cultural
consciousness of its own as the significant core of Russian society. Pushkin belonged to this class, and in *Eugene Onegin* he
was the first to present its contemporary image and inner life. To

estimate the uniqueness of his achievement, one would have to be aware of prior efforts which amount to so many sketches and crude copies rather than the imaginative re-creation of original art. With his realistic depiction of people, manners, and morals, Pushkin at once rendered laughably obsolete those prodigies of vice and paragons of virtue who had been the main staple of Russian readers of neoclassical and romantic poetry and prose. *Eugene Onegin* is a perfect expression of the landed gentry of Pushkin's time.

Though the polished world-weary hero is a product of the society to which he belongs, it would be a mistake to regard Onegin as a simple type. His is a complex nature which changes and matures as does that of Pierre Bezukhov or Prince Andrew over the years of the action of *War and Peace*. Onegin's early Byronic posing soon fades and the deeper traits of a type common enough in the society of the time begin to emerge. In reality he is alienated from his class, not because he rejects its values, although there is something of this in him, but because a lack of belief in himself prevents him from playing the part of a leader which inwardly he aspired to be. His cynical behavior is a product of this frustration which also explains his sudden retreat to the simple life of the country, his rejection there of Tatyana's passionate love, and his callous killing of Lensky in a duel.

Onegin is the first convincing full-length characterization in Russian literature. Pushkin, however, does not employ fine-spun analysis to bring out the complexities of his nature or to explain the motivation of his feelings, a technique which he must have observed in Rousseau's *Nouvelle Héloïse* and Richardson's novels. Though the limitations of a novel in verse may have rendered such an approach pecularily difficult, it was also alien to Pushkin's classical temperament and the objectivity and restraint which were touchstones of his art. The indirect realistic method he used was very much his own. The total image of Onegin emerges from an artistically contrived mosaic of impressions—the furnishings of his room, his toilet articles, the books in his study with special passages marked by the imprint of his finger-nail, his actions and statements as they affected others, and their reactions to him. Later Turgenev learned much from this method.

The importance of Onegin as a type for the future of Russian literature can hardly be overestimated. There is perhaps an element of distortion in the familiar claim of critics that he inspired a whole galaxy of so-called superfluous heroes in fiction, for the type was indigenous in Russian life, although the image altered with changing social conditions. But it is safe to say that, without Onegin, the introduction of the type might have been delayed for years, and the portrayals might well have lacked something in convincingness without the perfectly realized model provided by Pushkin.

The realism of Tatyana's portrait loses nothing in verisimilitude because Pushkin appears to idealize her, for like many romantic country girls of the landed gentry she herself idealizes life, often mistaking its sober prose for sheer poetry. Though she lives entirely in her own feelings, thoughts, and experiences, Tatyana possesses a strong individuality and a mind of her own. When Onegin appears in her rural solitude she falls ardently in love, for she sees in him her ideal hero, an image drawn from her reading of English and French romances. The cynical Onegin is momentarily touched by Tatyana's wonderful letter to him, but he fails to perceive in this anguished poetic outpouring of a young girl's heart the innate integrity of her nature and her infinite capacity for self-sacrifice.

The seemingly swift transformation of the shy, dreamy, provincial Tatyana into a majestic queen of Petersburg high society after her mother marries her off to the fat general has often been criticized as unfaithful to the reality of things. However, if one is attentive to the deeper spiritual and moral qualities of Tatyana, revealed particularly at the time of Onegin's rejection of her love, then the change is no less acceptable and comprehensible than that of Tolstoy's Natasha in *War and Peace* when she marries Pierre Bezukhov shortly after the tragic denouement of her love for Prince Andrew.

Similarly Pushkin has been blamed for contriving an unreal ending when he has Tatyana, in turn, reject Onegin, although she frankly admits her continued love for him, after he returns from his wanderings and discovers in this beautiful, matured society leader his ideal woman. However, Tatyana's declaration to Onegin on this occasion: "I have been given to another and I'll be true to him forever," is entirely in keeping with the logic of her developing personality. Back in the country she would have sacrificed anything she held dear because of her love for Onegin, like that other strong-willed woman Anna Karenina who did sacrifice everything because of her love for Vronsky. But Anna found out only too late that her idol had feet of clay and was unequal to her great love. A tragic conclusion was inevitable. Tatyana discovered this fact about Onegin before it was too late. If she could believe that he would return a love as profound and enduring as she was capable of offering, she might well have broken with society and its conventions. But she had learned much about Onegin's weaknesses, distrusted the genuineness of his motives now, and had become convinced of his incapacity to respond to her love in equal measure. And though she weeps nostalgically over his passionate love letters, over her former dreams and hopes, she now knows that he could never be the hero of her romance.

The relations of Onegin and Tatyana fed the imaginations of future Russian novelists in their creation of unhappy pairs of weak-willed heroes and strong-willed heroines. These charming women have served to convince readers that the female was the better half of the Russian race.

Though Belinsky's much-quoted declaration that *Eugene Onegin* is an encyclopedia of Russian life is quite preposterous, there can be no question that Pushkin's depiction of the country existence of the middle gentry and the city life of its more socially prominent members is realistically perfect and extraordinarily effective. In these respects he went far beyond the small beginnings in *The Gypsies* and *Count Nulin*, for he now drew heavily upon village life on his own estate at Milhailovskoe and on his varied experiences in Moscow and Petersburg salon society. One is fascinated not only by his uncanny selection of precise detail, but also by his amazing re-creation of the moral, emotional, and spiritual pattern, the moods and feelings, and the inner rhythm of this order of society.

One catches the beat of this inner rhythm, especially as it applies to the glittering worldly youth of Onegin's set, in the first stanza of the poem in which the hero contemplates the approaching death of his uncle whose country estate he will inherit:

> "My uncle's life was always upright
> And now that he has fallen ill
> In earnest he makes one respect him:
> He is a pattern for us still.
> One really could not ask for more—
> But heavens, what a fearful bore
> To play the sick-nurse day and night
> And never stir beyond his sight!
> What petty, mean dissimulation
> To entertain a man half dead,
> To poke his pillows up in bed,
> And carry in some vile potation,
> While all the time one's thinking, 'Why
> The devil take so long to die?' "*

* Alexander Pushkin, *Eugene Onegin*, translated into English by Dorothy Prall Radin and George Z. Patrick (Berkeley: University of California Press, 1937), p. 3.

Pushkin swiftly carries his readers through the early upbringing, education, passing love affairs, and social activities of this gilded youth, but he strives, and nearly always successfully, to combine the visual perception of things with their essential atmosphere, adding depth to the total realism of the picture. For example, Onegin visits the ballet theater and this is what he sees:

> The house is full, the boxes glitter,
> The pit is like a seething cup,
> The gallery claps with loud impatience,
> The curtain rustles—and goes up.
> There, half of air and all aglow,
> Obedient to the magic bow,
> Circled by nymphs in lovely bands,
> Istomina, resplendent, stands.
> Balanced on one toe, tremulous,
> She slowly whirls the other round,
> Then with a sudden leap and bound
> Flies as if blown by Aeolus.
> She winds, unwinds and, light as feather,
> In mid-air beats her feet together.*

With similar evocative power Pushkin portrays the simple life of the landed gentry on their country estates: that of the Larins—Tatyana's parents and her sister; the neighboring estate of Onegin which he had inherited from his uncle; and the smaller property of the idealistic, romantic poet Lensky whose quarrel with his friend Onegin ended in the fatal duel. Here nature adds its beauty and burden to daily living, and no Russian poet ever described it more realistically and sympathetically than Pushkin, especially when it is tricked out in winter's snowy splendor. The old-fashioned cultural interests of the Larins; the small talk of country folk when neighbors gather; their simple

* *Ibid.*, p. 12.

amusements such as the name-day party at the Larins where the condescending Onegin deliberately provokes Lensky by his excessive attention to the poet's betrothed, Olga, Tatyana's sister; the folk superstitions of provincial damsels and the enchanting wintry beauty and eerie terror of Tatyana's symbolic dream; her old peasant nurse's captivating account of how she was given in marriage at the age of thirteen; the duel scene with its exquisite lyric ending so strangely prophetic of Pushkin's own death in a duel—these and many similar scenes constitute an altogether convincing picture of a way of life hitherto unexampled in Russian literature. In truth, this impressive portrayal of the middle gentry became the source that fed the mainstream of Russian nineteenth-century realistic fiction.

6

That Russia's greatest poet should have eventually turned to prose does not seem so startling in the light of Pushkin's growing preoccupation with artistic problems of realism. To be sure, other factors were involved. It has been pointed out that by the end of the reign of Alexander I the popularity of poetry began to fade, and as the 1830's approached the public interest in Walter Scott and the historical novel intensified. Then, too, Pushkin's increasing financial worries, connected with his marriage, compelled him to turn to prose for which there was a growing demand. When he began his career poetry was still regarded in Russia as the leisure-time avocation of gentlemen who did not design to exploit their talent for money. Though Pushkin was virtually the first to make literature a profession in Russia, it was always difficult for him to overcome the feeling that writing poetry for gain was a violation of the nobleman's code. Necessity, however, forced him to compromise with his conviction, and he found a way out, equivocal though it may seem, that satisfied both his need and his pride. Once, in answering a pointed question of his brother, he declared: "I sing as the baker bakes, as the tailor sews . . . as the physician kills—for money, money, money. In my nakedness such is my cynicism." But more cogently he told Vyazemsky: "I write for myself and print for money. . . ." That is, he went on to explain, it was all right for an author to sell his manuscripts, but he must never sell his inspiration. And he sincerely lived up to this credo, for he wrote a number of things which he realized would never see the light of day because of the rigorous censorship. Even his masterpiece, *Eugene Onegin*, he began in the firm conviction that it could not be printed.

At the outset Pushkin expressed a scorn for prose. "How sorry are those poets who begin to write prose," he lamented to a friend. "I confess, if I were not obliged by circumstances, I would not dip my pen in ink for prose." During the last ten years of his life, however, he dipped his pen deep and often for prose and brought to the practice of it the same innovating power and artistic demands everywhere apparent in his poetry.

A combination of family pride on the defensive and the example of Walter Scott may well have prompted Pushkin's first effort in prose fiction—an unfinished historical novel about his black great-grandfather, *The Negro of Peter the Great* (1827-28). In the manner of Scott, Pushkin intended to provide a careful historical reconstruction of Peter's reign which would focus on the opposition of the old nobility to the Europeanized reforms of the tsar. In this respect, as well as in creating a prose style suited to the demands of historical fiction, he seemed to be on the way to success. The reticent Scott would have been somewhat shocked over the freedom Pushkin allowed himself in the realistic account of his ancestor's amorous adventures. But after a most promising beginning of seven chapters, Pushkin abandoned the work because, it is said, of his failure to find a solution to a radical change in the plot which he felt necessary.

In the third chapter of *Eugene Onegin*, in one of the many half-serious, half-joking digressions which constitute one of the poem's chief charms, Pushkin anticipates the time when he'll "dwindle into peaceful prose" and write "a novel in the old style" about the doings of a Russian family. And among the beginnings, sketches, and outlines of some twenty short stories and novels which he wrote down in his copybooks between 1829-36, there are several fragments that may represent attempts to fulfill this design of a family novel. One, for example, is "A Novel in Letters," which might have been inspired by the epistolary fiction of Richardson or Rousseau. Another, "A Russian Pelham," might have been suggested by Bulwer-Lytton's novel, although the few sample pages and rough plan bear little resemblance to the contents and style of the English *Pelham*. Yet these numerous fragments are evidence of Pushkin's keen interest in trying his hand at fiction during this period, and his failure to complete any of them perhaps indicates frustration in creating a style and treatment that would satisfy his artistic standards in writing a family novel of manners.

As a matter of fact, Pushkin's first completed effort in prose fiction, *Tales of Belkin* (1830), was a conscious experiment in artistic form and narrative approach at a time when both seemed inconsequential to Russian writers of fiction. His intention was to offer models of how a particular type of story ought to be told. The five tales in the collection *(The Shot, The Snowstorm, The Stationmaster, The Undertaker,* and *The Lady-Rustic)*, which have no connection with each other, are held together by the imaginary personality of the narrator, Belkin, a brief sketch of whose life is given in the preface to the collection. One reason for this mystification may have been a desire to create an illusion of reality, for in the preface each tale is represented as a true story told to Belkin by a real person, a device which Pushkin may have learned from Scott's *Tales of My Landlord*. Pushkin may also have wished to disguise his authorship—the collection appeared without his name—perhaps because of his uncertainty about critical reaction to a work so experimental in nature.

His concern was justified, for contemporary critics were baffled by a narrative method entirely unlike anything they were accustomed to, one conscientiously pruned of all the conventional ornaments of fiction writing. The stories are told in an extremely simple, direct style, with a paucity of description, dialogue, and authorial reflection or analysis. They are largely action stories, and in this type, Pushkin believed, nothing should be allowed to get between the reader and the forward progress of the action.

The *Tales of Belkin* are sometimes described, in the German sense, as *novellas*, and in several stories, especially in *The Snowstorm*, they contain the surprise ending that Goethe believed was essential in this genre. More precisely they are anecdotal short stories which Pushkin may well have heard from his friend Delvig, and he tells them with rare narrative skill and conscious restraint.

Apart from innovation in form, Pushkin also strikes a new note in his occasional emphasis on social tensions, as in the clash between the declassed officer and his aristocratic opponent in *The Shot*, and the seduction of the poor stationmaster's daughter by the wealthy hussar in *The Stationmaster*. But compassion for the lowly or the underdog does not lead to a distortion of reality. The declassed officer is not triumphant in the end, and the seduced girl, who would have been represented as the ruined victim of moral depravity by any contemporary treating the theme, happily marries her seducer at the conclusion of the story. Pushkin always perceives the irony of life as a possible solvent of its inequities. And though his and the reader's sympathies are clearly for the grief-stricken father of the seduced girl,

Pushkin does not humiliate him with pity, a fact that led Dostoevsky to value this tale higher than Gogol's famous story, *The Overcoat*, which in its concentration on the sad fate of a humble person may owe something to *The Stationmaster*.

The Tales of Belkin waited a long time before winning general recognition from critics, and one suspects that it was an undiscriminating acceptance connected with Pushkin's lofty position by then in Russian letters. However, a judge as perceptive as Tolstoy expressed his delight over these tales as perfect models of the art of narration. The work is the first piece of Russian fiction of enduring artistic value.

The social tensions which Pushkin had barely touched upon in *The Tales of Belkin* assumed a more central position in his next two works of fiction, *The History of the Village of Goryukhino* (1830) and *Dubrovsky* (1832). Perhaps the deeper, darker realism of his treatment of the subject explains why he never completed either novel, for they could hardly have been published during the "iron reign" of Nicholas I. It is most regrettable for both gave every promise of becoming outstanding novels on quite different themes.

It occurred to Pushkin to continue the development of Belkin, the fictitious narrator of the *Tales*, and in *The History of the Village of Goryukhino* he turns him, even in that incomplete portrayal, into a memorable character—a shy, lovable, wryly humorous individual with timid ambitions to be an author. With the aid of old records he has discovered, he sets out to write the history of Goryukhino, the village in which his estate is situated. Actually this is an amusing parody of *The History of the Russian People* by Pushkin's literary enemy Nikolai Polevoi, and at the same time an effective satire on the whole structure of serfdom. Behind Belkin's distorted historical account of the village and its inhabitants, reflecting the pomposity of pseudo-scholarship in his comic legalistic reverence for forms and titles, looms the somber reality of the ruination of the peasants because of the steward's calculated repressions. In his naive concentration on historical cause and effect, Belkin never perceives the harsh unchangeability of peasant life or the one peculiarity of his village, namely, that it has no history.

In *Dubrovsky* the tensions growing out of a different social situation are treated. Troekurov, a swaggering, powerful, and wealthy member of the landed gentry in the reign of Catherine the Great, persecutes and finally brings about the death of his neighbor Dubrovsky, who possesses fewer worldly goods but dares to show his independence. Pushkin finished only about half of this novel which is one of his best examples of sheer storytelling ability. There is perhaps more Scott-like romance than realism in the melodramatic action of a tale that involves the vow of young Dubrovsky to avenge his father's death; his leading a robber band to steal from the rich and help the poor; his secret love for his intended victim's daughter and his disguise as a French tutor to gain access to her; his beloved's forced marriage to Vereisky, another powerful but polished nobleman, and young Dubrovsky's attempt to foil it; and the attack on the robber band with which the fragment ends. But the plausibility of these romantic adventures is secured by a realistically conceived picture of the social milieu in which they take place—expansive daily life on huge landed estates, the absolute power of their owners over law courts and all who are socially inferior, and the stark horror of the murder of the drunken officer of the law in Dubrovsky's flaming manor house. Though the hero, young Dubrovsky, is the pure stuff of old-fashioned romance, the characterizations of Troekurov and the sinister Vereisky are among Pushkin's best and are harbingers of the great realistic portraits to come in Russian fiction.

Pushkin's zeal for experimentation in prose as well as in poetry, an important service in this early stage of Russian literature, continued during the last few years of his life when he wrote more prose than verse. Another such experiment, the long short story, *The Queen of Spades* (1834), was his most popular contribution to fiction during his lifetime. E. T. A. Hoffmann's tales of the supernatural may well have suggested the plot-line of *The Queen of Spades*, where the ghost of the old countess conveys to Herman the mysterious secret that will enable him to win at cards, but there is nothing of the German's romanticism in Pushkin's narrative manner. A carefully designed pattern of realistic effects compels a suspension of disbelief in the central supernatural device, and the swiftly moving action is heightened by a taut, terse, unadorned prose that subtly contrives an atmosphere of utter credibility. Though Pushkin had read Stendhal's *The Red and the Black*, Herman is hardly a Julien Sorel. However, the Napoleonic type, the man with an overweening thirst for personal success, had already begun to make its way into Russian literature, and Herman's cold, insatiable ambition is described as Napoleonic. But the retribution of madness that overtakes him in the end is the Pushkinian tragic fate that presides over the destinies of many of his heroes.

Nothing remotely resembling *The Queen of Spades* had appeared in Russian literature before Pushkin, and though its total artistic impact, more one of manner than of substance, was never successfully duplicated, the story greatly impressed and obviously influenced such writers as Gogol in *The Portrait* and Dostoevsky in *The Gambler*.

Once again the works of Walter Scott were in Pushkin's mind, especially *The Heart of Midlothian*, in his final effort at fiction—the historical novel *The Captain's Daughter* (1834)—a kind of by-product of his scholarly study of an event during the reign of Catherine the Great, *The History of the Pugachev Rebellion* (1834). Like everything he wrote, however, this novel also bears the stamp of Pushkin's originality. It is shorter and more compact than Scott's novels, and it is centered as much on the history of two families, the Grinevs and the Mironovs, as on the re-creation of the historical past. Though Pushkin is exact about historical details and local color, with his usual sense of measure he does not overwhelm the reader with an elaborate superstructure of antiquarian research. His interest is concentrated more on the manners and morals of people than on the dress and loose ornament of history. Perhaps this is why he succeeds so brilliantly in such portrayals as the comically henpecked Captain Mironov, commander of the remote Belogorsk fortress, who, in nightcap and dressing gown, drills his few soldiers without ever being able to teach them the difference between the left and right foot, and his strong-willed wife who with dignity and courage shares her husband's death at the hands of the rebels. And hardly less striking are the impetuous young Grinev and his stern father, who values a soldier's duty to his military oath above everything in life. Apparently Pushkin did not favor the institution of serfdom and the few individualized portraits of serfs in his writings reveal a deep and sympathetic understanding of them. One of the most remarkable of such creations is the old servant of the Grinevs, Savelich, whose integrity and cross-grained devotion to his masters illuminate a nature that is as attractively simple as it is morally beautiful. Pushkin is not so effective with the rebel leader Pugachev, no doubt because of the rigorous censorship, but even this necessarily restrained characterization suggests what Pushkin might have done with it if he had had an entirely free hand.

Pushkin has been criticized in *The Captain's Daughter* for allowing the interest in events to predominate over the interest in details of feeling. This is essentially true, particularly in young Grinev's love for Captain Mironov's daughter which hardly rises above the banality of Scott's treatment of affairs of the heart. But this criticism could also be applied, with only few exceptions, to the whole development of fiction in the West and in Russia from Cervantes to Pushkin. Of course, the modern critical understanding of realism was still lacking and its practice in fiction remained confused with romanticism with which, historically, it was related. In the chronicling of action, events were an end rather than a means in determining why characters acted or felt as they did. The analysis of feelings by Richardson and Rousseau and their imitators was too dominated by the cult of sensibility to become an effective instrument for probing the multifaceted aspects of human behavior.

In this respect it cannot be said that Pushkin contributed anything startlingly new to the novel. But in other ways—plot-making, situations, narrative methods, characterization, and prose style—he tremendously advanced the whole conception of Russian realism. That is, the life of the landed gentry which he described seemed to readers to be life as it is, free from the bookish stereotyped conventions and artificialities of the efforts of his native predecessors and contemporaries. And this achievement, as well as the finest characters he created, significantly influenced the subsequent development of Russian realism. Just as surely as Pushkin changed the whole context of Russian poetry, he also changed the context of Russian fictional prose. He initiated what is sometimes described in literary history as the "Classical School of Russian Realism." Indeed, if he had lived longer than his brief thirty-eight years, he might well have written the first great Russian realistic novel in prose, as, in *Eugene Onegin*, he did write the first great Russian realistic novel in verse.

II · GOGOL

□◆□◆□◆□◆□◆

Live or Dead Souls

IF THE ESSENCE of Gogol's creative art is a phenomenon of language, as some critics affirm, then a study of form and structure might be the key to an understanding of his total accomplishment. In this case the Aristotelian method of inductive classification of available material might seem to be the desirable approach. The trouble here is not with Aristotle's method, but with the modern classifier's frequent failure to realize that the development of literature has been subject to all the winds of change and that it may be a mistake to attempt to reduce its variables and imponderables to static patterns of illumination, to codify, so to speak, the uncodifiable, to impose order where no natural order can possibly exist.

With equal justification one could assert that the essence of Gogol's creative art is really a phenomenon of his developing personality. While this would have the enthusiastic support of psychoanalytically minded literary critics, it would evoke the wrath of Aristotelian methodologists and also that of formalists who deplore biographism in their emphasis on the certainties of verbal structure and the precise devices of art.

To be sure, the strange aspects of Gogol's realism and the

stranger facts of his life have served to create a climate of irresponsibility in the study of his fiction, a sort of open season in which more critical hunters have been slain than Gogolian prey. Leading Russian sociological critics of the nineteenth century—that is really what Belinsky and his followers Chernyshevsky and Dobrolyubov were—thought they had the matter well in hand in acclaiming Gogol as a novelist of social significance, concerned with exposing and satirizing the evils of Russian life. Though this position assumes that Gogol had in him more of the egalitarian spirit than he actually possessed and an antagonism to established authority quite alien to his conservative views, this interpretation has pretty much dominated the textbook image of Gogol and his works ever since.

At the turn of the century, Symbolist writers and critics, such as Bely, Bryusov, and Rozanov, attempted without much success to destroy this image by insisting on the absurdity of the contention that Gogol was interested in social reform and that *The Government Inspector, Dead Souls,* and *The Overcoat* were faithful transcripts of Russian life in the 1830's and 1840's. Instead they offered ingenious symbolic explanations, by way of throwing a dark light, so to speak, on the meaning of Gogol's art. Chichikov's traveling box was really his wife and Akaky Akakievich's new overcoat his mistress. And Bely saw in the emphasis on roundness of things and people the central symbol of *Dead Souls,* by virtue of which the novel became a whirling wheel with the rotund Chichikov as its hub, a kind of apex of the centripetal forces drawing all the action of the story to itself.

Perhaps somewhat inspired by the dissent of the talented Symbolists to the Belinsky-Chernyshevsky interpretation, a nearly contemporary group of academic pundits set out to explain the complexities of Gogol's art and creative personality in terms of the ambivalence of his nature. Kotlyarevsky saw the struggle as one between Gogol's romantic orientation and his desire to produce realistic fiction, as though these creative instincts were necessarily incompatible. For Ovsyanikovo-Kulikovsky, the abiding contradiction was rooted in the disparity between Gogol's soaring artistic genius and a weak intellect. Then Gippius argued that the ambivalence was an outgrowth of Gogol's obsessive desire to escape from the influence of his rather commonplace Ukrainian social milieu while at the same time being irresistibly attracted to it.

Soviet critics, on the other hand, with their admiration of Belinsky and Chernyshevsky as precursors of socialist realism, have accepted their views on Gogol after considerable Marxian face-lifting of them. In the process, of course, there has been some critical and moral shuffling. Not all of Gogol's writings, and certainly not the events of his life, exemplify critical realism, that invented preview of socialist realism, which prerevolutionary authors accepted into the fold of Soviet respectability are supposed to have practiced. Although it might appear to be about as difficult to find lurking Communist teachings in *Dead Souls* as in Laurence Sterne's *Tristram Shandy*, Soviet critics have a facile way of subjecting great writers of the past to a kind of Marxian rehabilitation. Thus we see the beginning of this transformation in Gogol's case in the early 1929 statement about him in the official *Literary Encyclopedia:* "However, despite the fact that Gogol was subjectively a representative and defender of reactionary interests of the landed nobility, objectively, in his artistic achievements, he served the business of the revolution, arousing among the masses a critical relation to their surrounding reality."

Since then Soviet appreciation of Gogol has been on an ascending scale, displaying more and more a tendency to minimize or even to disregard his ideological failings. Fine editions of his works and some brilliant Soviet scholarship on his life and writings have been published. This favorable interest reached new heights in the 1952 national commemoration of the hundredth anniversary of Gogol's death. At a large meeting in Moscow, one of the principal speakers declared that Gogol, after Pushkin, consolidated the glorious tradition of defending the common man, and that he was "indissolubly linked with all that is best and most progressive in mankind."

Nothing could represent a more striking contrast to this other-directed Soviet criticism of Gogol than the views of the few modern Western critics who have chosen to write about him at length. The aggressive, mocking antirationalism that occasionally enlivens Gogol's writings has a modernistic correspondence that intrigues some of our critics. *The Government Inspector* has been made to anticipate the current drama of the absurd, and novelists devoted to what they regard as the nightmare life of irreality today find in *Dead Souls* a familiar terrain of absorbing symbols and meaningful nonsense.

Some such reaction appears to dominate Vladimir Nabokov's book on Gogol,* a work of charm and originality diluted with more than a spoonful of Gogolian extravagance for which the author seems to have considerable affinity. For Nabokov, Gogol was anything but a humorist, he was completely uninterested in social reforms, and the Russia he wrote about was an entirely invented one, peopled by men and women who had no sensible existence except in their creator's imagination. In short, he asserts, Gogol was not at all concerned with real life. He "never drew portraits—he used looking glasses and as a writer lived in his own looking-glass world."

The Government Inspector, Nabokov declares, is not a comedy at all; it "is poetry in action, and by poetry I mean the mysteries of the irrational as perceived through rational words." This seems so to Nabokov because, as he says, Gogol's genius

* Vladimir Nabokov, *Nikolai Gogol* (Norfolk, Conn.: New Directions Books, 1944).

"deals not in the intrinsic qualities of computable chemical matter . . . but in the mimetic capacities of the physical phenomena produced by almost intangible particles of re-created life."

In the light of that beginning, we are not surprised when Nabokov next remarks that it would be ludicrous to search for an authentic Russian background in *Dead Souls*, just as it would be to form a conception of Denmark from *Hamlet*, which of course ignores the fact that Gogol was writing about existence in Russia during his own lifetime and Shakespeare about life in a foreign country lived long before the Elizabethan period. As for Chichikov, he is, in Nabokov's words, an "unpaid representative of the Devil, a traveling salesman from Hades," and the other characters of the novel are described as partaking of the same irreality. Further, the flavor of Nabokov's fascinating discussion of *The Overcoat* may be conveyed by his characterization of it as "a grotesque and grim nightmare making black holes in the dim pattern of life."

These few generalizations and quotations summarize briefly, and therefore perhaps unfairly, Nabokov's negative reaction to all who regard Gogol as a realist and his writings as a conscious artistic effort to portray more or less faithfully broad aspects of the Russian life of his time. Nabokov's positive analysis of Gogol's art is something else again and it is executed with penetrating insights that are sometimes as confusing as they are illuminating. In general, he believes that when Gogol wrote under the influence of literary traditions and attempted to treat rational ideas in a logical manner, his talent vanished. However, when he was concerned with his own private world of the absurd, which for Nabokov is filled with extraordinary and universal symbolic implications, then Gogol became Russia's greatest literary master.

This brief réchauffé of a century of critical opinions about Gogol, a writer often regarded as the initiator of the great stream of Russian realistic fiction, obviously creates more problems than it solves. It reminds one of the virtue of T. S. Eliot's observation on literary history that the whole body of tradition—the past no less than the present—is constantly being modified by fresh developments. In any event, the puzzling variety of opinion on the nature or even the very existence of realism in Gogol's art suggests the application of an old principle, namely, that an historical perspective is perhaps an essential prerequisite of sound judgment.

2

Gogol's literary career spans about twenty years, from 1830 to 1850 (he died in 1852), although what writing he actually did was probably confined to a much shorter period. In social and political, as well as literary, terms these two decades were of considerable importance in Russian history, for they mark the active beginning of that intellectual ferment which seethed and bubbled throughout the remainder of the nineteenth century and finally boiled over in the revolutionary events of 1917. Though we like to think of Gogol's masterpieces as peculiarly timeless, he himself was very definitely a product of his times and so was the Russia that appears in his writings.

The fear of popular opposition which Nicholas I experienced as a consequence of the Decembrist Revolt at the beginning of his reign was greatly intensified by the revolutionary activity that swept Western Europe between 1830 and 1848. With little cause morbid fear convinced him that revolution was at Russia's threshold, and it was fear rather than political self-aggrandizement that led him to take the military steps which earned him the title of "Gendarme of Europe." Fear again prompted such repressive measures as a perfected system of police spying, uncompromising censorship, and the demand for absolute acceptance of "orthodoxy, autocracy, and nationalism," the phrase that defined his limited conception of Russian patriotism.

Despite these stern measures, the severity of which was little mitigated by the tsar's few moderate reforms, Russia continued to change in the direction of progressive developments inherited from the preceding reign of Alexander I. Trade expanded, and with the growth of industry the country's feudal-monarchical structure began slowly to crumble, though this pattern of cause and effect would still require many years to reach its climax. Under such pressures one may observe the first stages in the alteration of the class structure—the economic decline of the landowning gentry, despite additional privileges conferred upon it by Nicholas I, and the corresponding increase in economic power of the small but growing middle class. Then the mounting restiveness of the peasants, who during the reign of Nicholas I perpetrated 587 outbreaks, many of which had to be put down by the military, underscored once again the fact that serfdom was still Russia's greatest unsolved problem.

One has only to read the memoirs and correspondence of this period to learn that the ugly picture of society in Gogol's works was not exactly drawn from a Russia that he had invented, as the Symbolist critics would have us believe. Civil service, education, and even the Church were overrun by a venal bureaucracy. Politics, in the sense that it functioned in Western Europe, simply did not exist in Russia. Turgenev, looking back at this time, when he was a beginning writer, remarks in his literary reminiscences that no one in the sixties could have any idea of the persecution to which the printed word was subjected under Nicholas I. There was no press, he writes, no public opinion, no personal freedom. To quote him: "You looked around: bribery was everywhere . . . the barracks dominated everything, no courts of justice, rumors that the universities would be closed . . . trips to Europe becoming impossible, no good books could be ordered from abroad, a dark cloud hung over the whole of the so-called department of learning and literature, and, to top it all, denunciations were whispered and spread on all sides."

The young Herzen, wandering through forsaken towns and villages of provincial Russia during his first banishment from Moscow in the late 1830's, provides us with a factual picture of parasitic gentry, rapacious merchants, and ignorant priests, which suggests that the corrupt provincial life described by Gogol in *The Government Inspector* and *Dead Souls* was an understatement of the reality of things. In one letter Herzen writes: "When will the Lord take pity on these people, who are as far from being humans as they are from being birds. It is really terrible to see how trivialities, nonsense, gossip swallow the lives of creatures who under different conditions might actually have been men."

It is necessary to identify this existence as an actuality and not a dream-world in considering Gogol's fiction from the point of view of realism. At about the time Gogol was working on *Dead Souls*, Herzen, in his *Notes of a Young Man*, tells of his reactions to the provincial society of Vyatka: "At first I wrote gaily, then I began to be depressed by my own laughter. I choked from the dust I raised and sought some human conciliation with the bottomless void, the filth, and looked for an escape even in despair." Gogol too, when first contemplating the Russian scene, had begun with laughter and then grew depressed. He said that when he read the beginning of *Dead Souls* to Pushkin, he, too, laughed uproariously, but as Gogol went on Pushkin grew gloomy and exclaimed: "God, how sad is our Russia!"

However, Gogol's Russia was not the Russia of Catherine the Great. Progressive Western European intellectual thought which had fed the catastrophic Decembrist Revolt of 1825 continued its heady influence despite government prohibitions. As always, reactionarism bred its opposite. Young people began to turn to intellectual pursuits of a freethinking nature during the last few years of the 1830's when Gogol's literary career was already under way. Attracted by certain European political and philosophical trends, students in Moscow University formed themselves into two groups. One, nicknamed the "Frenchmen," of whom Herzen was a leader, was devoted to the utopian socialism of Saint-Simon. The other, called the "Germans," to which young Belinsky belonged, was concerned mainly with questions of aesthetics and philosophy. In reality both groups espoused with different emphasis the dominant trend of European culture at that time—romanticism.

The secret police, which soon dispersed the "Frenchmen," somehow discounted the radical possibilities of German philosophy. "In that period," Belinsky recalls, "we felt through, thought through, and lived through the entire intellectual life of Europe, echoes of which were reaching us across the Baltic." Starting with the aesthetics of Schelling, the "German" group next turned to the ethics of Fichte, coquetted with the categorical imperatives of Kant, and finally came to a resting point in the revolutionary dialectics of Hegel, which, in the early forties, they combined with the revolutionary materialism of Feuerbach.

On the basis of this fused formulation of Germanic thought, the two foremost Russian intellectual leaders of the time, the philosopher and creative writer Herzen, then an exile abroad, and the literary critic Belinsky, joined forces in a program aimed at molding social consciousness by revealing objective reality which in belles lettres meant a faithful depiction of the harsh abuses of the regime of Nicholas I, especially serfdom, and their evil influence on national life. For good or ill, social significance had at last become a primary touchstone of Russian literature, which Belinsky and later thinkers and critics regarded as the center of all intellectual activity of consequence. In fact, creative literature had become the only form of public opinion in a police state, as well as a force capable of attracting, from all levels of society, like-minded and educated people who constituted a distinct and easily recognizable class which was eventually designated as "the intelligentsia." And it was Gogol, with his extraordinary grasp of reality, whom Belinsky hailed as the first writer in Russian literature to offer a devastating indictment of the evils of official bureaucracy and the serf-owning gentry.

3

To the impressionistic critic it may seem that Gogol is telling a pack of lies in his creative writing and—to paraphrase an aphorism of D. H. Lawrence, used in another connection—out of this pattern of lies his art weaves the truth. This would be to mistake for lies what was a conscious device of exaggeration, humorous or otherwise, which Gogol was as fond of as either Balzac or Dickens. Like both these near-contemporaries, Gogol may properly be described as a romantic realist whose liking for fantasy never allowed him to forget the fundamental connection between the art of the novel and the real life of society.

Because of the literary time-lag in Russia, Gogol grew up at the height of the romantic movement when his favorite reading was the early poetry of Pushkin and the historical novels of Walter Scott and his imitators. And a rich combination of romantic absurdity and realistic fun-making largely accounts for the immediate popularity of his first attempts at fiction, two volumes of Ukrainian tales, *Evenings on a Farm Near Dikanka* (1831-32). Although the humor of a precocious youth of twenty-two and the romantic activities of spooks and devils drawn mostly from Ukrainian folklore do not strike us today as either very funny or scary, in 1831 they introduced a new note into Russian literature. Two of these stories, however, contain a foretaste of the future Gogol—*The Terrible Vengeance*, a purely Gothic tale of incest devoid of humor and involving the horrible punishment of the wronged girl's father, and the sardonically amusing and erotically suggestive *Ivan Fyodorovich Shponka and His Aunt*, in which the undersexed nephew is terrified by his aunt's efforts to push him into marriage. The attractiveness of this whole collection rests primarily on the gay, breathless liveliness of the stories which is as much a quality of their varied style as of their content.

Pushkin hailed Gogol's first effort: "Here is fun for you, authentic fun of the frankest sort with nothing maudlin or prim about it. And what of the poetry and delicacy of sentiment in certain passages. All this is so unusual in our literature. . . ." Only ten years older, Pushkin took the adoring Gogol under his literary wing, although no two authors could have differed more in their approach to art. Perhaps this fact, as well as Gogol's discordant personality, prevented them from ever becoming intimate friends. However, during their four years of direct contact (1832-36), Pushkin, always generous to younger writers, acted as a kind of literary catalyst, for it appears that all of Gogol's major works were conceived during this period and some of them written. Gogol turned to Pushkin for subjects and evidence indicates that the poet supplied him with the themes of *The Government Inspector* and *Dead Souls*. "One has got to be more careful of this Ukrainian," Pushkin jokingly remarked to a friend, "for he'll plunder me and I'll be unable to cry out in protest!" So significant was the relationship in Gogol's eyes, that he declared, shortly after Pushkin's death in a duel in 1837: "My life, my greatest happiness died with him. . . . When I created I saw before me only Pushkin. Everything good in me I owe to him." Indeed, an essential stabilizing influence in Gogol's delicately balanced emotional nature vanished after Pushkin died.

When the youthful Gogol came up to Petersburg from the

Ukraine, he was neither well educated nor well read, and one of Pushkin's services was to provide him with a list of belles lettres, especially by foreign authors. The impression seems to exist in some quarters that Gogol's creative faculties were singularly uncontaminated by exposure to the writings of his contemporaries and predecessors. It is no disservice to his unquestioned originality to point out that he read, apart from many native Ukrainian and Russian authors, the works of French, German, and English writers. Scholars have demonstrated the influence on Gogol's writings of Homer's *Iliad* and of certain of the works of Cervantes, Molière, Le Sage, Sterne, Scott, Maturin, and the German romanticists, such as E. T. A. Hoffmann and Tieck.

For example, the influence of Homer and Scott is incongruously combined in *Taras Bulba*, Gogol's historical romance on the sixteenth-century Cossack Ukraine which appeared in his next collection of tales, *Mirgorod*, in 1835. History temporarily fascinated Gogol. The year before, through the efforts of a well-placed friend, he had obtained an adjutant professorship of history at the University of St. Petersburg. At this time he was still undecided on literature as a career, and with his insatiable ambition he now set out to storm the academic world with vast plans for writing a universal history and geography in two to three volumes, a history of the Ukraine in eight or nine volumes, and for good measure he threw in a project for a history of the Middle Ages.

Gogol began his academic career with a brilliant lecture in which the absence of factual information was compensated by glittering historical generalizations. But he soon ran out of them and had nothing to offer in their place. This creative artist as an academician suffered the fate of academicians who think they are creative artists. At the end of the first term Gogol pronounced an epitaph to his teaching career: "Ignorant I mounted my professor's chair and ignorant I descended."

The only completed work to emerge from all his projects on history was the novel *Taras Bulba*. Although descriptions of the glorious battle scenes between Poles and Cossacks echo the *Iliad*, all this is pure heroic romance, an historical period and events re-created by some process of divination rather than by careful historical reconstruction in the manner of Scott. Scenes tumble over one another in exuberant abandon, and the swift pace of the heroic parts is slowed down only by an occasional concentration on humorous incidents and a secondary love affair between the son of the old Cossack leader Taras and a beautiful Polish girl. Gogol handles this with all the unreality of Scott's treatment of love and in addition enervates the theme by his own peculiarly sexless idealization of the tender passion. In an indefinable way the sustained rhetoric of the style propels the narrative into life at the sacrifice of nearly every illusion of reality.

Gogol returns to realism in two other tales of the *Mirgorod* collection: *Old-World Landowners* and *The Story of How Ivan Ivanovich Quarreled with Ivan Nikiforovich*. But it is a particular phase of realism—Gogol has more than one—in which he engages life imaginatively to the end of intensifying it. The device he uses in the first story is to magnify the gluttony of the old pair by ironically rhapsodizing over it, and in the second he ironically exaggerates the friendship of the two Ivans in order to contrast it with the trifling incident that brings it to an end in hopeless litigation. Beneath the two humorous but different situations Gogol provides fleeting glimpses of a common way of life which, in its destructive absurdity, creates such situations.

Another phase of Gogolian realism turns up in the famous story *The Nevsky Prospect*, which appeared in *Arabesques*, a second collection of tales in 1835. Although there has been some critical mystification about its communication, at least the surface intention of the story is made quite clear at the end where Gogol observes that in a world of contrasting experiences fate unaccountably plays tricks on us, and in this sense he wonders whether we ever attain that for which our powers are specially suited. To illustrate this surmise he narrates the contrasting adventures, arising out of similar circumstances, of two young friends, a gay army officer, Pirogov, and a sensitive painter, Piskaryov. On an evening stroll together along Petersburg's Nevsky Prospect, the officer pursues a pretty blonde and the artist a beautiful statuesque brunette. Comedy and tragedy, realism and romance characterize their subsequent experiences. Though the dumb blonde fails to comprehend the purpose of Pirogov's advances, her husband comprehends it only too well and takes an amusing revenge on this officer who presumes to interfere in his married life. The sensitive artist timidly follows the lovely brunette and his idealizing nature has already invested her in an atmosphere of mystery and hallowed enchantment. But the pursuit ends in a brothel where she plies her trade. Crushed by this discovery, he returns home, falls asleep, and sees her in his dreams, the perfect fulfillment of his ideal woman. Eventually, he has recourse to drugs in order that he may live in this unreal world with his charming infatuator. In the end he is found a suicide in his dingy room, apparently preferring death to the intolerable reality of an unattainable ideal.

After awakening from one of his exotic dreams, Piskaryov exclaims: "My God! what is our life! An everlasting disharmony between dream and reality!" Indeed, disharmony was the fulcrum of reality on which Gogol's vision of life constantly teetered—the clash of appearance and substance, the real and the unreal, life as it is and life as it should be.

A limiting factor in this story, as in much of what Gogol wrote, is a kind of Poe-like "purity complex" that inhibits his treatment of the more intimate relation between men and women. It is a mistake, however, to translate this failing into an incapacity to cope artistically with feminine characterizations, for when he confines himself to their outward appearance and surface relations he is often brilliant. But love between the sexes is a sterile plant for him, reflecting his own physical sterility, and perhaps he found a sensuous compensation in idealizing feminine purity which sometimes led him into banal bombast in defense of its virtues. Thus the brothel in *The Nevsky Prospect* becomes one of "those dens in which man sacriligiously tramples and derides all that is pure and holy, all that makes life fair, where women, the beauty of the world, the crown of creation. . . ." Native and foreign critics have employed concepts drawn from Freudian psychoanalytic theory to solve the riddle of Gogol's sexual abnormality and demonstrate its influence on his writings. It would be captious to deny the relevance of this approach, even when applied to literary figures long since dead, but its success is seriously impaired by the lack of complete personal case histories, which the modern clinical psychoanalysts find so vital in dealing with living subjects.

Other stories in *Arabesques* which have their setting, like *The Nevsky Prospect*, in Petersburg extend the range of Gogol's commingling sheer fantasy with realistic effects and at the same time reveal an intensification and also a subtilizing of his rich vein of humor. In his *An Author's Confession*, Gogol observes that at about this point in his career he would imagine all sorts of amusing situations and funny characters in an effort to counteract fits of depression. Perhaps one should see no more than this kind of nonsense in *The Nose*, in which the government official Kovalyov wakes up one morning to find that his nose is missing. It turns up in a loaf of bread baked by the wife of Kovalyov's drunken barber—the only concession to realism in the tale—and next appears in a fine uniform wandering about the streets in a posture of defiance to the real owner. Whether Gogol's unusually long nose or Laurence Sterne's unusually long treatise on noses prompted this escape from depression into the comfort of the absurd, it is hard to say. To those who see in this story a castration fantasy with Freudian overtones of phallic symbolism, Tristram Shandy's premonitory caution to his readers may be offered: "I declare, by that word I mean Nose, and nothing more, or less."

This good-natured fun-making continues in *The Memoirs of a Madman*, with its talking dogs who also write letters to each other. But it ends on a poignantly realistic note when the poor copying clerk, frustrated in love, goes mad, imagining himself the King of Spain but at the same time praying to his mother to save him from the beatings and tormenting of his keepers in the insane asylum.

The Portrait, a Petersburg story of the supernatural, forces comparison with Pushkin's *The Queen of Spades* which may have inspired it, although Maturin's *Melmoth the Wanderer*, translated into Russian, may also have suggested the central theme of a portrait that comes to life. Like Herman in Pushkin's story, Gogol's artist is obsessed by ambition and acquisitiveness, and this passionate desire for wealth brings about the downfall of both through the medium of a supernatural agency. In nearly every respect, however, the two narrative methods differ. Pushkin's crisp, restrained style and carefully constructed realistic background compel belief in a supernatural experience. Gogol, on the other hand, fails to create an illusion of reality, even in the extensively revised 1842 version of this story, for his realistic details are swamped by rhetorical outpourings of romantic feeling.

The most celebrated of the Petersburg tales, *The Overcoat*, published in 1842 but no doubt drafted much earlier, brings to a focus all the lines of Gogol's amazing technique in the creation of a work that Tolstoy would have placed in his category of universal art, for the story of the poor copying clerk Akaky Akakievich appeals equally to the young and the old and to every layer of society. Here are realism and fantasy, humor and pathos, laughter and tears exquisitely proportioned in a symphony of fiction the perfect artistic unity of which is perhaps flawed, according to some tastes, only by the introduction of the supernatural at the end where Akaky's ghost seeks the stolen overcoat.

It is almost irrelevant to talk about realism in the ordinary sense in this famous tale, in which Gogol appears to be concerned with a primal relation of humanity and ultimate reality such that when once confronted reality is recognized for what it is. In man's struggle with life's adversities we all sympathize with the underdog's striving to obtain a moiety of happiness as he sees it. Many critics, however, have regarded *The Overcoat* as a deliberate realistic exposure of social inequities of the reign of Nicholas I and a satiric attack on the "circumlocution offices" of government bureaucracy. It is true that passages can be singled out which seem to amount to special pleading on behalf of the insulted and injured little people, such as the reflection of the new office worker who associates himself with others in tormenting Akaky Akakievich: "Long afterwards, at moments of greatest gaiety, the figure of the meek little clerk, with a bald patch on his head, rose before him with his pitiful words: 'Let me alone! Why do you insult me?' And in those heart-rending words he heard others: 'I am your brother.' And the unhappy young man hid his face in his hands, and many times afterwards in his life he shuddered, realizing how much inhumanity there is in man, how much vicious brutality lies hidden under refined, cultural politeness, and, my God! even in a man whom the world accepts as a gentleman and a man of honor. . . ."* This statement might almost stand as the manifesto of the "philanthropic fic-

---

* *The Overcoat and Other Stories.* By Nikolay Gogol, translated by Constance Garnett (New York: Knopf, 1923), pp. 14-15.

tion" that sprang up in Russia after Gogol's immensely popular story.

It would be idle to deny the subjective nature of this and similar passages, such as the elegiac valediction after the death of Akaky, or the satiric fun that Gogol has at the expense of government bureaucracy. These elements, however, are plainly subordinated to the artistic imperatives of the story; they play a functional part in setting the narrative tone and in developing the personality of Akaky Akakievich. That is, Gogol was not crusading for social reform in *The Overcoat*. He was not an artistic ideologue. In this tale the foibles and abuses of society were part of the pattern of reality which provided the material of his art. If there was any subjective emphasis, it was moral and not social. Later this concern with morality, especially in the Christian sense, loomed much larger in his vision of life and in his art.

4

However, it was *The Government Inspector*, written in 1835, produced the next year, and often regarded as Russia's greatest play, that initially won for Gogol the reputation as a realist of genius concerned primarily with exposing and satirizing social evils. No such portentous purpose presided over the play's origin. He wrote Pushkin: "Do me a kindness; give me some subject or other. . . . For God's sake, my mind and belly are famished." Pushkin obliged with the anecdote of a traveler who is mistaken in a small town for a government inspector, an experience which he had had himself in his travels.

The result was a comedy which, along with *Dead Souls*, drew from Gogol's contemporary Belinsky the emphatic declaration that these works "deal exclusively with the world of Russian life," and that Gogol had "no rivals in the art of portraying it in all its truth." Moreover, Belinsky saw in Gogol the most national of Russian writers, the first to be so regarded abroad in translation, and the first author in Russian literature who depicted ordinary people without idealizing them, guided—the critic said—by a belief in art as "the representation of reality in all its fidelity."

Elsewhere Belinsky qualified these opinions, asserting that Pushkin had anticipated Gogol as a national writer and also in the realistic depiction of Russian society. The important fact is that not only Belinsky, but other contemporary or near-contemporary figures, including both Turgenev and Dostoevsky, agree that Gogol's major works faithfully portray the social existence and people which these individuals knew from their own experience. Such unanimity of judgment by keen observers of Gogol's own day must stand as a refutation to later critics who refuse to see in *The Government Inspector* and *Dead Souls* an authentic picture of the Russia of that time and, in the characters, men and women drawn from real life. Additional support for this view may also be obtained, as previously indicated, from accounts of life in contemporary letters and memoirs.

On the other hand, Belinsky and his followers in criticism, especially Chernyshevsky in his study of the Gogol period in Russian literature, were wrong in asserting that Gogol deliberately set out to expose the harsh realities of the reign of Nicholas I, although they were correct in believing that his realistic writings helped to initiate a literary movement in fiction devoted to revealing and criticizing social and political abuses. Gogol was an artist of things rather than of ideas. When he concerned himself primarily with intellectual matters, as in his letters and in the volume *Selected Passages from a Correspondence with Friends,* he tended to think more feebly than justly. Revolution would have horrified him for, like Karamzin in the preceding age, he believed that the political and social order of Russia was ordained by God. A convinced proponent of serfdom, he was opposed to education for peasants who, he declared, should not even know of the existence of any book except the Bible.

"Do not chafe at the looking glass if your mug is awry" is the Russian proverb that Gogol set down as an epigraph to *The Government Inspector*. Nothing could more plainly indicate Gogol's intention in the play or the type of character he held the mirror up to. In the opening of the fragmentary second part of *Dead Souls* Gogol writes: "Why should we always describe poverty, wretchedness, and imperfections and unearth characters from wild and remote corners of our country? But what is to be done if such is the author's bent. . . ." He was not interested in the ordinary, the average, or in saints uncorrupted, but in rogues who, he apparently believed, were all too numerous in Russian life. And he wanted enough of them to fill a comedy in five acts which—he told Pushkin in the letter already quoted— would be "funnier than hell." And so it is. There is not a sympathetic character in the play; they are all addicted to the roguery of Russian life.

Except for the awkward asides, one of the conventions of eighteenth-century satiric comedy that influenced Gogol, *The Government Inspector* is a gem of pure art in its perfect fusion of form, content, and treatment. Its aim is a persuasive picture of living life and not a pot of social message. Nicholas I, who overrode the censor's rejection of the play, is reported to have remarked after the first performance: "Everybody got his due, I most of all." Unlike many of the critics, he was wise enough to realize that Gogol's comedy was not an attack on his government, but a rollicking exposé of abuses in the body politic which any ruler would want to see eliminated.

In all the boisterous action of the play there is hardly any point in querying whether we have a fantastic product of the imagination or something truly real. It is like so much dough, kneaded and pummeled by Gogol, charged with copious portions of his yeasty brand of realism, and emerging from the creative oven in an odd-sized baked shape but always recognizable as a large loaf of good Russian black bread, the staff of life. One likes to think that he approached his caricatured men and women very much as Dickens did those zany creations in *Pickwick*, that is, in a spirit of pure fun. But in Gogol's case there is nearly always an element of human negativeness about the people who inhabit his artistic world. From the lowliest citizen to the highest official in this little town everybody seems to be swindling everybody else. Bribery has become institutionalized. It is an extravaganza in civic waywardness. With irony which in the circumstances borders on the morbid, that arch pair of dissemblers, the Mayor and Khlestakov, solemnly agree that they don't like two-faced people, which is of a piece with the darkly humorous slip of the Trustee of Social Welfare Institutions who explains that in his hospital the patients "all get well like flies." And the same individual, when arranging for the collective bribery by the town officials of Khlestakov, who is mistaken for a government inspector, insists that it be done properly, the way it is "done in a well-run society." In the play's matchless final scene the dreadful truth of this society's complete corruption is driven home by the Mayor, the greatest scoundrel of the lot. As each gulling official in turn laughs at the exposure of his colleagues in the letter of Khlestakov, who had gulled them all, the Mayor furiously shouts: "What are you laughing for? You're laughing at yourselves!" *The Government Inspector*, which makes sport of evil, symbolically suggests what Gogol directly expressed in the well-known words at the end of his early humorous tale about the quarrel of the two Ivans: "It is gloomy in this world, gentlemen."

In general, Gogol's realistic method failed to stress the development of self-knowledge in his characters, even when he refrained from turning them into caricatures. They explode into life, as it were, by virtue of the extraordinary force of his imaginative creativeness, in which salient features are magnified to the point where reality is on the edge of but never quite tumbles over into unconvincingness. Whenever the action skirts irreality, Gogol's superb dialogue, alive with the naturalness of living speech, saves the situation. Nearly all the characters in *The Government Inspector* are of this type, and especially the Mayor and the central figure Khlestakov, one of the very great characters in Russian literature.

5

This much attention to a play in a study of fiction seemed necessary, not only for the light it throws on Gogol's developing realism, but also because *Dead Souls* is a kind of extension of *The Government Inspector* with the difference that the author's increased maturity over the seven years he took to write it and his changing outlook clothed the world of the novel in darker hues in which evil is tempered more by judgment than by comedy. However, there is no lack of the comic in *Dead Souls*, and Gogol also projects some of his recently learned dramatic technique into the novel: he structures his great scenes the way a playwright might, and some of his most amusing characters are really "character parts" in the theatrical sense.

Gogol appears to have begun *Dead Souls* in the autumn of 1835, that is, preceding the performance of *The Government Inspector*. But in June 1836, after the production of his play, he went abroad and remained there during nearly the whole period of the writing of *Dead Souls*. He returned to Russia in 1841 to see his novel through the press. It was published the next year.

Dead Souls may be approached on any one of several levels

of conscious or unconscious artistic intention. But a careful reading of both the first part and the fragment of the second leaves little excuse for regarding the whole as a nonrealistic symbolic work, a kind of vast metaphor of the evils of Russian life, articulated in language symbols and images that are personifications of universal sin. That is, to seek for the novel's ultimate design in what Henry James called the author's "deep well of unconscious cerebration" seems quite unnecessary.

The derivation of *Dead Souls* from the picaresque tradition in the works of such writers as Le Sage and Bulgarin requires no substantiation, however much Gogol's story of a rogue and his travels transcends *Gil Blas* and *Ivan Vyzhigin* in moral conception, imaginative inventiveness, and artistic treatment. In these respects *Dead Souls* bears comparison with *Don Quixote*, although the hero Chichikov has his wits about him and pursues a plausible if illegal objective in a real world, whereas the mad Don is in quest of a defunct ideal in a romanticized world. Cervantes deals with the lost illusion of knight errantry by way of ridiculing the foibles of the present. Gogol is concerned with the greed that corrupts man, a human condition which serves as a vantage point from which to satirize the failings of his countrymen.

If the hero of Balzac's *Human Comedy* is the franc, that of *Dead Souls* is the rouble. Though Gogol, unlike Balzac, does not attempt to create a philosophy of accumulation, he is determined, in a land where bribery is endemic, to exemplify the moral wisdom of the Biblical injunction that the love of money is the root of all evil. It was the main theme of *The Portrait;* its ramifications touched nearly every character of *The Government Inspector;* in *Dead Souls* it is a persistent offstage voice that humorously pokes fun at the evil of acquisitiveness, and in the fragmentary second part it rings out stridently in moral homilies. Failure to recognize the wisdom of the precept is

Chichikov's chief weakness. "It would be more just," Gogol writes in the novel, "to call him simply a proprietary and acquisitive man. Acquisitiveness is the sin behind everything. . . ."

The wonderful opening of *Dead Souls* would have lost much in artistic effectiveness if Gogol had substituted for it the last chapter which is the natural chronological beginning of the novel, for it is there that we learn of Chichikov's early years and initial waywardness so necessary for an understanding of his complete personality. And here also, in an amusing rejection of the virtuous romanticized heroes of previous Russian fiction, Gogol declares that "the time has come at last to put the rogue in harness," that is, to move closer to the reality of things as Gogol saw them. For the young unloved Chichikov life was sour and uncomfortable under the stern guidance of a pinched, narrow-minded father of obscure gentry origin who mingled frequent punishment with pious exhortation. The boy had no friends or playmates, and his father's parting advice, on sending him off to school for the first time, was not to gad about, be subservient to teachers and superiors, and guard the few kopecks he gave him because—he said—"with money you can do anything in the world," advice which the son never forgot.

To overlook this and similar evidence is to ignore the degree to which the faulted nature and insensate ambition of the mature Chichikov were formed by the unhappy circumstances of his childhood. Certainly Gogol himself stresses the point, for he returns to it in a passage of major emphasis in the incomplete last section of the fragmentary second part, incidentally an indication of planned continuity in the characterization which is all too frequently ignored. There, when disaster finally overtakes Chichikov because of inability to resist temptation, Gogol represents him as reflecting on the reasons behind this lost opportunity: "Feelings which had hitherto been unknown, unfamiliar, and inexplicable welled up within him, something belonging to the grim, dead precepts of his early childhood with its lonely joylessness—the desert-like emptiness of his home life, his isolation in the family, and those first impressions of poverty and misery...."

Though Chichikov is a model worker in the positions he assumed in government service after his schooling and exercised every form of self-denial in an effort to save, he soon falls into the peculation and bribe-taking generally practiced by civil servants. One is reminded of the eager advice which Gogol's fatuous mother wrote him when as a young man he entered the civil service in St. Petersburg, namely, that since everybody was doing it he should try to supplement his income by taking bribes! But Chichikov plays this game with a charm, dignity, and discrimination beyond the abilities of his bungling competitors in the nice art of getting ahead by illegal means. Gogol is perhaps being more realistic than ironic in suggesting that his hero simply goes along with the generally accepted order of things in endeavoring to satisfy his ambition. But what is this ambition? To possess what his father was unable to bequeath to him—an income-bearing landed property, the status symbol of the gentry. He yearns after a well-equipped house, a carriage, good food, and ultimately a wife and children. Chichikov reasons that others had risen from nothing, so why shouldn't he? However, Gogol stresses that Chichikov, despite his ambition, does not love money for its own sake and is not at the mercy of meanness or avarice. He is neither harsh nor callous, writes Gogol, nor devoid of pity or compassion.

When Chichikov is detected in shady dealings, he uses all his wiles and bribery to escape prison, although on each such occasion he is compelled to slip back to the bottom again in his efforts to climb the civil-service greased pole of success. In a bureaucracy where dishonesty is the rule rather than the exception, it is little wonder that he eventually begins to think of himself as a victim of circumstances beyond his control. As he whimsically puts it, he suffers "in the cause of justice." And Gogol, satirizing these warped moral values of Russian society, has his hero comically protest, after repeated exposures of his chicanery: "Why was I picked out? . . . they are all stuffing their pockets. I've made no one unhappy, I didn't rob a widow or turn anyone into the streets. . . . If I had not profited, others would have done so. Why then are the others flourishing and why must I perish like a crushed worm?"

It is at this low point in his fortunes that Chichikov takes up the rather dubious calling of a legal agent. One of his first jobs is to arrange the mortgage of serfs of a bankrupt estate. After performing what Gogol describes as the necessary "oiling" of the officials concerned, Chichikov honestly admits to one of the bribed functionaries that half the serfs of the mortgage list are dead, and the official jovially wonders why he worries about so trifling a matter. This comment suggests to Chichikov the idea which Pushkin is reported to have conveyed to Gogol as the basic plot line of the novel. Chichikov plans to visit various estate owners and obtain from them, by regular legal transfer, their dead serfs or souls, as they were called. He is convinced that the owners will be glad to part with them for nothing or for a mere token fee, for they have to pay a head tax on every registered serf until the next census catches up with the dead ones. Chichikov gleefully estimates that he can easily obtain a thousand dead souls, mortgage them at two hundred roubles each as living serfs, and with this capital of two hundred thousand roubles realize his dream of buying an estate, marrying, and living comfortably with his future wife and children in what the old-fashioned novelists called connubial felicity.

This account of Chichikov's early career in the last chapter of *Dead Souls* explains much about the hero's behavior and thoughts throughout the whole course of the novel and it also adds a good deal to the unity and direction of the characterization. In the last pages of this chapter, Gogol, by way of insisting upon the realism of the portrayal, begins by twitting the patriotic reader for resenting the scalawag of a hero as representative of the Russian people. But the author, Gogol insists, must speak the truth and nothing but the truth, because readers are afraid of looking too profoundly into anything. What disturbs him, however, is the type of reader who will actually be pleased with his hero. In moments of communion with himself, writes Gogol, this reader will ponder the weighty question in the depths of his soul: " 'Is there not also something of Chichikov in me?' he will ask. Of course there is! Yet if any acquaintance of his, neither too exalted nor too low, should pass by at that moment, he would take him by the arm and, barely restraining a guffaw, would say to him: 'Look, look, there goes Chichikov, Chichikov has arrived!' And then, just like a child, forgetting the respect due to rank and years, he will run after him, teasing and shouting: 'Chichikov! Chichikov! Chichikov!' "

In any event, shortly after he conceived his get-rich-quick scheme, this middle-aged gentleman, dressed in immaculate but conservative attire, his total savings locked up in a traveling box, took to the road in a chaise, a troika, such as a well-appointed bachelor favors, accompanied by his smelly valet Petrushka and his irresponsible coachman Selifan, and eventually arrived at the town of N., his initial base of operations in the mysterious business of buying up dead souls.

6

The provincial town of N. is larger than the one in *The Government Inspector*, but its various officials are every bit as corrupt, only they play the national game of bribery with much more sophistication. And Chichikov, who has nothing in his makeup of the bravado, crudity, and outrageous lying of Khlestakov, easily wins his way into the affections of the town fathers and their wives with his genteel manners, oily flattery, and the appearance and appointments of a Petersburg gentleman.

Towns for Gogol are centers of concentrated human folly and he brings them to life with a creative gusto that is positively Rabelaisian. Cobblestone streets, traffic, fences, houses, hotels, office buildings, and meetings, dinners, card games, balls, and a variety of typical townsfolk and their conversation are described in a bewildering combination of reality and exaggeration. It has been asserted that the world of *Dead Souls* is sheer invention, that Gogol, living abroad so long, was largely ignorant of provincial Russian towns and country estates. Nothing could be more erroneous. Only when art and nature join forces, he declares in one place in the novel, does description achieve the impossible. Gogol possessed what Coleridge called the "ebullience of the creative faculty" which in the art of description enables him to realize the Aristotelian doctrine of the impossible rendered probable or not improbable. If existence in the town of N. strikes one at times as a bit bizarre, it is owing to Gogol's familiar device of intermingling the strictest realism of detail with the unreal. His notebook, which is crammed with precise data about the appearance, the social life and official administration, and the typical inhabitants of provincial towns, testifies to his zeal for the correctness of such details.

In the cause of objective realism, another stricture may be made against those who believe that Gogol's satire is a subjective "exteriorization of the fauna of his own mind," a kind of unconscious catharsis or purgation of his real or imaginary defects. On the other hand, it is also unlikely, as the sociological critics claimed, that *Dead Souls* was designed as a broad attack on the institution of serfdom. Although the novel's preoccupation with the unsavory business of buying and selling human beings, even dead ones, no doubt suggested this conclusion, it is obvious that Gogol regarded the theme simply as a convenient device for writing the kind of picaresque novel he had in mind. After all, he plainly accepted the institution of serfdom as a fact of Russian life.

What he does satirize is the real world of the landed gentry, the bungling, inefficient, and impractical way in which they organize their existence and that of the peasants on their estates, and the corruption, snobbery, extravagance, and false posturing they fall into when assuming office in town or city government. There is nothing subjective or introspective about such satire, which is often accompanied by comic, caricaturing touches to heighten the element of ridicule. For example, when the "well-born agreeable lady" of the town of N. calls on her friend, the "agreeable lady in all respects," for a gossip session on Chichikov, we have a lengthy delightful scene entirely satiric in intent. The opening lines illustrate Gogol's method: "As soon as the lady agreeable in all respects learned of the arrival of the agreeable lady, she at once ran into the hall. The ladies clutched each other by the hands, exchanged kisses, and cried out as do two girls meeting not too long after graduation from boarding school, but before their mothers have had time to explain to them that the father of one is poorer and of lower rank than that of the other. Their kisses had a resounding smack to them and made the dogs bark, and for this they were spanked with a handkerchief. . . ."

The part of the novel devoted to Chichikov's visits to the five estate owners outside the town of N. to purchase their dead souls is the core of the work and perhaps its finest contribution to literature. Here Gogol's method of characterization deepens and even alters to some extent. Like Sterne, from whom he may have learned the device, Gogol is very fond of digressions. They may be chatty monologues of instruction to readers in the manner of Thackeray, or vivid rhetorically poetic passages on the joys of the road, or the beauties of the Russian language, or that famous concluding digression of the novel where Chichikov's galloping troika, its bells filling the air with their wondrous pealing, symbolizes the headlong progress of Russia.

In one such digression in the seventh chapter, Gogol explains to his readers that there are two types of authors. One type becomes celebrated by drawing exceptional characters embodying the highest values of humanity. Such characters, declares Gogol, cloud men's eyes with the smoke of illusion and obscure the sadness of life by showing man as a thing of beauty. The other type, among whom Gogol includes himself, is the author who dares to concentrate on everyday characters and present them roundly and clearly for the benefit of all. Contemporary judgment, Gogol insists, does not recognize that great spiritual depth is required to illuminate a picture drawn from depressed life and to make of it "a pearl of creation." And he concludes that he is destined to wander together with such heroes and to observe the whole vast movement of life—"to observe it through laughter which can be shared by all and through tears which are unknown and unseen."

No one would deny that Gogol has elevated these five landowners to pearls of creation by the sheer force of his art. Like certain characters in *Pickwick*, they are not types but "humors" in the Ben Jonsonian sense—the slothful, sentimental, saccharine Manilov, living in a fool's paradise completely unrelated to reality; the congenital liar Nozdryov whose gross fictions are psychological manifestations of his need to quarrel and bully; that epitome of stolid self-sufficiency, the huge bear-like Sobakevich, who regards every endeavor as a challenge to self-aggrandizement; the greedy old widowed Korobochka in her tiny pumpkin-like coach who must first find out the nonexistent going rate on dead serfs before she will sell hers; and finally the miser Plyushkin, a monster of avarice, who owns a thousand serfs yet continues to cram his bulging storehouses with all the abortion of life and uses a yellowed toothbrush in the family since before the time of Napoleon.

In another sense one may regard these pearls of creation as allegorical personifications of various failings of the landed gentry as Gogol sees them. Though caricature is pushed to the extreme in these portrayals, they are not puppets; a mimetic degree of actuality is always present. In one of his asides in *The Overcoat*, Gogol protests that "there is no creeping into a man's soul and finding out what he thinks," an effort that was to become a major concern of Dostoevsky in characterization. But with minor exceptions it is true that Gogol's realism in the projection of characters is devoid of psychological analysis of thought and feeling.

To transform everyday characters into pearls of creation and still not produce unbelievable emblematic creatures, Gogol relies heavily on massive realistic details. His inspiration is mainly the inspiration of detail, and no Russian author ever employed it as abundantly and as effectively as Gogol, unless it be Tolstoy who, before he renounced the technique, always used much more restraint than Gogol in the practice of it. In the thirty pages of the chapter on Plyushkin, more than half of it is devoted to meticulous description of the approach to the estate, then to its immediate surroundings and the village, the external appearance of the manor house, its interior, and finally a minute detailing of the looks, dress, and habits of the master. Much of this effort is designed to build up a unified picture of the total correspondence between the "humor" of the character in question and his appearance, behavior, and all his surroundings.

As indicated, realistic descriptive touches are frequently enlivened by comic exaggeration. Chichikov's heart "flutters like a quail in a cage" after his quarrel with Nozdryov. Sobakevich's face has "a tempered and glowing look such as is to be seen on a copper coin," and in keeping with the hugeness of everything in this huge man's ménage, the turkey served up for dinner is "as big as a calf." The wooden planks on the road to Plyushkin's home "rise and fall like piano keys" when Chichikov walks over them. And in the copying office in the town hall, Gogol observes that there is "a great deal of pen-scratching and the noise of it is like the passage of carts loaded with brushwood through a forest several feet deep in withered leaves."

A favorite technique is to pyramid a simple description into digressive proportions which in a curious way contributes to the atmosphere of a given scene. To illustrate this practice by a very short sample—when Chichikov drives up to Sobakevich's porch he notices two faces at the window: "one was a woman's, long and narrow as a cucumber, crowned with a bonnet; the other a man's, broad and round as a Moldavian pumpkin, called gourds, from which Russians make balalaikas—light two-stringed balalaikas, the pride and amusement of some smart twenty-year-old lad, saucy-eyed and jaunty, winking and whistling at the white-breasted and white-throated maidens who gather around to listen to his soft strumming."

Not a little of the humor of *Dead Souls* is of the picaresque variety, springing from the daily give and take of Chichikov and his two servants who were part of the meager inheritance from his niggardly father. Their relations represent the closest that Chichikov ever comes to dealing with live peasants, and in them he reveals himself as a typical serf-owner. Though Petrushka and Selifan are of the breed of Sancho Panza, their behavior is that of real Russian peasants and Gogol portrays it with a realism in which the humor is little exaggerated. Like most peasant coachmen, Selifan has the habit of singing and talking to his horses, the lazy dapple-grey on the right that never pulls its weight, the bay in the center, and the fallow-bay on the left, nicknamed Assessor because it had been bought from one. When Selifan is tipsy, as is the case on the return trip from his master's visit to Manilov's, his horse-talk soars to heights of purple eloquence and his driving to recklessness that ends with an overturned chaise and Chichikov in the mud.

" 'Cunning are you, cunning! There, I'll out-cunning you!' said Selifan as he stood up and whipped the lazybones. 'Learn to work, you German pants-maker! The bay's a respectable horse, he does his duty. I'd willingly give him an extra of oats because he's a respectable horse, and the Assessor, too, he's a good horse. . . . There, there! Why are you twitching your ears? Listen, idiot, when you're spoken to! I shan't teach you nothing wrong, you lout. What d'ya mean, crawling like that?' Then he again applied his whip, adding: 'Ah, you barbarian! You damn Bonaparte, you!' And he urged on all three: 'Giddap, you darlings!' and he flicked them all with the whip, not by way of punishment, but just to show that he was pleased with them. Having given them that pleasure, he again addressed the dapple-grey: 'Do you think I don't see the way you're carrying on? No, you must live in truth if you want to be respected. Now the folks we just visited were fine people. It's a pleasure to talk with a good man; with a good man I'm friends always, the best of pals, whether it be to drink tea or eat a bite—with pleasure, I say, if he's a good man. A good man has everyone's respect. Now take our master, everyone respects him, because, do you hear, he was in the government service, he's a collegiate councilor. . . .' "

Selifan is right; everyone in the town of N. respects Chichikov. And when the news gets around that he is buying large numbers of serfs—at first it is not suspected they are dead ones—he is regarded as a millionaire and the catch of the season for some marriageable lady. The most prominent people invite him to their homes, and he behaves toward all with courtesy, modesty, and quiet charm. In the light of a reputation of this sort, the reason for his eventual ostracism is a laughable commentary on the intelligence of the townsfolk: it is caused not so much by the rumor, which is never proved, that he is purchasing dead souls, but by the entirely groundless rumor that he plans to elope with the governor's young daughter. However, the discreet Chichikov, fearing a real exposure of his past, promptly sets out again on his travels, moderately pleased with the notarized lists of dead souls legally transferred to him.

In this first part of the novel Gogol endows Chichikov with the essence of universal comedy—he is a liar, dishonest, and a racketeer in the modern sense, while at the same time he fully believes in his own pretensions to honesty, justice, and the good life. But Gogol never for a moment leaves him without redeeming features, however ironic they may seem juxtaposed to his human failings. His heart is compassionate, Gogol repeats, and he is shocked at the haggling of some of the owners in selling their dead serfs. Sobakevich's trickery in slipping into his list the name of a nonnegotiable female serf pains him. And he even complains—to himself to be sure—of the expensive finery worn by the women at the governor's ball: "To think of it, some of them had a thousand roubles of rags on them! And all squeezed out of the peasants or, worse still, at the expense of their conscience." If it is difficult to judge him harshly in this first part of the novel, it is because he seems, in comparison with all the other characters, more attractive in appearance and behavior, as well as more intellectual and moral, if we construe this latter quality not absolutely but as one of degree.

The fantastic element, an attribute of Gogol's special brand of realism—a contrast between the real and the unreal—accounts for much of the novel's charm, which is further enhanced by an amazing vividness of perception and the most intense verbalizing style in Russian fiction, a torrential, engulfing outpouring which varies from grandiloquent poetic rhetoric to evocative mimetic dialogue and elaborately structured description, never dull, never dead.

The life resurrected in *Dead Souls*, according to Gogol, is observed through laughter and also through tears. Though the comic spirit prevails, below the surface there is always the infinite sadness of Russian life, its corruption, its inequities, its endless stagnation.

7

When Gogol first thought of *Dead Souls* in 1835 he did not appear to have had any concrete plan in mind for the novel's development. Presumably it was to be an effort in one volume, written in the humorous, carefree vein of *The Government Inspector* on which he was then working. His later assertion that he was prompted by Pushkin's advice at this time to concern himself with serious themes has no support.

On the other hand it seems clear that public and critical reaction to the opening performance of *The Government Inspector* in 1836 deeply disturbed Gogol and no doubt activated religious and moral fixations which had always been a part of his complex personality. Though the play was actually successful and repeatedly performed, he was distressed by the mixed praise and blame it aroused. Some critics hailed his civic courage in exposing corruption and others condemned him for attacking the tsar's government.

Always highly sensitive to criticism, Gogol's immediate reaction was to leave his native land, which he did in 1836 shortly after the first performance of his play. From abroad he was soon writing friends back in Russia that he had drawn up a comprehensive plan for *Dead Souls*, as though he wished to confound hostile critics by undertaking a work of major artistic proportions compared to *The Government Inspector*, and to please

favorable critics by contemplating a large novel that would reflect his true opinions of Russian society and offer it a message
of social significance. The novel will be "enormous," he wrote,
several volumes in length, in which "all of Russia will appear,"
and he plainly hints at its social and accusatory contents. It
would be a huge comic-satiric novel—or poem, to use Gogol's
word—realistic in form and moralistic in purpose, which in three
separate but thematically connected parts would be concerned
with important stages in the adventurous career of his hero as
observed against a varied background of Russian life.

This larger purpose, which Gogol seems to have formulated
over 1836-38, is reflected in the completed first part of *Dead
Souls* as it was published in 1842. Moreover, in this first part
there are allusions to his plan for the continuation, and in the
last chapter he directly informs readers that "two long parts of
the poem are still to come, and that is no trifle." Contemporary
critics acclaimed the first part, praised its realism, and saw in
Chichikov a typical representative of innumerable Russians who
were not particular about the means they used to amass money.
One critic also described the novel as an "epic" because it em-
braced all the important aspects of Russian life, and he eagerly
looked forward to its sequel. Opposition critics, however, denounced the novel for its coarseness and its concentration on
low characters.

Any measure of praise for the extant fragmentary second part
of *Dead Souls* is hard to come by. It is customary, especially
among Western critics, to dismiss it with a shrug and expression
of regret that Gogol ever attempted it. The usual judgment is
that the fragment contains a few good bits but on the whole
represents a marked artistic falling off from the first part. To
support the contention that it was impossible for Gogol to continue his masterpiece on the same high level, critics cite the sad
facts of his psychological and spiritual crises during the last ten

years of his life. To this end are mentioned his growing religious mania, the strange obsession that he was destined to perform an artistic mission of universal significance, and his disturbing attempts to discover in works he had already published an ethical content designed to reform his sinning countrymen, a notion that led him to revise *Taras Bulba* and *The Government Inspector* to conform to this pattern. Also mentioned as indications of incompetence are his pathetic appeals from abroad to friends and readers for ideas on the further development of the plot of *Dead Souls* and for detailed information about life in Russia to aid him in piecing out the imperfections of his waning imagination. Additional evidence of intellectual deterioration is found in his book *Selected Passages from a Correspondence with Friends*, that amazing concoction of moral and practical precepts upholding the political and social order of the regime of Nicholas I which so infuriated the dying Belinsky and provoked his celebrated letter of denunciation. Further, critics point out examples of confused thinking in Gogol's *Selected Passages*, *An Author's Confession*, and in various letters, where he speciously endeavors to "update" his earlier works in terms of his altered views—that in his heroes he really exposed the banality of his own soul and thus his readers, in laughing at his characters, were actually laughing at him which enabled him to free himself of odious features; that his works were not so much a reflection of social vices of society as of his own vices, for he sought self-chastisement or to be chastised by others because his soul was an unworthy receptacle of divine inspiration. Finally, critics maintain that in burning the manuscripts of the continuations of *Dead Souls*, one in 1845 and the other shortly before his death in 1852, Gogol was prompted by a moment of artistic truth, realizing that the sequel was a failure, although it could just as cogently be argued that he burned the last version in a moment of religious self-mortification, urged on by the preaching of his spiritual advisor, Father Matvei, who believed that literature was the work of the devil.

However, one may approach this difficult problem of the continuation of *Dead Souls* with a different perspective and one for which some evidence exists. That is, despite his illness and worsening psychotic state, Gogol never lost sight of the total design of his novel, clearly implicit in the complete first part, and that his continuation of it, to the extent that we can judge his efforts on the basis of the extant fragmentary second part, is consistent with this design and is effectively realized, without any marked failing of artistic power.

A clear hint of the future development of his hero occurs in the last chapter of the first part where Gogol treats the subject of passions. He writes that there are good passions which bring boundless bliss, but there are evil passions, and one of them has taken hold of Chichikov—an insignificant urge in a man "born for better deeds, forcing him to forget high and sacred duties and to see in worthless baubles something great and holy."

If this intention is kept in mind, certain puzzling features of Chichikov's personality and behavior in the first part of the novel are easily clarified. For example, Gogol's baffling stress on Chichikov's attractive personal aspects and dormant moral capacities was deliberate, for he intended to suggest the possibility of his later moral reformation, to emphasize even this early that so striking a change was not at all alien to the logic of the developing personality of his scamp of a hero.

In short, the extensive design of the novel was hardly an afterthought, as is sometimes supposed, inspired by public reaction to the published first part and Gogol's mounting religious mania and morbid psychopathic condition. If he designed the proposed three parts of *Dead Souls* to parallel the Inferno, Purgatory, and Paradise of Dante's *Divine Comedy*, the first part of the novel is Chichikov's inferno and its final chapter announces that the hero's "existence held the secret of what would later bring him to his knees and reduce him to ashes before the wisdom of heaven. . . ." And Chichikov is reduced to ashes, figuratively speaking, at the end of the fragmentary second part, where also the theme of the "wisdom of heaven" is caught up in the Christian precepts of old Murazov who prepares Chichikov for his new life.

One might deplore a certain moral emphasis in the continuation as a betrayal of Gogol's major talent as a humorist, which would amount to ignoring the moral element in his early works and the humor in the second part of *Dead Souls*, as well as the enriching influence of time and maturity on the artistic growth of an author. And though one might also question the judgment involved in Gogol's total design for *Dead Souls* and the baleful influence of his religious "sickness" on the sequel, there can be no doubt of the sincerity of his tremendous spiritual struggle. Whether such an experience was inevitably inconsistent with artistic fulfillment is purely a matter of opinion. Gogol tells us in *An Author's Confession* that in order to portray positive aspects of Russian life he had to have an intimate knowledge of the human soul, and that this could be achieved only by a study of the soul's greatest master—Christ. In his self-appointed mission to reintroduce the teaching of Christ through the medium of artistic literature, Gogol was simply a predecessor of Dostoevsky and Tolstoy. Indeed, his religious experience bears some similarity to that of Tolstoy, who continued to create great fiction after his spiritual revelation although many regarded him as insane.

Fluctuating between the claims of personal religious devotion and those of literature, Gogol's struggle to make one serve the other undoubtedly intensified his neurotic state, a condition that may well have driven him in 1845 to burn nearly all that he had written of the second part of *Dead Souls*. But it would be a mistake to imagine that thereafter he succumbed entirely to the inner turmoil of his mind. Rejecting his spiritual advisor's plea to seek calm by retiring from the world, Gogol once again took up the task of continuing his novel. We have glimpses of him at this time recopying sections of the second part of *Dead Souls* with pleasure and ardor, laughing over funny passages, and asserting that he never felt better. Almost to the end of his life Gogol did not lose faith in the power of literature to serve the moral and Christian destiny of Russia.

8

What has survived of the second part of *Dead Souls* is not so much of a "fragment" as its usual cursory critical handling would indicate. In the Gogol edition of the Soviet Academy of Sciences, this "fragment" runs to slightly more than half the length of the completed first part.

If the transformation of the cunning rogue Chichikov into a positively good man, like Dostoevsky's Prince Myshkin in *The Idiot*, would seem to be a more suitable task for a Salvation Army worker than a literary artist, the process is not exactly foreign to the experience of life or, for that matter, the endeavors of novelists. The fact is that Gogol does not attempt to describe this process until the very end of the second part of *Dead Souls*, and there Chichikov is represented as merely experiencing a change of heart because of the misfortunes he has suffered. The real transformation was to take place in the third part, of which nothing has come down to us, and hence the bulk of the fragmentary second part is devoted to a continuation of Chichikov's efforts to lengthen his list of purchases of dead souls.

If in these efforts one expects more of the gusto and grotesquerie of the first part, then there is bound to be some disappointment. But it must be realized that such an emphasis was quite out of place in terms of Gogol's overall plan of the novel. In the second part the quality of the realism changes. There is less stress on the fantastic, more on actuality. A different set of characters and different experiences in the context of an equally real but different slice of Russian life were necessary to bring about the slow dawning of a Christian moral conscience in Chichikov. And an element of didactic moralizing was inevitable, but it is no more offensive in this scheme of things than it was later in some of the greatest novels of Turgenev, Dostoevsky, and Tolstoy.

Throughout most of the fragment there is no falling off in the further characterization of Chichikov. He pursues his travels, now in southern Russia, with Petrushka and Selifan, still bent on buying up dead serfs and an estate. His initial encounter is with Tentetnikov, the first thoroughly honest landowner to appear in the novel and a brilliantly realistic portrayal. The image may have been suggested by Pushkin's Onegin and certainly looks forward, in some of its traits, to Goncharov's Oblomov. Tentetnikov, like Prince Nekhlyudov in Tolstoy's later story, *A Landlord's Morning*, tries to run his own estate only to discover that the peasants do not understand him any more than he, with all his book knowledge, understands them. In his failure, he slips into complete inactivity and boredom, weakly justifying himself by endless plans to write a book which he never manages to begin.

Chichikov next boldly calls at the magnificent neighboring estate of Tentetnikov's friend, General Betrishchyov, where, as always, his gracious deportment makes him a welcome guest. Only once does he slip in lying to his host that Tentetnikov is writing a book about generals. When the host demands to know what general in particular, Chichikov in confusion answers "about generals in general." The wealthy, pompous Betrishchyov, drawn in Gogol's best caricaturing manner, readily believes Chichikov's fabrication that an old uncle has offered to leave him in his will three hundred serfs if the nephew can match them with an equal number. And when Chichikov explains that it would be a good joke if he met the demand with dead serfs, the general laughs uproariously and at once offers to help him accumulate them.

Friends who heard Gogol read from a much longer version of the second part than has survived have left enthusiastic accounts of further developments in the characterizations of the general and Tentetnikov, who becomes betrothed to Betrishchyov's daughter, is exiled to Siberia for a political offense, and marries his beloved who follows him there. These accounts are, in part, supported by extant discarded fragments of the longer version.

Betrishchyov falls in with Chichikov's suggestion that he visit the estates of the general's relatives in the surrounding countryside, apparently with the intention of procuring more dead souls. This device provides occasions for encounters with a group of landed gentry that parallels the amazing group in the first part of the novel. The contrast is striking for now Gogol has a different purpose to serve. The moral unpleasantness of the first group is replaced by moral goodness in the second, although each is a type and has his oddities and failings which reflected those Gogol professed to see in the whole class. It would be hard to find the likes of the first group anywhere in Russian literature, but reasonable facsimiles of the second appear frequently in later fiction. They are realistically individualized, occasionally flecked with comic caricatured traits, but they never possess the grotesque features of the first group. They include the gloriously described mountain of fat Petukh, the type of wasteful landowner who lives only to eat; the intelligent Platonov who is utterly bored with everything and especially with the idea of managing his estate; the cracked Colonel Koshkoryov, an addict of foreign expertise in efficiency and agriculture, who compels Chichikov to file his request for dead serfs in the estate office, Bureau of Reports and Petitions, from which comes the reply that there are no dead souls for souls are immortal, and that anyway all the serfs on the estate have already been mortgaged twice over; and Khlobuyev, a highly cultured landowner who has allowed his estate to fall into ruins simply because he lacks the will to do anything about it.

The one exception to this group is Kostanzhonglo, obviously Gogol's answer to what he regards as the national weaknesses of the whole class of landed gentry. It is at this point that Gogol first introduces a didactic moralizing element in *Dead Souls*. Kostanzhonglo is a model, self-made estate owner who has achieved remarkable success and much wealth through hard work and business acumen. He willingly offers the enraptured Chichikov an exposition of his methods and philosophy of life. In the course of stressing the doctrine of hard work, honesty in all dealings, and the charm of country existence, he attacks the stupidity, laziness, and lack of thrift of Russian landowners and the waste, corruption, and snobbishness of those who desert their estates for the city. In condemning the growing tendency of landowners to substitute for Russian initiative the latest European ideas and agricultural techniques, he echoes the Slavophils, and his insistence that the farmer's simple existence is the only natural life and that on the land man is morally purer, nobler, and higher, he anticipates the thinking of Tolstoy. In fact, some of the views and agricultural practices of Kostanzhonglo reappear in Tolstoy's future characterizations of Levin in *Anna Karenina* and Nikolai Rostov in *War and Peace*.

Chichikov is in ecstasies over these revelations and regards Kostanzhonglo as the most intelligent man he has ever met. Though he dreams of owning such a model estate and managing it in this expert manner, his mind is primarily concerned with profits, with how his wealthy host "rakes it in" as he phrases it.

When he puts the question on how he can get rich quickly on the land, his host harshly tells him that he must work not only for his own prosperity but for that also of all around him. However, Chichikov confesses his inability to believe that one can acquire a fortune without sin, but his host assures him that it can and must be done by the most honest and just means, by starting with kopecks at the bottom and working with and getting to know the common people.

On Kostanzhonglo's advice and with a loan from him and Platonov, Chichikov buys the bankrupt estate of Khlobuyev. After the purchase he reflects on the "patience and work" he will need to develop his estate. He had grown to know such virtues, he ponders, ever since he wore baby clothes, but he wonders whether he possesses them now in middle age. Other less commendable ways of exploiting his property occur to him, and the thought even flits through his cunning brain that he might bolt and get out of paying his loans. As he drives away from his estate, this man, who had traveled over much of Russia scheming, planning, contriving, obsessed by what Gogol calls an evil passion, glories in the fact that he now owns land, property, and serfs, not just imaginary serfs, but real, existing ones, and he begins to jump up and down on his carriage seat, rubbing his hands, winking at himself, and then, putting his fist to his mouth, he blows a march on it as on a bugle.

This measure of success, however, fails to work a moral change in Chichikov. On the contrary, it intensifies his instinct to accumulate more in dishonest ways. At this point five or six chapters which must have followed have not survived, but their story line may be roughly reconstructed from hints in the last extant section of the second part of the novel. Chichikov apparently visits other landowners, obtains more dead souls, and makes the acquaintance of the fabulously wealthy Murazov, who is Kostanzhonglo's ideal of a man who amasses a fortune honestly by hard work, uses it to help others, is deeply religious, and lives according to Christian ideals.

Then it appears that Chichikov takes up residence in one of the principal cities of the province and duplicates, on a more elegant and expansive scale, the social success he achieved in the town of N. in the first part of the novel. If anything, the city officials are more corrupt than those in the town of N., and it seems that Chichikov becomes involved with them in fraudulent activities, one of which is arranging the falsification, to his own advantage, of the will of the rich old aunt of Khlobuyev. In all these manipulations he has acquired a sum of three hundred thousand roubles, two estates, and a long list of dead serfs.

The last section of the fragment* opens with Chichikov preparing to set out on his travels again before the law catches up with him. While he is admiring himself in the mirror in a new suit of silky material in his favorite lingonberry red, the police arrive. Brought before the Governor General of the province, who had arrived to clean up the city's scandalous corruption, and confronted with accusations and proofs of wrongdoing, Chichikov's poise vanishes and he is reduced to an abject, cringing seeker for mercy. He ends his pathetic plea: "My whole life was like a whirlwind or a ship tossed among the waves at the mercy of the winds. I am a human being, Your Highness!" But this uniquely honest official promptly sends him to prison.

In his dirty, stinking cell, the purgatory that Gogol has destined for him, Chichikov is visited by the kind, religiously minded Murazov, who sees in him admirable qualities that have been wasted in a blind pursuit of property. In his utter despair Chichikov does not so much try to justify as to explain his behavior to Murazov. The statement illuminates further Chichi-

* This final section, apparently an unfinished last chapter of the second part, was apparently the only section of the 1845 burned manuscript that survived. The other chapters that have been summarized here belong to a later version of the second part of the novel.

kov's amoral personality as Gogol had conceived it from the very beginning of the novel: "I can claim that I earned my kopecks with bloodsweating patience, by toil, toil, and not by robbery or by absconding with public funds as some people do. And why did I save my kopecks? In order to spend the remainder of my days in comfort; in order to be able to leave something to my children whom it was my intention to acquire for the good of my country. That is why I wished to save. I've been a little crooked, I won't deny it, I have been crooked. That can't be helped now. But I became crooked only when I saw that I could not get anywhere along a straight road and that the crooked road led more directly to the goal. But I toiled and used my wits. If I stole, I did so from the rich. But what about all those scoundrels who hang around the courts, taking thousands of roubles from public funds, robbing the poor, stripping the last kopeck from those who have nothing! . . ."

Is Gogol telling us here that in a country of crooks the way to hell is paved with good intentions? Is this the purpose he had in mind when he first hit upon the vast design of *Dead Souls*—to present Chichikov as a kind of Russian Everyman, transgressing the moral and civil laws of the land, to take him through stages of crime and punishment, and in the end to lead him to redemption as a object lesson to his countrymen to go and sin no more? Was Gogol, dealing with a lesser but more typical Russian criminal than Raskolnikov in *Crime and Punishment*, anticipating Dostoevsky's doctrine of salvation by suffering? However that may be, the good Murazov, after delivering Chichikov a sermon on Christian ethics, obtains his release and sends him on his way with the final practical advice to find a quiet retreat as near as possible to a church and a community of simple people, and then marry and forget the noisy world and its temptations. "I will, I will!" the grateful Chichikov cries. And Gogol adds, as Chichikov once more sets off on his travels. "He was no longer the former Chichikov. He was like the ruin of the former Chichikov. The inner state of his soul might be compared with a building that has been taken to pieces in order to make out of it something entirely new. . . ." In short, Chichikov, who had traversed the long road of his inferno and purgatory, was now prepared to seek his salvation by good deeds—the paradise of the unwritten third part of *Dead Souls*.

It seemed desirable to dwell at some length on this substantial fragment, so often scanted by critics, not only to demonstrate the impressive scope of the total conception of *Dead Souls* and the profoundly unified and realistic treatment of its remarkable hero, but also to suggest that if this second part had only come down to us in complete and finished form, its artistic impact would probably have been as great as that of the famous first part.

III · DOSTOEVSKY

"A Realist in the Higher Sense"

SPEAKING FOR HIS OWN generation of fiction writers, Dostoevsky is reported to have declared, although the statement may be apocryphal: "We have all sprung from Gogol's *Overcoat*," and with an important qualification to be mentioned later, this generalization could stand. On the strength of Dostoevsky's first story, *Poor Folk* (1846), Belinsky had designated him an adherent of the "Natural School," a new trend in realism which, according to Belinsky, had been started by Gogol. Actually, this label was first used by Faddei Bulgarin in the early 1840's to disparage writers who imitated Gogol's lowly characters and his satire of government bureaucracy. With scorn Belinsky pointed out the immeasurable chasm that separated Bulgarin's picaresque novel *Ivan Vyzhigin*, in 1829, and Gogol's *Dead Souls*, in 1842. The difference was that between a clever hack writer and a literary genius, between a period floundering in prose fiction and one that had acquired a sense of direction and momentum that carried the movement to the end of the century and even beyond into the Soviet period.

The adjective "Natural" was obviously used by Belinsky as a synonym for "realistic," a word that had not yet come into vogue in Russian literary criticism. What he had in mind was the old-fashioned imitation of nature—a fiction that was not rhetorical or idealizing but one based on a faithful representation of life. The Natural School was in no sense an anticipation of the Naturalism of Zola, who proposed to substitute novels of observation for novels of imagination in which the form would become a kind of scientific laboratory where the writer conducted objective, controlled experiments. Although it might occur to Soviet socialist realists today, as it apparently did to Zola, that fiction should be informed with a bright affirmation of progress to be achieved through man's ability to control his environment, it would hardly have entered the thoughts of great Russian realists of the nineteenth century.

Yet similarities and dissimilarities between French and Russian realism compel notice. The major works of Stendhal, Balzac, Flaubert, and Zola were known in Russia and to a limited extent influenced novelists. Dostoevsky paid eloquent tribute to Balzac and his first published effort was a translation of *Eugénie Grandet*, although he no doubt found the works of Victor Hugo, Eugene Sue, and especially George Sand more to his liking. By the end of the nineteenth century his own novels began to influence French fiction and by the twentieth they played a major role in the development of the literary intelligence of France.

Belinsky did not live long enough—he died in 1848—to grasp that French realistic fiction was fundamentally the characteristic expression of bourgeois society. One of his few lapses in critical discernment was his failure to appreciate the worth of Balzac, who has been described as "the sociologist of the novel." On the other hand, he seemed determined to turn Gogol and his followers, including Dostoevsky, in the new Natural School into sociologists of the Russian novel. In June 1841 he wrote his friend V. P. Botkin: "I have developed a sort of wild, frenzied fanatical love for freedom and independence of human personality which are possible only in a society founded on truth and virtue." And three months later he informed Botkin: "And so, I am now at a new extreme—the idea of *socialism*—which has become for me the idea of ideas. . . ."*

Belinsky gathered under the umbrella of the Natural School the unusually rich outpouring of fiction during the two years 1846-47, all of it, with one exception, consisting of the first works of new young writers. The list included Dostoevsky's *Poor Folk* and the first stories of Turgenev's *Sportsman's Sketches*, as well as A. I. Herzen's *Who is to Blame?*, A. V. Druzhinin's *Polinka Saks*, I. A. Goncharov's *A Common Story*, D. V. Grigorovich's *The Village* and *Anton Goremyka*, and A. F. Veltman's *Adventures from the Sea of Life*. Belinsky evaluated this fiction, not as a class-conscious Utopian socialist, but rather as a sociologically minded critic searching for artistic treatment, in realistic terms, of the social problems that beset his country. He approved the rejection of idyllic scenes of happy peasants and descriptions of lovely exteriors and interiors and praised the concentration on real peasants, house porters, cabbies, and clerks as heroes, pictures of the haunts of the starving and dens of immorality, and the poverty, suffering, and ugliness of Russian life.

Though Belinsky maintained the right of art to serve the public interest, he always insisted on the primacy of art in this commitment, a fact too often overlooked by Soviet expositors of his ideas. It is difficult to say how far his political convictions would have swayed his literary judgment if he had not had to contend with the severe censorship of the reign of Nicholas I. Alluding to this fact, he wrote Botkin: "I am . . . obliged to act against my nature and character. Nature has condemned me to bark like a

* Quotations from V. G. Belinsky are from his *Selected Philosophical Works* (Moscow: Foreign Languages Publishing House, 1948).

dog and howl like a jackal, but circumstances compel me to mew like a cat and wave my tail like a fox." However, he sternly warned against a spirit of partisanship and sectarianism in literary criticism. There is a danger, he wrote, that "the influence of contemporary social problems will vitiate art." Though he believed that literature must be an expression of society, he also affirmed that "art undoubtedly must first be art as such and only afterwards can it be an expression of the spirit and drift of society in a given epoch." In the case of the novelist, he saw clearly that there was something beyond realism, something that was involved in the relation of the writer's world to the real world. As Belinsky put it: "One must be able to pass the facts of reality through one's imagination and endow them with a new life."

The social factors that concerned writers of the Natural School were different in degree and intensity from those that preoccupied French novelists. The defeat of the revolutions of 1848 in Western Europe, the consolidation of the bourgeoisie, and the swift rise of capitalism created the social patterns of life that were so strikingly reflected in French realistic fiction. In Russia there was no revolution, a middle class and capitalism were still in an early stage of growth, and the resolution of the age-old problem of serfdom would not take place until the Emancipation Act of 1861. However, the collapse of the repressive rule of Nicholas I after the debacle of the Crimean War, his death in 1855, and the reforms which his successor Alexander II was virtually compelled to introduce, brought about an upsurge of democratic thinking in the freer climate of opinion that was then permitted.

The intelligentsia, which had barely begun to sprout in the suffocating atmosphere of the 1840's, now positively flourished. It had split into two rival groups, the Slavophils and the Westernizers, and though both believed equally in Russia's destiny of future greatness, they offered different programs for its realization. The Slavophils preached a return to indigenous Russian virtues before the Westernizing reforms of Peter the Great. The Westernizers saw nothing in Russia's past that was worth reviving and advocated that the country intensify its practice of absorbing the best in Western European education, culture, and institutions.

Though both groups praised Russia's supposed freedom from class strife, it is curious that the Westernizers split into two factions that suggest a positive class differentiation. For in the late fifties and in the sixties the *raznochintsy*, that is, men from various strata of society—poor, struggling students, sons of priests, traders, petty officials, and peasants—who had obtained status with higher education and membership in the intelligentsia, tended to oppose the landed gentry among the Westernizers. In actuality, the basic social and political struggle of the time was between these aggressive intellectual commoners, the so-called radical democrats, who demanded the abolition of serfdom and progressive changes in the whole feudal agrarian structure, and the conscience-stricken liberals belonging to the landed gentry who sought these same goals but hoped to achieve them without causing any conflict within their own class or with the bureaucracy or autocracy. This struggle was reflected in every intellectual and artistic endeavor, and the leading mouthpieces of the radical democrats were those two members of the *raznochintsy*, the ideological heirs of Belinsky—Chernyshevsky and Dobrolyubov.

This social pattern, so different from that of the West, produced a literature with quite a different realistic emphasis. Unlike French realism, Russian realism, created by novelists from the landed gentry, failed to come to grips with society as a whole and it was often much less objective as a reflection of life. These Russian writers did not stress economic determinants of human action, like Balzac and Zola, but were more concerned with intellectual and moral growth or failure among the landed gentry. Such emphasis accounts for the unique educative or "teaching" aspects of Russian realistic novelists whose typical approach was to join social and historical problems with those of individual fitness and behavior. If French realism of the nine-teenth century is preoccupied with the greatness and decline of the bourgeoisie, the characteristic concern of the Russian is with the greatness and decline of the landed gentry.

A familiar observation is that political and social criticism in Russia, driven underground by government persecution and rigid censorship, was forced to incorporate itself in the dramatic imagery of fiction and that this in turn affected the quality of its realism. There is some truth in this observation but it perhaps ought not to be pushed too far. During the twenty-six years of the reign of Alexander II (1855-81), a period of reforms and relatively enlightened censorship, all of the great works of Turgenev, Dostoevsky, and Tolstoy were published and the best of Goncharov and Saltykov-Shchedrin. In these many novels, including nearly all the masterpieces of Russian fiction, there is really very little overt criticism of the regime or the so-cial structure, only an indirect criticism of the stagnation of the kind of life, mostly that of the landed gentry, which these novel-ists largely depicted. Yet during these years an expanding and occasionally violent revolutionary movement developed, there was much pungent journalism, and Chernyshevsky's tenden-tiously radical novel, *What Is to Be Done?* (1863), appeared. In fact, Turgenev, Dostoevsky, and Tolstoy, who nurtured a higher personal view of art, were opposed to the utilitarian posi-tion of the radical democrats that literature's primary function was to serve the crying needs of the people for social change.

Years later Gorky, evaluating the attitude of these novelists to the harsh realities of their own day in his article, "Notes on the Petty Bourgeoisie" (1905), condemned their passive attitude toward life, especially Dostoevsky's doctrine of patience and Tolstoy's preaching of nonresistance to evil. "For the two world geniuses," he declared, "lived in a country where the abuse of people had already reached dimensions shocking in their licentious cynicism. Despotism, drunk with its own impunity, turned the whole country into a dark torture-chamber where servants of the regime, from the governor to the village policeman, arrogantly plundered and tortured millions of people, playing with them like a cat with a mouse it has caught. And they said to these tormented people: 'Do not oppose evil!' 'Have patience!'"

Chernyshevsky and especially Dobrolyubov drew attention to this passivity, this do-nothing attitude of the great novelists reflected in their pictures of Russian life. Though these two critics of the fifties and sixties have often been stigmatized for their antiaestheticism and one-sided insistence on the social significance of literature, in which a work of art is always regarded as a specific objective form of mirroring reality, actually they contributed important insights for our understanding of trends in the fiction of the time. If Dobrolyubov, in his famous article on Goncharov's *Oblomov*, conceived too narrowly the actionless hero who sees no purpose in life, there can be no doubt that he identified a pattern of reality reflected in Russian literature from Pushkin's *Eugene Onegin* through the fiction of Gogol, Lermontov, Herzen, Goncharov, Turgenev and beyond. Speaking of the estate of Goncharov's hero, Dobrolyubov declares: "No, Oblomovka is our own motherland, her owners are our teachers. . . ." What Dobrolyubov failed to observe was that these novelists were primarily concerned with portraying faithfully the life they knew best and with distilling from it, to the greater glory of their art, the essence of eternal, universal problems and not the transient news of the day. If these novels may sometimes be called problem novels, they are so because they are devoted to humanity's great problems of good and evil, of life and death.

Dobrolyubov's article, however, suggests an orientation in the development of Russian realism different from that popularized by Belinsky as the Natural School. In short, there is good reason to place Gogol in the Classical School of Russian Realism begun by Pushkin and including such great continuators as Lermontov, Turgenev, Goncharov, Tolstoy, and Chekhov, to mention only the most prominent names. From Pushkin to Chekhov something is held in common which is passed on from one writer to another. The style and form of each seem to make a logical transition from one to the other, changing of course over the years but essentially the same throughout. They all begin with disharmony and attempt to find harmony. The milieu they treat is largely that of the landowning gentry in their existence in the country and the city. In general, the chief protagonists are ineffective, often weak men and strong-minded women, the prototypes of which were Pushkin's Eugene and Tatyana. Family life is the focus of interest, indeed often the only solid element of plot; moral and philosophical problems are stressed; and the characters, who are typically introspective and more or less unhappy, are treated with sympathetic understanding. Description is emphasized, even to the point of the superfluous, and style is artistically restrained and kept unobtrusive.

Now Gogol's fiction undeniably fits into this pattern, but it also reveals certain sharp differences. The most striking are his highly individualistic, rhetorical style, romantic elements involving much exaggeration, extreme caricaturing, a predominance of satire, and his occasional introduction of lowly characters.

There can be no doubt that some of these differences influenced a development in the forties and for years later of a body of so-called "philanthropic fiction" that stood apart from the mainstream of Russian classical realism and concentrated on humble characters with the deliberate intent of exposing social evils.

It was this last aspect of Gogol's art that initially attracted Dostoevsky, as well as other "philanthropic" writers, and prompted his statement that he and his immediate contemporaries in the forties had all sprung from Gogol's *Overcoat*. Apart from this, however, there is little else in Gogol that reappears in Dostoevsky. Nor in any significant sense does he have anything in common with the other writers in the Classical School of Russian Realism. Some of his earliest critics were quick to point out this fact. Dostoevsky was unique in Russian realistic fiction and established his own school.

2

From the outset of his literary career Dostoevsky seemed aware that he was adding a new dimension to the conception of realism in fiction. *The Overcoat* of Gogol was in Dostoevsky's mind when he conceived his first work, the short novel *Poor Folk*, but so was Pushkin's *The Stationmaster*. In commenting on both of them in *Poor Folk*, the hero Devushkin no doubt states Dostoevsky's opinion. Devushkin prefers Pushkin's tale because the old stationmaster is portrayed in such a simple, life-like manner, and he dismisses the whole situation in *The Overcoat* as an insignificant action drawn from vulgar, everyday life. Besides, he adds, it is a work of an evil tendency, untrue to life, "for there cannot have been such a clerk" as Akaky Akakievich.

As early as the end of 1846, by which time Dostoevsky had published only his first three tales, *Poor Folk*, *The Double*, and *Mr. Prokharchin*, some critics had already discerned his originality and the special emphasis of his art. In 1847, for example, V. N.

Maikov wrote: ". . . Mr. Dostoevsky's creative method is original in the highest degree, and he is the last person to be designated as an imitator of Gogol. . . . Both Gogol and Mr. Dostoevsky portray actual society. But Gogol is primarily a social writer and Mr. Dostoevsky a psychological one. For Gogol the individual is significant as representative of a certain society or circle; for Dostoevsky society is interesting only to the extent that it influences the personality of the individual."*

As a matter of fact, Dostoevsky's letters at this time to members of his family, as well as other data, suggest that *Poor Folk* has more autobiography in it than Gogolian inspiration. Whatever influence Gogol may have had, Dostoevsky soon surmounted it as is indicated by his amusing parody of the master's style and personality in the character of Foma Opiskin in the early work *The Village of Stepanchikovo*. From the young Dostoevsky's point of view, Gogol's characterization of Akaky Akakievich was a mere externalization that sacrificed probing the soul in depth to brilliant surface effects. It was precisely an analysis of Devushkin's soul that Dostoevsky was primarily interested in, as he rather bumptiously informs his brother in a letter shortly after the publication of *Poor Folk*: "They (Belinsky and others) find in me a new and original spirit in that I proceed by analysis and not by synthesis, that is, I plunge into the depths, and while analyzing every atom, I search out the whole; Gogol takes a direct path and hence is not so profound as I. Read and see for yourself. Brother, I have a most brilliant future before me!"

On the perceptive but slight foundation of initial commentary, a superstructure of criticism of staggering proportions has been erected over the years, both in Russia and the

* Quoted, with slight alterations, from the translation in Vladimir Seduro's *Dostoyevski in Russian Literary Criticism, 1846-1956* (New York: Columbia University Press, 1957), p. 11.

West, in the course of which every major and minor aspect of Dostoevsky's life, thought, and art has been minutely investigated. It is a quality of his genius that he has meant all things to all peoples, but if his personality, as well as those of the great characters of his fiction, are still discussed in print as unfathomable riddles, it is to be attributed more to the human passion for conundrums, real or imaginary, than to the dubious complexity of his life and art.

So numerous and varied have been the Russian critics that it is possible to organize them into schools identifiable by the special emphasis of their approaches: comparative-historical, sociological, political, symbolic, decadent, mystical, psychological, linguistic, impressionist, religious, formalist, polyphonic, early Marxian and later Marxian.

The mass of Western criticism cannot be so precisely differentiated, although a considerable body of writing has accumulated which could be properly designated as a "psychoanalytical school." In the West the frequent lack of Russian among investigators has tended to shift the emphasis from studies of form, style, and language to nonliterary matters. Although a literary artist is concerned essentially with creating life and not systems of thought, a surprisingly large amount of Western criticism of Dostoevsky's fiction is devoted to appraisals of him as a prophet, a philosopher, a psychologist, and a political, social, or religious thinker. Some of this is perhaps understandable in our day of hard choices in philosophical and political loyalties, for many of the intellectual problems that have disturbed generations between two catastrophic world wars and since then are most effectively dramatized in Dostoevsky's celebrated novels. This is one reason why these works are more popular today than they were in their author's lifetime. We are aware that Nietzsche, whose philosophy has been recently resurrected, admitted to learning his psychology from Dostoevsky. Nietzsche's central doctrine that he who wishes to be a creator of good or evil must first destroy all values resembles closely that of Shigalyov in *The Possessed*. Sartre too has paid his tribute to Dostoevsky whose condemnation of the tyranny of reason may well have furnished some inspiration for the French thinker's existentialist belief that human action becomes simply the expression of a biological urge to self-assertion. And Camus also, in one of his last books, *L'Homme révolté*, draws heavily upon the agonizing questions raised in *The Brothers Karamazov* in elaborating his thesis that the mistaken belief in reason in modern times has led to a loss of all sense of values and to the cynical seizure of power by dictators.

Despite some Western opinions to the contrary, the Soviet contribution to our understanding of Dostoevsky has been of the first magnitude. To be sure, the official Party line on him has been much influenced by the views of Lenin and Gorky. When asked what he thought about the novels, Lenin is reported to have replied: "I have no time for such trash." And Gorky repeatedly condemned Dostoevsky's irrationalism, passivity, and his doctrine of salvation by suffering. But both were peculiarly ambivalent about the novelist and their uncertainty has infected all subsequent Soviet reaction. Lenin early authorized a statue in Dostoevsky's memory, and he is quoted on excellent authority as esteeming his talent. Nor could Gorky refrain, in his "Shop Talk," from listing Dostoevsky's works among the greatest novels of all time, those marvelously fashioned from the "thought, feeling, blood, and the bitter, burning tears of the world."

Though a number of Soviet analyses have tried, quite unconvincingly, to prove that features of Dostoevsky's novels were socially predetermined, other Soviet Marxian and non-Marxian studies—literary, stylistic, linguistic, and ideological—amount to major contributions. However, the most significant and useful

Soviet publications are those which have provided a mass of fresh factual information on Dostoevsky's life, his creative art, and the development of his thought. These include biographical studies, annotated editions of his fiction and magazine articles, four volumes of letters, a number of notebooks, and the correspondence, memoirs, and diaries of members of his family and friends. In addition, a series of investigations on the influence of native and foreign authors has underscored the fact that European adventure novels more than once served Dostoevsky in the fantastic incidents and construction of his plots.

To mention the existence of this large body of factual material is perhaps salutary, for a comprehensive knowledge of it helps dissolve the attractive mystery which has nurtured so much of the highly imaginative criticism, especially in the West, of Dostoevsky's life, art, and thought. For it is now possible to establish the extent to which his fiction is autobiographical, the prototypes of some of his principal characters, and the influence of foreign models on the form, plots, and incidents of his novels. Then the publication of the rich material in the notebooks bearing on the composition of all his major novels takes us into the writing laboratory of Dostoevsky and allows us to study, in unexampled detail, the whole process involved in the creation of these masterpieces. This process, as well as the abundant information about the conception and plans of his works which Dostoevsky often provides in his letters, may in turn be most fruitfully checked for fulfillment of artistic intentions against the finished novels. Finally, the vexed question of the correspondences of Dostoevsky's thought and ideas and those of his characters may be substantially resolved by correlating his views, fully expressed in the pages of his two magazines, *Time* and *Epoch*, in *The Diary of a Writer*, and in his letters, with those of the characters in the novels.

None of this is meant to suggest that one can explain the deep mystery of genius in the creation of enduring art but simply to warn critics of the futility of attempting to do just that. Conscious that he was an innovator in fiction, Dostoevsky was not disposed to keep his future commentators in the dark about it. He did not consider himself a writer of any definite social group. Rather he regarded his work as of universal significance, an effort, he said, "with complete realism to find man in man." He defined his innovation as an attempt to represent in fiction spiritual phenomena above and beyond social practices, to resolve the psychological contradictions of man in terms of true and eternal "humanness." "They call me a psychologist," he wrote in his notebook. "It is not true. I am only a realist in the higher sense; that is, I portray all the depths of the human soul."

3

Such a claim reminds one of the observation that the art of fiction is by its very nature irrational. Being a realist in the higher sense may seem a little bit like being more equal than equal, and it raises a suspicion that Dostoevsky, like some modern realists in fiction, was more in contact with himself than with life. Yet he had definite ideas about realism and they seem to articulate the kind of fiction he wrote.

Compared with his landed-gentry rivals, Turgenev, Goncharov, and Tolstoy, Dostoevsky regarded himself as an intellectual proletarian with an entirely different outlook on life. They were novelists of the countryside, he was a poet of the city. In their works they chronicled the biographies of members of their class, whereas he wrote about off-center city dwellers living in off-center worlds of their own. He thought that their realism, at its best, dealt with the typical and surface features of existence, at its worst, with the irrelevant, whereas he was completely immersed in the realities of the spiritual life of men. That is, he preferred to shift the action from the external world to that of the mind and heart of his characters. For him art was a medium for conveying the wisdom of life, the emotions of the soul.

Confronting the issue of realism squarely, Dostoevsky wrote to one of his correspondents: "I have an understanding of reality and realism entirely different from that of our realists and critics. My idealism is more real than theirs. Lord! To relate sensibly all that we Russians have experienced in our last ten years of spiritual growth—indeed, do not our realists cry out that this is fantasy! Nevertheless, this is primordial, real realism!" And by way of clarification he wrote another correspondent: "I have my own special view on reality in art; what the majority call almost fantastic and exceptional sometimes signifies for me the very essence of reality. . . . In every issue of a newspaper you meet accounts of the most real facts and amazing happenings. For our writers they are fantastic; they are not concerned with them; yet they are reality because they are facts."

In his notebooks and elsewhere Dostoevsky reiterates this stand that fantastic but actual happenings, usually involving misfortune, have a deeper reality for the artist because they embody a tragic vision that is the quintessence of life. And in *The Diary of a Writer* he gives an example of how he and Tolstoy would differ on this question of realism. There he retells an incident in Tolstoy's *Childhood, Boyhood, and Youth* of how a child, in an unhappy moment, thinks of killing himself and of the consternation this act would cause among his family. Then Dostoevsky repeats a recent newspaper report of a twelve-year-old boy who does commit suicide after having been punished for doing poorly at school. For Dostoevsky the fantastic, tragic event is the more real one, not only because it happened, but also because it challenges the writer to probe all the psychological factors that compelled the boy to kill himself.

Certainly "fantastic realism" well characterizes many of the striking actions of Dostoevsky's heroes and heroines. He was an avid reader of newspapers, and he drew on them, as well as upon Gothic tales and adventure stories, for some of the seemingly bizarre elements of his plots and the stranger lineaments of his characters. It gave him no little artistic satisfaction, in terms of his convictions on "fantastic realism," to read in a newspaper, shortly after the appearance of the first part of *Crime and Punishment*, an account of the murder of a pawnbroker by a Moscow student under circumstances that resembled closely those connected with Raskolnikov's murder of the old pawnbroker.

It is illuminating to observe how Dostoevsky directly transmutes one of these "fantastic facts of reality" into the pure gold of art. He read in the newspaper of a young woman who, clasping an ikon to her breast, jumped four stories to her death. The incident inspired his exquisite tale, *A Gentle Creature*. Starting with the suicide, the bare facts of the press release pass through the alembic of his uncanny analytical imagination as he works backwards in an effort to build up a frame of action that is consistent with psychological realism and the truth of the tragedy.

Dostoevsky's literary style and method were fairly well formed by 1849, when he was sentenced to prison in Siberia for revolutionary activities in connection with the Petrashevsky Circle. In the course of this first period, besides *Poor Folk*, twelve more pieces appeared—sketches, short stories, a novella, and the unfinished novel *Netochka Nezvanova*. Most of the surface aspects of the great literary artist of the future may be detected in these early writings. In one of the short stories, *A Faint Heart*, he describes his narrative approach. He begins with the action, *in medias res*, avoiding the long build-up in characterization or in events so common with his great contemporaries in fiction. At the outset this technique may cause some confusion for the reader and it creates at once an atmosphere of foreboding or expectancy. Chronology and logical sequence are dispensed with as incidents occur before the conditions governing them; the relations between characters are told or their behavior described before they themselves appear on the scene. The air of mystery which surrounds his tales at the beginning is largely a result of these devices; it eventually vanishes and the world of reality appears. The method, of course, is consciously dramatic and has led some critics to assert that Dostoevsky actually blocked out his novels as a dramatist might plan a play, a notion that loses credibility in the light of the structure, psychological analysis of the characters, and the length of the novels. The use of dramatic devices in prose fiction was already an established technique which Dostoevsky could have learned from foreign Gothic tales and stories of adventure which he obviously relished. Even this early in his fiction one perceives detective story elements, action that develops swiftly unimpeded by long descriptions, and the characters, mostly wretched clerks and poor students dwelling in the unsavory corners of St. Petersburg, fall into definite psychological types who live through their feelings, in the chaos of passion.

Dostoevsky spent nearly ten years as a convict at Omsk and in compulsory service as a soldier in Siberia before he was permitted to return to St. Petersburg and once again resume his literary career. There was no essential change in his creative methods, as is commonly maintained, only a steady development of established techniques. If anything, prison defined and deepened his creative urges. But his harsh experiences in Siberia did markedly alter his outlook on life and profoundly influenced the content and spiritual quality of his fiction. His youthful, radical yearning for social reform had been sublimated in a renewed faith in the teachings of Christ and in the power of the Orthodox Church to bring surcease to the troubled existence of Russia. In prison he had constantly read the New Testament, the only book allowed, and it had taught him, along with his own unhappy experiences, the doctrine of salvation by suffering. Shortly after his release, he wrote a woman who had befriended him as a convict and told her of his new faith, a statement that illuminates the spiritual change he had undergone: "Here it is: to believe that there is nothing more beautiful, more profound, more sympathetic, more reasonable, more manly, and more perfect than Christ, and not only is there nothing, but, I tell myself with jealous love, there can be nothing. Besides, if anyone proved to me that Christ was outside the truth, and it *really* was so that the truth was outside Christ, then I should prefer to remain with Christ than with the truth."

The importance of this credo in the development of Dostoevsky's future thought and for the spiritual content of the great novels to come is self-evident. Finally, in prison he had got to know the common people of Russia as never before, and in their natural gifts and their infinite capacity for patient suffering he saw more hope for the future of Russia than in all the efforts of the intellectuals. Dostoevsky left Siberia with a mind crammed with rich material for further study and future writing.

4

Between 1859, when he resumed publishing, and 1862 Dostoevsky wrote the long short story *Uncle's Dream;* a novelette, *The Village of Stepanchikovo; The House of the Dead,* a book based on his prison experience; and his first completed full-length novel, *The Insulted and Injured.* The fiction represents a continuation in form and content of his pre-prison stories but with some advance in the delineation of character. Though *The House of the Dead,* which Tolstoy for reasons of his own placed at the head of his rival's works, is usually regarded as a piece of superb reporting, it is obviously much more than this. In the grim, detached realism, the selection of detail, and especially in the imaginative apprehension and psychological analysis of leading personalities among the convicts, Dostoevsky is every bit the literary artist. In the early tales he had evinced a passing interest in the criminal type, such as Bykov in *Poor Folk* and old Murin in *The Landlady*. Now, in *The House of the Dead*, he manifests a keen psychological interest in the incorrigible criminal, such as Orlov and Petrov, who kills on instinct rather than by reason and thus reveals a positive connection between criminality and the dominance of self-will. This more penetrating understanding of the criminal type served Dostoevsky well in the creation of similar characters in the great novels.

In 1861, the year Dobrolyubov died, he published a comprehensive critical review of all Dostoevsky's fiction up to that time. Though the article is essentially a treatment, from the radical-democratic point of view, of Dostoevsky's compassion for the downtrodden "little people," Dobrolyubov also pointed out the tendency of the principal characters to fall into two easily recognized types which he called the "embittered" and the "meek." And one of these embittered heroes, Golyadkin in Dostoevsky's second story *The Double*, he further described as a "split personality."

This early singling out of types, supported later by their repetition in the great novels, has provided a special focus for a wealth of critical analysis, in which the structural unity and philosophical ambience of Dostoevsky's fiction are sometimes regarded as deriving from the inner significance of type personalities. In much of this critical literature nowadays two or even three well-defined types are recognized—the Double, the Meek, and the Self-Willed criminal type.

These types, especially the Double with its often puzzling psychic ambiguities, have attracted psychologists and psychoanalysts who have published a number of interesting case studies which in general attempt to relate the complex behavior patterns of the characters to the unconscious drives of their creator. In these efforts methods of investigation and conclusions have varied somewhat. Freud saw Dostoevsky as a victim of parricidal impulses and a consequent guilt complex reflected in Ivan and Dmitri Karamazov. P. C. Squires decided that "Dostoevsky was an epileptic, schizophrene, paranoid type, complicated by hysterical overlay." J. Neufeld reached the startling conclusion that the Slavophilism projected in the novels was owing to an Oedipus complex which represented Dostoevsky's impassioned love for his "mother," the "mother" in this case being Mother Russia. W. Stekel explained the theft of a pair of pants in the short story *The Honest Thief* as a transformation of homosexuality into kleptomania! S. O. Lesser based the fatal relations of Myshkin, Rogozhin, and Nastasya Filipovna in *The Idiot* on the strong homosexual bond between the two men. Of two investigators of *Crime and Punishment*, one concludes that "Raskolnikov was an autistic personality with traces of the manic depressive," and the other that his murder of the old moneylender "was the result of efforts to appease unconscious guilt due to an incestuous attachment to his sister."

In *The Brothers Karamazov* Dostoevsky once remarked that psychology cuts both ways. One suspects that he would have happily agreed with Jung's observation that that which constitutes the essential nature of art must always lie outside psychology's province. Long before the advent of Freud he had become a brilliant amateur psychologist with the profound insights of a literary genius, and before Proust he had learned to explore the unconscious in depth, but with an artistic purpose quite different from that of the great French novelist. While he was still doing his enforced military service in Siberia, Dostoevsky planned to collaborate with a friend on the translation of the work of a German physician and zoologist C. G. Carus, *Psyche: Zur Entwicklungsgeschichte der Seele* (1846). Though the project was dropped, Dostoevsky no doubt absorbed ideas from this book which were later used in his fiction, such as the theory that an abnormal state of mind may be the gateway to supernormal experiences, a process which seems to be reflected in the behavior patterns of Raskolnikov, Myshkin, and Stavrogin; the notion of the periodic throwback of conscious activity into the unconscious which illuminates the actions of several characters and is directly echoed in *The Idiot* by Myshkin; and the idea that magnetism is the intermarriage of nervous systems insensibly drawing two people together, which may account for the emphasis Dostoevsky places on the magnetic attraction of such pairs as Raskolnikov and Svidrigailov, Myshkin and Rogozhin, Pyotr Verkhovensky and Stavrogin, and Ivan Karamazov and Smerdyakov. Then, too, Carus' theorizing on the symbolism of dreams may have encouraged Dostoevsky's frequent use of this device in his fiction.

In general, however, Dostoevsky seemed to be opposed to systematic psychology. His method is to dramatize the psychopathic experiences of his characters without indulging in extended psychological comment. Intuition and self-observation, as well as observation of others, largely account for his astounding knowledge of the workings of the conscious and unconscious mind. In terms of the recent theory of "intentional fallacy" in fiction, which has understandably encouraged psychiatric speculation about the creative process, Dostoevsky's novels fail to support the proposition that a work of art cannot be evaluated according to its manifest intention, that what really matters is not what the author intends, but what he actually writes in the finished novel. There is little need to guess at Dostoevsky's intentions. They are abundantly expressed, in the case of the major novels, in notebooks, letters, and other documentary material and they appear to be amply fulfilled in the printed works.

Some psychoanalytic literary critics admit that it is impossible to realize scientific conclusiveness in such investigations, since characters in novels are not real people and biographical information about their authors is hardly ever sufficiently complete for case-study purposes. Added to this uncertainty is the fact, which Freud asserted in his study of *The Brothers Karamazov*, that every author is free to borrow from the treasury of world literature various standard situations of psychiatric import.

Despite Dostoevsky's assertion that he was not a psychologist but a realist in the higher sense, his fiction conforms in part to Freud's description of the psychological novel as one in which modern writers split up their ego into component egos through a process of self-observation and in this way personify in many heroes the conflicting trends in their own mental life. This definition, however, fails to suggest Dostoevsky's artistic skill in allowing even his most dialectically minded Doubles to speak only their own thoughts. Or, it might be better to say, he creates this illusion.

Though Dostoevsky's experiences and self-examination enter into portrayals of the fascinating series of Doubles, he was perfectly aware of the psychopathological aspect of the type even though he lacked the technical refinements of modern novelists who follow a master such as Freud. As early as *The Double*, where he carries the development of the type to the extreme of insanity and of projecting a second self, Dostoevsky's comments reveal his knowledge of the abnormal manifestations involved in the characterization of Golyadkin. And *A Raw Youth*, written much later and ranked artistically below the four famous novels, is nevertheless intensely interesting for the student of Doestoevsky's method and for its direct statements

on the ambivalence which had dominated many of his characters up to this point. Speaking of the personality of the major
figure, the Double Versilov, his son Dolgoruky remarks: "It
has always been a mystery, and I have marvelled a thousand
times at that faculty of man . . . of cherishing in his soul his
loftiest ideals side by side with the greatest baseness, and all
quite sincerely." Versilov frankly confesses to such feelings:
"Yes, I am split in two mentally and I am terribly afraid of this.
It is just as though your double were standing beside you; you
yourself are sensible and rational, but this other person beside
you wishes without fail to do something senseless and occasionally something funny, and God knows why; that is, you
want to against your will, as it were; although you fight against
it with all your might, you want to do it." And at the end of
the novel, his son says of his father's dualism: "But the Double
I do accept unquestionably. What exactly is a Double? The
Double, at least according to a medical book of a certain expert . . . is nothing other than the first stage of a serious mental
derangement, which may lead to something very bad."

The part self-observation may have played in the conception
of the Double type is suggested in a letter that Dostoevsky
wrote to a female correspondent who sought his advice on her
dual impulses which, she feared, led her to commit reprehensible acts. He answered: "That trait is common to all. . . . that
is, all who are not wholly commonplace. Nay, it is common
nature, though it does not evince itself so strongly in all as it
does in you. It is precisely on this ground that I cannot but regard you as a twin soul, for your inner duality corresponds
exactly to my own. It causes at once great torment and great
delight. . . . Yes, such duality is a great torment. . . . Do you
believe in Christ and in His Commandments? If you believe in
Him (or at least have a strong desire to do so), then give yourself wholly up to Him; the pain of your duality will be thereby

alleviated, and you will find the true way out—but belief is first of all in importance." This is a key statement in support of Dostoevsky's complete awareness of what he was about in the artistic creation of those famous characters that fall into the category of the Double. And belief in Christ, as he told his correspondent, was also his solution, however unconvincing, for the resolution of their tormenting dualism.

In a recent article an expert in psychology has properly pointed out that the divided selves of Dostoevsky's Doubles do not correspond to psychiatric notions of the "split personality," nor to the commonly accepted symptoms of schizophrenia. "Dostoevsky's consciously 'split' characters," he writes, "do present classical symptoms of the obsessive-compulsive character, however. The 'split' is not a separation of selves, it is an obsessive balancing or undoing of one idea or force with its opposite."* This really seems to describe the invariable state of mind of the Doubles. They are men and women obsessed by contending forces such as love and hate, pride and meekness, belief in God and disbelief, and the struggle for dominance determines the actions of the characters and defines their personalities. At times it appears that the Double combines in its makeup the traits of the other two types—the Meek and the Self-willed.

Before *Notes from the Underground* (1864), the Double was clearly adumbrated in a number of tales, but these early characters reveal little self-knowledge of their personalities and never analyze in any depth their dualistic feelings and convictions. The nameless hero of *Notes from the Underground*, however, is a profound analyst of his own ideas and feelings as

* Lawrence Kohlberg, "Psychological Analysis and Literary Form: A Study in the Doubles of Dostoevsky," *Daedalus*, 92 (Spring 1963), p. 352. The evidence assembled in this excellent article has been very helpful in the formulation of my own views on the problems connected with Dostoevsky and psychology.

well as those of others. He is a "thinking Double" and in this respect marks a significant advance in Dostoevsky's essentially realistic method of characterization.

In fact, this remarkable work, which employs a concentrated power of psychological analysis unique in literature at that time, signalizes a turning point in Dostoevsky's creative art. A series of happenings in his life shortly before writing *Notes from the Underground* probably contributed to its misanthropic tone. Trips abroad disillusioned him about the political and social structure there and strengthened his faith in the future high destiny of Russia if it could be kept free of the materialistic poison of the West. These experiences parallel a shift from the mild liberalism he had been expressing in his magazine *Time* to the conservatism that shortly appeared in his new magazine *Epoch*. Then an unsuccessful love affair with that strange woman Polina Suslova deeply affected him both emotionally and creatively. The love-hate feeling of this female Double in real life enriched his understanding of the type in fiction. Finally, the death of his wife and older brother, so closely associated with him in his journalistic endeavors, scarred his mind at the time of writing *Notes from the Underground*.

This short work is a kind of prologue to the great novels to come for it contains their basic motifs in attenuated form. Its first part is often regarded, on a purely metaphysical level, as an early and amazing foreshadowing of modern existentialism. The fullest expression of man's individuality characterized in all its most revolting aspects emerges triumphant in the end as a manifestation of the highest good. Dostoevsky himself was not an existentialist, but the first part of *Notes from the Underground* is a remarkable overture to that philosophy in which may be found the major themes that have concerned existentialist thinkers from Kierkegaard to Sartre.

However, Dostoevsky was writing fiction and not a philo-

sophical tract. The underground man takes his place among the
Doubles. Every positive human attribute of his nature seems to
inspire its negative quality. He thirsts for power and is power-
less, he desires to torture and be tortured, to debase himself and
debase others, to be proud and to humble himself. He is an
antihero like nearly all Dostoevsky's major figures, a rebel
against the constituted order of things. These very catchwords
suggest the modernity of Dostoevsky and why he has influenced the novel and thought of our own time. The underground man, for example, would fit very well into the tragic
and absurd condition of life which Sartre allots to man. There
is, of course, an overriding difference in the approaches.
Dostoevsky's emphasis is on the spiritual life of dislocated man
in a real and acceptable world, whereas the antiheroes of not
a few novelists today are concerned solely with anxieties and
contradictions of their inner life growing out of daily battle
with an unreal, dislocated world whose irrational responses
seem to leave them no alternatives other than sex and alcohol.

But the underground man, unlike earlier characters of this
type, is fully aware of his dualism and subjects all the contradictions of his distorted personality to a searching analysis. He concludes that his fundamental conflict is based on an opposition
between will and reason. Will negates reason and in turn is
negated by reason. He inveighs against socialists who think that
man can be governed by rational self-interest, a position that
Dostoevsky himself had taken shortly before in an article in his
magazine. Reason no more determines the path of man's life
than the path of history, argues the underground man.

There is some evidence that Dostoevsky had offered a substitute for the evil of reason in *Notes from the Underground* and
that it had been deleted by the censor. However, he had earlier
advocated this substitute in his magazine article, "Winter Notes
on Summer Impressions," namely, man must have religion to

fall back on. That is, the underground man would have to achieve faith in a love of Christ in order to find peace of mind and ultimate salvation. This way out is plainly indicated in the second part of *Notes from the Underground* where the prostitute, who possesses pity and love, can be saved, whereas the underground man has only reason to fall back on and hence is cut off from life.

It is little wonder that Nietzsche's "joy was extraordinary," as he expressed it, when he first read *Notes from the Underground*, and he discovered in it "music, very strange, very un-Germanic music." No work of fiction had ever previously analyzed the complexities of the human personality so completely. Moreover, in *Notes from the Underground*, Dostoevsky had taken a long step forward in intellectualizing his favorite type character, the Double, and in involving it with philosophical, political, and social ideas of great importance in his future novels.

5

In the series of celebrated novels beginning with *Crime and Punishment* (1866), Dostoevsky stressed a feature that had been only hinted at in his earlier writings and was new in Russian and European fiction in general. Ideas now began to play the central role in his novels. His chief figures are often embodied ideas and he appears to be concerned not so much with the life of his characters as with the ideas they represent. Such a process, of course, leads to the disintegration of the ordinary world of the novel and in its place we have a world of men and women organized according to the ideas that possess them. The characters have no biography, for they are exempt from the cause and effect of daily life and the only verisimilitude is their inner word about themselves.

In Russia in the 1920's excellent critical studies were devoted to the significance of ideas in the structural complex of Dostoevsky's fiction, but all were agreed that he wrote not philosophical or purpose novels, but rather novels about ideas. The essential conflict in these investigations was whether Dostoevsky synthesized the ideas of his characters into a philosophical position of his own or whether he refrained from resolving their conflicting ideas, allowing them to coexist as a perpetual dramatization of the internal contradictions of man. In the latter case the assumption would be that the hero was given complete freedom to develop his ideas because Dostoevsky was not interested in him as a typification of a way of life, as an object of reality, but only as a special point of view on the world and on himself.

If these scholars had been able to make full use of Dostoevsky's notebooks, letters, and journalistic writings, the extent of his conscious control over the characters and ideas they embody would have been much clarified. To be sure, the character's integrity and self-awareness of ideas deriving from his total personality are always artistically sustained, but it is a mistake to imagine that Dostoevsky did not consciously work out in advance a concrete system of thought for a major character, although he may have elaborated the plan set down in his notebooks and letters in the course of writing the novel.

For example, in the notebooks and in letters to his publisher Katkov, Dostoevsky provides us with a comprehensive outline of *Crime and Punishment* and much information about the nature of Raskolnikov and the basic ideas he embodies. He wishes to present his hero at the moment of the birth of a terribly destructive idea which is the fruit of his rebellion against society. Raskolnikov's theory of ordinary and extraordinary people and the crime that results from it are products of what Dostoevsky considered the distorted thinking of the young revolutionary-minded generation. They are people who think it possible to organize a social system on a rational plan, that reason can take the place of human nature, of the living process of life. In his journalistic writings, as well as in *Notes from the Underground*, Dostoevsky had already expressed a negative position on these claims which he associated with the pretensions of socialism, for he believed that life would not submit to mechanical rules or the living soul to logic. This is the central idea of *Crime and Punishment*—to portray a man who is the victim of "incomplete ideas" going the rounds, as he explained in his letter to Katkov, a person who tries to order his life on a self-willed plan of reason. In addition, Dostoevsky further explains to his publisher, he wants to demonstrate through his hero that the legal punishment inflicted for a crime intimidates a criminal infinitely less than lawmakers think, partly because the guilty person morally demands punishment.

In the notebooks as Dostoevsky analyzes the idea in terms of the hero, he recognizes a persistent ambiguity deriving from the dualism of Raskolnikov whom he has cast as one of his thinking Doubles. Of this there can be no doubt. In the novel Razumikhin says of his friend Raskolnikov: "In truth, it is as though he were alternating between two opposing characters." And a striking jotting in the notebook not only identifies the fact of dualism in the characterization, but also reflects Dostoevsky's image of the Doubles as containing the opposing traits of two other character types—the Meek and the Self-Willed. For he writes: "Svidrigailov is desperation, the most cynical. Sonya is hope, the most unrealizable. (These must be expressed by Raskolnikov himself.) He is passionately attached to them both."

It is the inner contradiction of self-will and submissiveness in Raskolnikov's nature which, when expressed in action, creates the intense drama of the novel. This dualism undermines

his self-willed theory of murder and in the end leaves him completely confused about his motive for killing the old pawnbroker—a miracle of psychological perception on Dostoevsky's
part. And after the murder Raskolnikov is similarly torn between Sonya's path of submissiveness to expiation of his crime
and his self-willed pride which convinces him that the murder
was a crime only because he failed in his purpose.

Interestingly enough, the notebooks indicate that Dostoevsky, having originally launched his hero with a single-minded
motive for committing the murder, also got momentarily lost in
Raskolnikov's dualistic crosspurposes. In a fragment of dialogue
in the notes Raskolnikov argues a specific motivation for the
crime: "There is one law—a moral law. Agreed, agreed! Well,
sir, and this law? Why, if conscience does not accuse me, I seize
authority, I acquire power—whether money or might, and not
for evil. I bring happiness. Well, then, because of a paltry
screen, to stand and look over to that side of the screen, to envy
and hate and to stand still. That's ignoble." On the margin,
opposite the passage, Dostoevsky wrote: "Devil take it! This is
partly right."

Similarly, Raskolnikov's arguments for and against revealing
his crime and accepting punishment obviously began to raise
doubts in Dostoevsky's mind that the denouement which he
had long since conveyed to his publisher was the artistically
logical one. Entries in the notebooks show his fluctuations on
this score. Should Raskolnikov, a facet of whose nature is endowed with satanic pride, seek the way out of suicide, the only
possible solution of the wholly self-willed character Svidrigailov? And under the heading "Conclusion for the novel," Dostoevsky set down in one of the notebooks: "Raskolnikov goes
to shoot himself." But in the end Dostoevsky sacrificed this
aesthetically satisfying conclusion to the original idea of the
novel which was his own idea rather than that of his hero—

Raskolnikov must reveal his crime, accept his punishment, and having discovered faith in Christ, will learn in prison that happiness cannot be achieved by a reasoned plan of existence but must be earned through suffering. Dostoevsky had applied the balm, salvation by suffering, which he had learned in his own prison experience, to resolve the dualism of his hero and dissipate the dangerous "incomplete ideas" which had led him to crime as, in a sense, they had once led Dostoevsky to commit a crime against the state. It is a most lame and impotent conclusion.

From this point on the remaining novels reveal a pattern of uniformity in dramatized ideas, type characters, and Dostoevskian philosophy cast against a background of extraordinary diversity of action. There is no lack of individualization in heroes and heroines, but increasingly all reality becomes only an element in their self-knowledge. As in the case of *Crime and Punishment* at the end, the other masterpieces irresistibly reach out more and more to the chief question that consciously or unconsciously profoundly troubled Dostoevsky's mind—the existence of God.

6

A long stay abroad with his second wife (1867-71) served to crystallize Dostoevsky's opinions concerning the religious and political opposition between Russia and Western Europe. Many letters back home show his growing conviction of the mission of Russia and its Orthodox Church to save Western civilization whose decay, he imagined, was being brought about by bourgeois materialism and socialist chicanery. He worried acutely over the influence of Western radicalism on revolutionary-minded Russian youths. During these years and later he dreamed of a vast artistic work that would involve a treatment of the theme of the ultimate salvation of a civilization at war with itself, in which Russia and its Christian faith would be the instruments of grace. While he was writing *The Idiot*, he worked away under the shadow of this cosmic idea which, he felt, would require three to five connected novels bearing the general title, "The Life of a Great Sinner." Though he never wrote this huge work, for which he has left behind some rough plans and notes, he borrowed from it in creating several novels in which he depicted the tragedy and pain Russia would have to suffer before it could achieve world leadership and the salvation of Europe envisaged in the sweeping design of "The Life of a Great Sinner." Facets of the design shine most brightly in *The Possessed* and *The Brothers Karamazov*, but *The Idiot* must be regarded as an initial contribution to a fictional project concerned with an artistic synthesis of universal salvation.

In this work the towering love-hate motif involving Myshkin, Rogozhin, Ganya, Nastasya, and Aglaya; the rebellion against God of the ambivalent Terentev, whose philosophizing develops that of Raskolnikov and anticipates the ideas of Kirilov in *The Possessed* and Ivan Karamazov; the noisy protests of the young radicals; and the confusing activities of the Epanchins, Ivolgins and their hangers-on—all tend to obscure the central idea of *The Idiot*. Its successful realization was regarded by Dostoevsky as the principal aim of the work. He wrote his friend Strakhov: "In the novel much was composed in haste, much is prolix and has not succeeded, but something has succeeded. I do not stand behind the novel. I stand behind my idea."

Through many pages of eight separate outlines of *The Idiot* in the notebooks, one may follow Dostoevsky's frustrating search for the identity of his hero. Without a clear image of him and the idea he represented the novel remained mired in false starts. Interestingly enough the original conception of

Myshkin is that of a Double and his dominant traits resemble those of Rogozhin in the novel rather than those of the Idiot Prince. In one of the notes in the sixth plan Dostoevsky pinpoints his chief characteristic as "The dualism of a profound nature." But certain Christian features are opposed to the titanism and morbid pride of his dual personality. In the plan Dostoevsky developed these softening traits much further in still another character whom he later discarded. This preoccupation with Christian attributes very likely caused him to connect them with the image of the hero which so persistently evaded him. For toward the end of the seventh plan a sudden inspiration flashed through Dostoevsky's brain. He set down a cryptic note, pregnant with meaning in terms of the finished characterization of the hero of the novel: "He is a Prince. An Idiot Prince (he is with the children)?!"

Actually, Dostoevsky claimed that the idea represented by Myshkin had been in his mind for a long time, and apparently it required only a clear image of his hero to bring it to realization. "The chief idea of the novel," he wrote his niece, "is to portray the positively good man. There is nothing in the world more difficult to do, and especially now. . . . The good is an ideal, but this ideal, both ours and that of civilized Europe, is still far from having been worked out. There is only one positively good man in the world—Christ." Further, for Dostoevsky the idea was also concerned with the larger problem of ethical and moral good in the Russian nature.

Dostoevsky was aware of the difficulty of convincingly portraying a character endowed with the perfect moral beauty of Christ, for he realized that human perfection in any form did not exist in real life. We find him confronting the problem in the notebooks and offering his own solution: "How to make the figure of the hero appealing to the reader? If Don Quixote and Pickwick, as virtuous figures, succeed in gaining the sympathy of the readers because they are laughable, the hero of the novel, the Prince, if he is not laughable, then he has another appealing feature—innocence!" In the further interests of realism, Dostoevsky also felt it wise to introduce the human flaws of epilepsy and idiocy in the otherwise perfect white marble surface of Myshkin's moral beauty.

Myshkin is the first of the Meek characters to become the hero of a novel, and unlike the others—Sonya Marmeladova, for example—he has the capacity to analyze his feelings and thoughts and develop what might be called the Meek personality's philosophy of life. He has a kind of sixth sense, mentioned by Dostoevsky in his notes, which enables him to see through the thoughts of others. His social and religious views, in their positive or negative meaning, anticipate those of characters in *The Possessed*, *A Raw Youth*, and *The Brothers Karamazov*, and they are very close to Dostoevsky's if we may judge from the personal opinions he expressed in letters and journalistic articles. In brief, Myshkin asserts that the authoritarian path of both the Roman Catholic Church and socialism leads to the destruction of society in which they seek to impose the equality of despotism. Myshkin, on the other hand, calls on all to accept the Russian Orthodox faith which, he insists, aims to bring about universal harmony by preaching submission and service to one another and thus achieve a true equality.

Like all the Meek characters, Myshkin is passive, but the greedy, sensual, sinning society in which he moves is intensely active. His influence is exercised solely through the spiritual perfection of his own life and the force of his radiant personality. Despite his great religious faith, which calls for an enraptured unification with the highest synthesis of life, he fails in his mission. He finds it difficult to comprehend the passionate love Nastasya and Aglaya offer him, for what his morally perfect nature seeks is a spiritual, not an earthly, union of man and woman. At the conclusion of the novel nearly all the sinning people he has influenced are rendered unhappy. Nastasya has been murdered, and Myshkin himself has lapsed into idiocy. Perhaps Dostoevsky intended the outcome to symbolize Christ's failure on earth among those of little faith.

Unlike *The Idiot*, *The Possessed* is not dominated by a central, all-pervading idea, or perhaps it might be more correct to say that if Dostoevsky began the novel with such an idea, it got lost in the conflicting action of the work. It was the only novel he ever wrote with a deliberate didactic purpose in mind, and its inadequacies may be attributed to this fact.

In the second half of 1869 Dostoevsky began to write a novel the subject of which we have no way of knowing. Shortly after he started he was electrified to read in the press of the murder of a young Moscow student who belonged to a secret political society organized by S. G. Nechaev, a disciple of the revolutionist Bakunin. The student had been slain because of suspected treachery to the group. Dostoevsky promptly seized upon the Nechaev affair as the main theme of the novel he was trying to write. Apparently he originally thought of it as a quick fictionized version of the political conspiracy and the murder which would enable him to pay off a long overdue debt in accumulated advances to his publisher. Besides, he saw an opportunity to speak out more directly and forcefully against radical tendencies which he believed were undermining Russia.

Dostoevsky's creative process did not operate in this manner. The more he worked on *The Possessed* the longer and more complicated it became. The notebooks shed light on some of his difficulties, especially the fact that the Nechaev affair soon began to attract into its orbit certain of the situations and at least one major character from the plan of the unwritten "Life of a Great Sinner," as well as profound questions of religion and morality implicit in that projected work. More so than in any previous novel, characters in *The Possessed* are modeled on real people—the political conspirators on the participants in the Nechaev affair, old Verkhovensky on T. N. Granovsky, a piously liberal professor of history in the 1840's, Karmazinov on Turgenev. Dostoevsky had turned against his own liberal youth, and these satirical portraits of older liberals reflect his growing conviction that they were responsible for the revolutionary activities of murderous young radicals such as Nechaev and his followers. Eventually he managed to integrate, though not always successfully, the two main strands of his plot—the romantic element built around Stavrogin and suggested in part by the plan of "The Life of a Great Sinner," and the political conspiracy headed by the bloodthirsty young Verkhovensky, modeled on Nechaev.

Dostoevsky declared that the main character in *The Possessed* is Stavrogin and the wealth of material on him in the notebooks indicates that no other figure caused him so much uncertainty. With some prescience he wrote his publisher: "It seems to me that this figure is tragic, although many will no doubt say, after reading: 'What is that?' " Critics, perhaps seduced by the charm of bafflement, have written much about Stavrogin, preferring to see in the curious evasiveness of the characterization occult significance, psychoanalytical denotations, or profound symbolic truths. In searching for a striking symbolic correspondence, a recent critic proposes that the birth of Christ is relevant to the birth of Stavrogin's illegitimate son by Mariya Shatova!

More than once Dostoevsky has been charged with failing to preserve logical coherence in the projection of his complex characters. Pressures of illness, time, deadlines of serial publication, and the urgent need for money may account for some of his lapses in this respect. Although an author ought never to mystify himself, to say nothing of his readers, it is possible to discern an artistic purpose in what might be paradoxically described as the logical incoherence of Stavrogin, for certainly in terms of the story of *The Possessed* his enigmatic nature seems definitely to have contributed to his extraordinary fascination for the reader.

The evil model in the plan of "The Life of a Great Sinner" seems to have been the starting point of the characterization of Stavrogin, but in adapting him to the plot of another novel ambiguity set in. Although at least two real persons have been mentioned as models, it is clear from the notebooks—as Dostoevsky worked away at Stavrogin—that the image began to attract some of the typical traits of the Byronic hero, such as Pushkin's Eugene Onegin and Lermontov's Pechorin. In one place in the notes Dostoevsky actually describes him as "Byronic."

It is interesting, however, that there is much clarifying material in the notebooks on the career, personality, and motives of Stavrogin's strange actions, yet Dostoevsky studiously avoids working it into the finished novel. In fact, in one place in his notes he reminds himself "not to explain the prince [Stavrogin]," and in another, "to keep the reader in a quandary." And under the caption "Very Important" in the notes, he jots down: "The prince reveals himself to no one and is everywhere mysterious." Instead of Stavrogin becoming the typical Dostoevskian hero who is a bearer of ideas, the author cautions himself in the notes: "The prince does not have any special ideas. He has only an aversion to his contemporaries, with whom he has resolved to break. . . . But there are no ideas."

Finally, though his publisher refused to print the famous section, "The Confession of Stavrogin," which contains the account of his violation of the little girl and much other important information about his actions and thoughts, there is no evidence that Dostoevsky protested this exclusion, nor did he ever attempt, as he could so easily have done, to include it in subsequent editions of the novel. Yet the facts in this omitted section concerning Stavrogin's past life and the emphasis upon the crime against the girl which torments his conscience contribute much toward explaining his unaccountable behavior in *The Possessed*. On the whole, it seems clear that Dostoevsky deliberately strove to make Stavrogin a mysterious, enigmatic character because he believed that this kind of portrayal would best serve the artistic purpose of his novel.

Though the personal magnetism of this strange man draws all to him and he exerts a powerful influence over such individuals as young Verkhovensky, Shatov, Kirilov, Liza, and others, in the end they recognize the deception and pitiful emptiness of their hero. Stavrogin, in his struggle between good and evil, reaches the bottom of psychological amoralism where he is finally unable to distinguish between good and evil. Eventually even the struggle ceases, and as a complete moral and spiritual bankrupt he takes the only way out—suicide.

It is the world of revolutionary conspiracy, in which Stavrogin plays a rather passive role, that provides most of the action of *The Possessed*. The whole handling of the conspiracy is, of course, a grotesque parody of Russian radicalism of the time. But Dostoevskys' bitter satire of the participants is sincere, inspired by fierce ideological opposition and deep anxiety over the use of violence to achieve political ends. Here realism is sacrificed to didacticism, and the characters in question, instead of being driven by their own ideas, are driven by those imposed upon them by their creator.

A different matter are Shatov and Kirilov, both of whom are in the process of breaking away from the conspiracy. They represent brilliant ideological projections that strangely complement each other in their polarity. Shatov believes in a God who is a man and Kirilov in a man-God. For Shatov faith in the world destiny of Russia and its people requires faith also in the

Russian Orthodox God. Kirilov believes that it is man who has created the world and God and that they exist only to the extent that the individual wills them to exist.

At the end of *The Possessed*, it is that charming and amusingly satirized old liberal Stepan Trofimovich Verkhovensky who carries the real message of the novel—Dostoevsky's answer to the radicals. For driven to hysteria by the crimes of his son, the old man wanders off in a quixotic search for Russia, and he finds it in his new faith in the religion of the masses whom he had always scorned.

7

It was in *The Brothers Karamazov*, however, that Dostoevsky offered a final answer to the problem of faith, of God, which had encroached on all his previous major novels and had obviously troubled his own dualistic thinking for years. The search for God is the central idea of *The Brothers Karamazov*. In no other novel has the white-hot intensity of his ideological world glowed so brightly or has he spiritualized ideas so arrestingly. And nowhere else has he employed so compellingly his wonderful artistic capacity to evolve ideas of universal significance from the sordid stuff of life as in this story of the terrible crime of parricide and clashing passions of love and hate.

The taint of old Karamazov, a monster of lust and debauchery, exists in all his sons. It is less apparent in the saint-like Alyosha, perhaps because his image is incomplete in the novel. Dostoevsky's notes and the novel itself indicate that the portrayal of Alyosha would continue in one or more sequels, for like the projected hero of the plan of "The Life of a Great Sinner," who undoubtedly influenced the conception of Alyosha, he was destined to go out into the world and live through a stormy period of sinning and revolutionary activities before he achieved salvation by suffering. But Dostoevsky had only a few months to live after completing *The Brothers Karamazov*. In the novel Alyosha is the only one of the brothers who loves life more than the meaning of life. He has the intuitive wisdom, selfless compassionate heart, and radiant personality of the meek Myshkin, and like him he morally influences all with whom he comes in contact.

The Karamazov taint of carnal sensuality is strongest in Dmitri, who in some respects may be regarded as the hero of the novel for its story is largely his. Simplicity and deep feeling are the essence of his nature. He acts on instinct rather than on calculation. Dmitri earns the right to forgiveness of all the evil in him by his capacity to repent and suffer. He admits to a certain moral guilt when falsely accused and convicted of the murder of his father, and conscious of his baseness, of having sullied his honor, he declares at the trial, "I accept the torture of accusation and my public shame. I want to suffer, and by suffering I shall purify myself."

The notebook and letters, however, indicate that Dostoevsky thought of Ivan as the hero. He is easily the most absorbing character in the novel and in certain respects he reflects the mental image of his creator. In the notebooks Ivan is actually mentioned as the murderer of his father, thus conclusively establishing the full import of his moral guilt in implanting the idea of the slaying in the twisted mind of his illegitimate half-brother Smerdyakov.

Ivan is the last and the most fascinating of Dostoevsky's series of Doubles, and his ambivalence takes the highest form of a cosmic struggle of man with God. He begins with an act of rebellion and ends in complete metaphysical insurrection against God's world. The Karamazov taint in him takes the form of intellectual pride. When his pride asserts itself, he dreams, like Terentev and Kirilov, of becoming a man-god; when the sub-

missive side of his nature predominates, he is dejectedly prepared to accept the world-god, for he cannot understand the
higher harmony between man and the world of God.

The resolution of Ivan's struggle, as well as the whole ideological emphasis of the novel, is concentrated in the section
entitled "Pro and Contra," one of Dostoevsky's greatest artistic
achievements. Evidence has been provided in this study to
demonstrate that the leading characters and their ideas are not
unconsciously symbolic creations or uncontrolled manifestations of "intentional fallacy." On the contrary, they are very
consciously controlled creations of a great literary artist who
carefully shaped his material to fit prepared designs and did
not hesitate to use his characters as mouthpieces of his own favorite ideas, although this is nearly always contrived with consummate art and realistically adjusted to the intellectual and
spiritual horizons of his protagonists. In the notebooks, for example, and in a long letter to his editor on "Pro and Contra,"
Dostoevsky emphatically states that his main intention in this
section, which he regards as the culminating point of the novel,
is not so much a denial of God as a repudiation of the meaning
of His creation. He connects this position of Ivan with socialism which, he declares in the letter to his editor, "sprang up
and started with a denial of the meaning of historical actuality
and arrived at a program of destruction and anarchism." And he
pleads with the editor not to change a word in Ivan's recital of
the shocking sufferings of little children, for these are all true
accounts, he explains, which he has taken from newspapers and
other authentic sources. Then he pointedly insists that Ivan's
contention, based on the senseless sufferings of innocent children, that the whole of historical actuality is an absurdity, is an
unassailable argument.

Moreover, Dostoevsky resolves the uncertainty of readers as
to whether or not Ivan really agrees with the Grand Inquisitor's

condemnation of Christ for preaching man's freedom of choice in the knowledge of good and evil. He writes his editor: "But my socialist (Ivan Karamazov) is a sincere man who frankly confesses that he agrees with the Grand Inquisitor's view of mankind, and that Christ's religion (as it were) has raised man much higher than man actually stands. . . . They [the socialists] bring to mankind the law of chains and of subjection by means of bread." Here is plain proof that in the Legend of the Grand Inquisitor Dostoevsky's intention was to identify Roman Catholicism and socialism, as Myshkin had done in *The Idiot*.

In another letter to the editor Dostoevsky elaborates the argument which he will place in the mouth of the old monk Zosima as an answer to Ivan's denial of God's world. He not only associates himself with this answer, but he explains rather naively how he will turn it into an artistic statement. "*I will compel people to admit*," he writes, "that a pure, ideal Christian is not an abstraction, but a vivid reality, possible, clearly near at hand, and that Christianity is the sole refuge of the Russian land from all its evils. . . . You will understand that a great deal in the precepts of my Zosima (or rather the manner of their expression) belongs to his character, that is, to the artistic presentation of his character. Although I myself hold the same opinions which he expresses, yet if I expressed them personally [as coming] *from myself*, I would express them in a different form and in a different style."

Indeed, Zosima's answer to Ivan, expressed in Dostoevsky's own voice, appears in various pages of *The Diary of a Writer*—that equality is to be found only in the spiritual dignity of man; that suffering does not destroy the harmony of life but is a fulfillment, an act of Godly justice which corrects transgressions for the sake of the whole; that the secret of universal harmony is not achieved by the mind but by the heart, by feeling and faith; that if one loves all living things, this love will justify suffering, and all will share in each other's guilt, and suffering for the sins of others will then become the moral duty of every true Christian.

The great debate between Ivan and Zosima reflects the anguished dialogue that went on in Dostoevsky's doubting dualistic mind in his own search for faith. Shortly before his death he unwittingly exposed these overriding uncertainties in reacting to radical critics, who condemned the conservative ideology of *The Brothers Karamazov*, and to conservative critics who berated him for atheistic tendencies. He wrote in his notebook: "The villains teased me for my ignorance and a retrograde faith in God. These blockheads did not dream of such a powerful negation of God as that put in the [mouth of the Grand] Inquisitor. . . . Even in Europe there have never been atheistic expressions of such power. Consequently I do not believe in Christ and His confession as a child, but my hosanna has come through a great *furnace of doubt*." He seems more proud of Ivan's Negation of God than of Zosima's faith in Him.

Though no art, not even the most abstract, can completely reject reality, some exasperated critics deny any reflection of it in Dostoevsky's novels; others have perceived in them an awareness of a world outside the realm of human consciousness, the source of the higher realism he claimed. To be sure, there is little in human experience that quite satisfactorily explains the behavior patterns and exaggerated motives and actions of Raskolnikov, Myshkin, Stavrogin, and Ivan Karamazov, and one could add many other characters to this list. Yet these characters seem real and vital, they win our sympathy, and we have little difficulty in identifying ourselves with this or that aspect of their natures.

Yet Dostoevsky, unlike Flaubert who hated being called a realist, valued this attribute of his art even to the extent of being on the defensive whenever he anticipated charges that he had violated reality. We find him writing his editor that however unconvincing Ivan Karamazov's arguments against the absurdity of historical actuality may seem to the readers, "I know that the figure of my hero is real in the highest degree." And suspecting that some critics will regard his portrait of the Russian monk Zosima as unfaithful to life, he protests to his editor: "I think I have not sinned against reality: It is true not only as an ideal, but it is true as reality."

In a sense, this was one of Dostoevsky's principal difficulties —he constantly fluctuated between the real which reveals life and the ideal which exposes the soul. In any event there was nothing in him of the conventional realistic novelist who strives to reproduce reality in its immediate aspects. He well understood that to write is to choose. Dostoevsky preferred to think that the higher realism which he took as his province, so different from any manifestations of realism in fiction that had preceded him, was like that of Shakespeare—not restricted to mere imitations of life but concerned primarily with the mystery of man and the human soul. In truth his men and women seem to be part of a region of experience from which all the circumstances of ordinary life have been banished and only the soul survives. In that region earthly reality tends to approximate more and more closely to spiritual reality. He sought reality not in the mundane facts of daily existence but in the tragic absurdity of life, and by his art he imposed on it a spiritual or ideological unity which transfigures it and creates a higher realism.

IV · TOLSTOY

"My Hero is Truth"

MUCH HAS BEEN WRITTEN about similarities and dissimilarities in Dostoevsky and Tolstoy, but no two great novelists differed so fundamentally in their conception and practice of realism in the art of fiction. Though both authors, ideologically speaking, had a vested interest in Christ's teachings, Dostoevsky was peculiarly spiritual and Tolstoy completely earthbound.

Like Gogol, whom he preferred as a storyteller, Tolstoy believed that a work, in order to be good, must come singing from the author's soul. But he criticized Gogol for a pitiless and unloving attitude to his characters, a charge from which he absolved Dickens, and he could quite justly have absolved himself. Though in *What is Art?* he failed to admit any of Dostoevsky's writings to his category of "universal art," which conveys feelings of common life accessible to everyone, he did include the tales of Pushkin and Gogol.

Tolstoy had the greatest admiration for Pushkin, although as a young writer he complained of the bareness of his prose and criticized *The Captain's Daughter* because the interest in events predominates over interest in details of feeling. But the account is well known, although its veracity has been questioned, of how his enthusiasm for the opening of a Pushkin short story, which plunged directly into the action, inspired him to begin *Anna Karenina* in the same manner.

The derivation of Tolstoy's fiction from the Classical School of Russian Realism begun by Pushkin can hardly be doubted. However, this colossus of a genius, who took all knowledge for his province, read omnivorously in foreign literatures as well as in Russian, and one may trace in the rich unrolling tapestry of his art threads from the works of English eighteenth-century writers, especially Sterne, and, in the nineteenth century, Thackeray and Dickens, whom he regarded as the greatest novelist of the age, and also the French realists, particularly Stendhal. If literature is the memory of culture, Tolstoy seems to have remembered it all, but so original was his artistic nature that anything he may have borrowed, he completely assimilated and made his own. The realistic tradition he inherited he greatly expanded and enriched in practice so that the finished product became the despair of imitators.

No novelist was more acutely aware of the reality around him than Tolstoy or more exhaustively absorbed, through the intellect and senses, in all its manifestations. Unlike Dostoevsky, who creates a world of his own in the image of the real world, Tolstoy accepts the real world, and his picture of it is fresh and interesting because he sees so much more of it than his readers, but its commonplaces, observed through the prism of his imagination, take on new meaning. That is, he is able to perceive genuine poetry in the average which so often embodies the reality of man's dreams and hopes. Man needs hope as much or more than he needs knowledge, Tolstoy declared in answer to a speech of Zola who advised a group of French students to accept science as the road to a new faith rather than build their living faith on the debris of dead ones, for, he warned, reality

becomes a school of perversion which must be killed or denied
since it will lead to nothing but ugliness and crime. Tolstoy
countered: "It is commonly said that reality is that which exists,
or that only what exists is real. Just the contrary is the case:
true reality, that which we really know, is what has never
existed."*

That reality is so often different from what men and women
hope and dream, that life often disappoints them because they
have confused the imagined with the real, is a central problem
with Tolstoy's more reflective characters. In *The Cossacks*
Olenin's conception of the romantic existence of these people
in the Caucasus is shattered by the reality of it; in *War and
Peace* Prince Andrew's exaggerated notions of a career in the
army and in politics are harshly corrected by experience; and
in *Anna Karenina* Levin's idealistic hopes about marriage are
soon disillusioned. In such cases Tolstoy usually demonstrates
that the reality of things is richer, more affirmative and life-
giving than the reality imagined by such characters. But he does
this through their active experiences, although reflection plays
its part, for he never forgets that realistic literature should portray human beings in action. Disillusionment with reality is not
resolved in metaphysical quests as in Dostoevsky's fiction and
in that of not a few novelists today. Tolstoy's alienated man
does not ask himself the everlasting question: Who am I? but
rather: Why am I here and where am I going? At least the
matter of self-identification is already resolved. The different
emphasis is fundamental and it is a quality of Tolstoy's realism.

---

* Quotations of belles lettres and essays are from *Tolstoy Centenary
Edition*, translated by Louise and Aylmer Maude (21 vols.; London: Oxford University Press, 1928-37): "Sevastopol in May," vol. 4, p. 152; *War
and Peace*, vol. 6, pp. 13-14, 516; *War and Peace*, vol. 7, pp. 8, 59; *War and
Peace*, vol. 8, pp. 321, 486; *Anna Karenina*, vol. 9, p. 127; *Anna Karenina*,
vol. 10, p. 357; "Non-Acting," vol. 21, p. 166.

2

The great poet Pushkin and not Tolstoy stands as the brightest and foremost symbol of Russian literature in that country very much as Shakespeare does in English literature. However, if Tolstoy is regarded, not only as a literary artist, but also as a religious philosopher and modern reformer, then he was possibly the greatest single moral force in the world in the second half of the nineteenth century. Certainly no Russian writer is better known outside his country than Tolstoy. Yet it is probably true that his various religious, moral, and philosophical works would never have received the wide hearing they did if Tolstoy had not already been the author of *War and Peace* and *Anna Karenina*.

During his lifetime the tremendous popular impact of these novels and other purely literary works placed him at the head of all Russian writers. Even his two chief rivals acknowledged his supreme position. Dostoevsky, with his feeling of inferiority about Russian culture, joyfully hailed *Anna Karenina* as greater than any Western European novel in the nineteenth century. Turgenev, who could never get along with Tolstoy as a man and on one occasion narrowly avoided fighting a duel with him, profoundly admired his genius and on his deathbed pleaded with him, in the famous phrase, "great author of the Russian land," to return to writing belles lettres.

By the last two decades of the nineteenth century what might be called the "saturation realism" of Tolstoy encountered a mixed reception in Western Europe. The current French naturalist dicta in criticism, and perhaps also some of Tolstoy's extreme religious and moral views which had begun to filter into the West, hindered an unprejudiced appreciation of his fiction. Upon reading a French translation of *War and Peace*,

Flaubert wrote Turgenev: "It is of the first rank! What painting and what psychology! . . . It seemed to me at times that there were things worthy of Shakespeare! I uttered cries of admiration during the reading!"

In general, however, French critics compared Tolstoy's works, especially *Anna Karenina*, unfavorably with *Madame Bovary* and its impeccable form, tailored style, and naturalistic detail. Their tendency was to express bewilderment over the vast mass of reality reflected in Tolstoy's major novels and to regard them as peculiarly formless and artless—the chaotic outpourings of some super-reporter of life. Nor did Matthew Arnold in England clarify the situation much by basing his preference of *Anna Karenina* to *Madame Bovary* partly on the conviction that Tolstoy's novel was not really a work of art at all but a piece of life, and that what it lost in art it gained in reality. And Henry James' nearsighted discovery of "large loose baggy monsters" in Tolstoy's fiction, his lament over the absence of "a deep-breathing economy of an organic form," and later E. M. Forster's comment on *War and Peace* as an "untidy book" have contributed to this notion of formlessness and artlessness which has clung to so much Western criticism of Tolstoy. In its application to serious fiction, Arnold's dichotomy of life and art is a spurious conception. Not "a piece of life" but life in all its manifestations crowds the huge canvas of Tolstoy's masterpieces. Their patterns of human relationships are always carefully planned, and plot is a poetic form of reflecting reality rather than a contrived frame on which to stretch events. If the transformation of reality into art has been effected with equal skill in, let us say, Stendhal's *The Red and the Black* or Flaubert's *Madame Bovary*, in no novel has so much reality been transformed into art as in *War and Peace*.

In the Soviet Union Tolstoy is venerated and his works have been published in millions of copies. The ninety-volume Jubilee

Edition of all his writings is in completeness, textual accuracy, and scholarly annotation one of the most magnificent tributes ever paid to a great author. Soviet scholarship on Tolstoy is extremely copious and much of it of high quality, but where interpretation is required, it is more often than not dominated by Lenin's Marxian formulations, especially by his article, "Leo Tolstoy as a Mirror of the Russian Revolution." Lenin, more modest than Stalin as a literary critic, made the sharpest distinction between Tolstoy the artist, whom he praised in the highest terms, and Tolstoy the thinker whose doctrines of moral perfectibility and nonresistance to evil he contemptuously dismissed. Lenin did laud Tolstoy's stubborn opposition to tsarist oppression and viewed such activities as an important factor in the developing revolutionary movement. Tolstoy, of course, abhorred the violence of revolution, and he once declared in his diary that "Socialists will never destroy poverty and the inequality of capacities. The strongest and most intelligent will always make use of the weaker and more stupid. . . . Even if that takes place which Marx predicted, then the only thing that will happen is that despotism will be passed on."

Such a statement, and others like it, have not discouraged Marxian investigations of Tolstoy's fiction. An outstanding one, illustrative of most in interpretation but differing from those of Soviet critics in the author's deep knowledge of Western European literature as well as Russian, was contributed by George Lukács, the brilliant Hungarian Marxist literary critic who spent a number of years in the Soviet Union.* Despite his wide and illuminating frame of reference, Lukács, like Lenin, narrowly argues that Tolstoy created his literary masterpieces on the basis of an essentially false philosophy, but as a political reactionary he unconsciously dramatized the revolutionary

* "Tolstoy and the Development of Realism," *Studies in European Realism*, translated by Edith Bone (London: Hillway Publishing Co., 1950).

forces of his time. It is hard to imagine Tolstoy ever doing anything unconsciously, particularly in his writings. He would
fully have agreed with Chekhov that nothing happens by
chance in art.

In order to overcome the unpoetic nature of a society per-
meated by capitalism, Lukács maintains, Tolstoy makes the exploited peasant, either consciously or unconsciously, the central
problem of his fiction. "The poetic starting-point in the presentation of each character by Tolstoy," Lukács writes, "was the
question: in what way was their life based on the receipt of
ground-rents and on the exploitation of the peasants and what
problems did this social basis produce in their lives."

In these terms Anna Karenina's fatal passion for Vronsky,
which is not unlike many great love stories in literature, becomes for Lukács another tragedy growing out of "the contradictions latently present . . . in every bourgeois love and marriage." Even the famous mowing scene in this novel, when
viewed in terms of Levin's un-Marxian attitude toward the
peasants, is set down as "a sentimental attitude to physical
labor." In a review of *Anna Karenina*, Dostoevsky, unlike
Lukács, censures Tolstoy for making the central problem of
all his writing not the exploited peasantry, but the landed
gentry. The ineptness of this kind of criticism is unwittingly
limned by D. H. Lawrence in his poem, "Now It's Happened":

> But Tolstoy was a traitor
> to the Russia that needed him most,
> the clumsy, bewildered Russia
> so worried by the Holy Ghost.
> He shifted his job on to the peasants
> and landed them all on toast.

The vital point missed by Lukács is that Tolstoy, whenever
he dwells upon man's inhumanity to man in his fiction, is never
directly attacking a political system, but rather man in general

for placing his own egotism ahead of the common needs of humanity. Even toward the end of his life, when he excoriated the tsar's government for its abuses, he was in effect denouncing all governments whose abolition he devoutly hoped for in terms of his doctrine of Christian anarchism. The radical democrats of the 1860's, such as Dobrolyubov and Chernyshevsky, and the revolutionists who followed were all profoundly distasteful to Tolstoy. He was an aristocrat by birth and never ceased to be one in temperament however much his humanitarian instincts led him to advocate the cause of underprivileged peasants and workers. Actually peasants play a relatively small part in the total corpus of his fiction and he rarely stresses their feelings of class opposition to the landed gentry. Anticipating the objections of readers of *War and Peace* to his concentration on members of his own class, he wrote in the draft of an unused foreword: "The lives of officials, merchants, seminarists, and peasants do not interest me and are only partly understandable to me; the lives of the aristocrats of that time, thanks to the documents of the period and other reasons, are understandable, interesting, and dear to me." He is more forthright on his prejudices in a note to himself in one of the draft versions of *War and Peace* where he flatly states that the lives of all people not in his class, including peasants, seem boring and monotonous and all their actions stem from the same motives: envy of their superiors, self-interest, and material passions. And he concludes: "I am an aristocrat because I cannot believe in the lofty intellect, the fine taste, or the complete honesty of a man who picks his nose and whose soul communicates with God."

3

All four of Russia's most celebrated novelists began their literary careers with short stories and novelettes, and in Tolstoy's case these early tales are important, not only for their intrinsic worth, but also for an understanding of the development of a realistic narrative art which found its fullest expression in the great novels. Tolstoy really began his apprenticeship at the age of eighteen when he started his diary which he continued, with interruptions, during the rest of his life. An intense interest in hidden motives of behavior characterizes entries dealing with his youthful experiences, and a fondness for classifying all manner of human attributes suggests his later talent for conquering the subconscious by an application of penetrating analysis.

These techniques are carried over in Tolstoy's first piece of fiction, *A History of Yesterday*, a short fragment written when he was twenty-two and unpublished during his lifetime. It is an account of an evening with friends, the drive home, and the hero's thoughts as he falls asleep—a youthful exercise in style and narrative form. Like so many authors, Tolstoy had to struggle for clear expression and was often ungrammatical as his wife testified later, for she frequently corrected mistakes in recopying his manuscripts. In general, he labored to purge his prose of stereotyped bookish language and to create a style that would approximate as closely as possible the speech of his own cultured class. Eventually he developed the capacity to adapt his prose to the subject at hand and, in dialogue, to catch the idiom of the speaker. It is therefore all the more surprising to find him, in *A History of Yesterday*, imitating the mannered style and analytical method of Sterne's *Sentimental Journey* which he had been reading and soon partly translated. Sterne's influence is obvious not only in the young Tolstoy's language, but also in his concentration on odd details, in his posturings and digressions, and in the analysis of conscious and subconscious thoughts and feelings of characters reacting to particular situations. Perhaps aware of his imitativeness, Tolstoy never returned to this exuberant abandon in fiction.

The next year (1852) appeared his first published work, the

delightful short novel *Childhood*, to which he later added the sequels *Boyhood* and *Youth*. In this effort sure instinct rather than trial and error seemed to guide his early encounter with the exacting demands of art. As he labored over the manuscript, repeated diary entries record the fact that the writing goes badly and the rewriting worse. "Without regret," he reminds himself, "I must destroy all unclear places, prolix, irrelevant, in a word, all things that are unsatisfactory even though they may be fine in themselves." Without compunction he adhered to his rule, in the course of accumulating four separate drafts of *Childhood*, that no addition however talented could improve a work as much as a deletion.

Tolstoy's skill in evoking forgotten childhood memories, which, when recalled with feeling seem infallibly true and charming, is quite original. The quality of realistic descriptions, especially of nature, and his subtle analysis of the actions and thinking of characters are nothing short of miraculous in a young man of twenty-four. Although *Childhood* draws heavily upon his recollections, there is a great deal of sheer invention in the work. This divided concentration underscores the fact that perhaps more so than other major novelists Tolstoy's fiction is unusually autobiographical. Such a generalization must not be construed as a reflection on his imaginative powers, but the reality he transformed into art was largely his own life of re-corded experience and observation rendered doubly effective by acute psychological analysis and meticulous selection of significant detail. In many respects the convincing realism of his fiction is rooted in autobiography.

In addition to *Childhood*, for example, nearly every one of the Caucasian group of short stories, written or conceived during his two-year stay in that region, is an outgrowth of personal experience in fighting with the Russian forces against the hill tribes or some adventure on his furloughs. Within the limitatations of the short-story form, the principal characterizations of military figures are studies of varying depth, and the significant action is often narrated with a realism quite fresh for that time. The rightness or wrongness of war, a subject which played a large part in his future thinking, is at least touched upon, and in *The Raid*, and to a certain extent in *The Wood-Felling*, there is more than a suggestion of his later ruthless analysis of the conventional worship of military glory.

On the way home from the Caucasus, ultimately to join the Russian forces in the Crimean War at Sevastopol, he encountered a fierce blizzard which inspired his memorable story, *The Snow Storm*. Repeated motifs of snow and wind have almost the quality of incremental repetition of a folk ballad, and the theme of the storm is so vividly realized that it takes on the human attributes of an intensely imagined character. Tolstoy is rarely content with the realistic perfection of a still-life in visualizing inanimate objects of nature, for he nearly always draws sentient overtones from such descriptions in stressing the relation of nature to man or man's environment. At the end of *The Snow Storm* the elements seem to retreat and glower in the face of man's indomitable courage in struggling against them. In *Three Deaths* the moral beauty of the death of the ancient tree, in perfect harmony with nature's law, is contrasted with the stubborn, ugly death of the querulous old lady. And the gnarled oak in *War and Peace*, described first in its leafless, autumn state and then in its spring greenery, is clearly connected with a deep psychological change going on in Prince Andrew. Something of the same emphasis is manifested in Tolstoy's treatment of animals. Even the dogs in *War and Peace*, exclaimed one critic, are individualized. The realistic manner in which he projects himself into the consciousness of the poor, old piebald gelding in *Strider: the Story of a Horse* gains in effectiveness by the implied conclusion that the animal is more dignified and useful than its owners. These extra effects extended the limits of earlier realism in Russian fiction.

The three Sevastopol "sketches," as they are sometimes erroneously labeled, are not merely a reporter's narration of what Tolstoy saw and experienced during the terrible siege of that city, for he immeasurably enhances their appeal by employing fictional devices. In short, they are often deftly contrived art. The first one, with its swiftly limned portraits of typical inhabitants of the city and its moving accounts of the self-sacrificing heroism of the Russian defenders, raised Tolstoy to a position of popular fame as a writer. Patriotism had claimed him in his first contact with the siege, and he entered in his diary: "Have now reached a period of real temptation through vanity. I could gain much in life if I wished to write without conviction."

He turned his back on this temptation in the second Sevastopol piece when he points out the human folly of the war and indulges in forthright criticism of those Russian officers whose "patriotism" is translated into terms of personal gain. And at the end he added the famous statement which may be regarded as his credo for the rest of his long life as a writer and thinker: "The hero of my tale—whom I love with all the power of my soul, whom I have tried to portray in all his beauty, who has been, is, and will be beautiful—is Truth." The piece was hopelessly mangled by the censor, and the outraged editor wrote Tolstoy: "You are right to value that side of your gifts most of all. Truth—in the form you have introduced it into our literature—is something entirely new among us." The treatment of war and the characterization of military figures in the Sevastopol pieces anticipate *War and Peace.*

After Tolstoy's return to civilian life and during his first trip to Western Europe, his literary interests shifted from war to moral problems. The change was brought about not only by a new order of experiences, but also by his negative reaction to demands of Petersburg liberals and radical democrats connected with *The Contemporary*, the magazine he had been publishing in, for political and social significance in literature. In 1856, he jotted down in his diary: "How I long to have done with magazines in order to write the way I'm beginning to think about art—awfully lofty and pure." But efforts in this new vein, such as the fragment of a novel, *A Landlord's Morning*, and the short stories, *Lucerne, Albert,* and *Three Deaths,* took on the aspect of fictionalized moralistic tracts, in which the voice of Rousseau is heard in Tolstoy's determination to argue the baleful influence of political laws and organized government on nature and art.

A return to his former autobiographical manner in the novelette *Family Happiness* (1859), the first part of which is a beautiful evocation of romantic love in a girl whom he might have married, and the second part his rationalization that the marriage, if it had taken place, would have failed through no fault of his, did no more than the previous moral tales to improve his literary image with public and critics, who now began to write about his failing powers.

Discouraged and out of sympathy with the current literary taste, for the next three years Tolstoy turned his incredible energies to the exciting field of educational theory and practice. In a speech, in 1859, to the Moscow Society of Lovers of Russian Literature, he deplored those who believed that the only concern of literature was to denounce and correct evil, and to promote the growth of civic feeling in society. On the contrary, he concluded, "There is another literature, reflecting eternal and universal human interests, the most precious, sincere consciousness of the people, a literature accessible to every people and to all times. . . ."

Marriage in 1862 brought an end to Tolstoy's educational experiments and reawakened the urge to resume creative writing. The next year he brought out his brilliant novelette, *Polikushka*, where he reveals the hard features of peasant life, but in a tone of refined humor that aims to ridicule the false and insincere in art—a new note in his fiction. This same year appeared his short novel *The Cossacks* which he had been working on for some time. It is undoubtedly the finest masterpiece of this early period. The hero Olenin, a cultured, highly civilized man from the city, is if anything less interesting than the Cossacks, the natural men with whom he is so strikingly contrasted. Tolstoy was fond of the natural man, and such Cossacks as the young daredevil Lukashka, the untamed girl Marianka, and the incorrigible old reprobate Eroshka are among his truly memorable characterizations. The natural beauty of Cossack existence transforms Olenin in the end into a philosophical reasoner searching for personal happiness, a kind of Rousseauistic "natural man," a type that became a favorite of Tolstoy in later fiction.

The Cossacks helped to win back some of Tolstoy's popularity with the reading public, but the radical-democratic critics, sensing the implied condemnation of all modern society in the story, gave it only grudging praise. This work brought to a superb close Tolstoy's first literary period. Sometimes characters in these early tales come close to being merely emanations of himself, and only the best of them are psychologically alive. Whether he is treating war, family happiness or exemplifying moral truths, both in subject matter and in his method of conquering reality by a fresh, uninhibited analysis of human thought and action, Tolstoy moved artistically in the direction of the famous novels to come. He was ready, in 1863, for the long, hard task that led to his greatest contribution to Russian literature—*War and Peace*.

4

The desire to write a novel about the historical past occurred to Tolstoy shortly before his marriage. Its hero was to be a participant in the Decembrist Revolt of 1825 who, in 1856, returned to Russia from exile. Tolstoy took up this theme in 1863 and wrote three vivid chapters and then put them aside because he felt it necessary to study the period of his hero's youth. The realization that the Decembrist conspiracy had its roots in events connected with Napoleon's invasion of Russia, historical accounts of which had long interested Tolstoy, brought about a new concentration on this earlier period. For in the autumn of 1863 he wrote a close friend that he was absorbed in a novel "covering the years from 1810 to 1820" (actually *War and Peace* extends chronologically from 1805 to 1820). A discarded early foreword suggests that originally Tolstoy may have had a trilogy in mind, in which *War and Peace* would be followed by a sequel focused on the events of 1825 and another on 1856. As additional support for this conjecture, one may cite the "open" ending of *War and Peace* where Pierre Bezukhov has already begun to manifest an interest in the political movement which five years later culminated in the Decembrist Revolt.

From the outset of the work Tolstoy was concerned with Napoleon's struggle against Russia and its relation to historical problems, as well as with the peaceful elements of family life, but early drafts and notes fail to indicate that at this stage he had worked out a comprehensive plan that would involve the vast epic sweep and elaborate philosophy of history of *War and Peace*. Nor did the publication, in a magazine in 1865, of the first thirty-eight chapters under the simple title *1805*, corresponding roughly to the first twenty-five chapters of the definitive text, suggest that he had hit upon his larger and final design. By the

next year, when a second installment appeared which took the
story only through 1805, Tolstoy's design does not seem to
carry the action beyond Napoleon's retreat from Moscow.
Notes at this point hint that the ending was to be a happy
one—Prince Andrew, who recovers from his wound, nobly
gives up his love for Natasha in order that she may marry
Pierre whose changed outlook on life is uninfluenced by Platon
Karataev's simple philosophy; and Sonya, inspired by Prince
Andrew's renunciation, gives way to Princess Mary's love for
Nicholas. Pierre and Nicholas marry on the same day and
Nicholas and Prince Andrew leave to rejoin their army units.
In fact, in 1866 Tolstoy was confident he would finish the novel
the next year and publish it as a whole under the title, *All's
Well That Ends Well!**

We have no certain knowledge of just when Tolstoy's pre-
liminary and inconclusive plans were brought into focus on a
final vision of vaster design and inner harmony, the details of
which were undoubtedly developed as the writing continued.
At least one clear indication of the kind of insight that fired his
imagination and illuminated the huge potentiality of his subject
while at the same time giving it some direction and aim is an
entry in his diary, March 1865: "I read with delight the history
of Napoleon and Alexander. At once I was enveloped in a cloud
of joy; and the consciousness of the possibility of doing a great
thing took hold of my thoughts—to write a psychological novel
of Alexander and Napoleon, and of all the baseness, empty
words, folly, all the contradictions of these men and of the
people surrounding them." Further jottings in his diary reaffirm
his delight with this purpose and his determination to carry it
out. At about this same time and later Tolstoy attended evening

* For some facts on the chronology of the composition of *War and
Peace* and supporting evidence drawn from the drafts and notes on the
novel, I am indebted to the excellent study of R. F. Christian, *Tolstoy's
War and Peace* (London: Oxford University Press, 1962).

gatherings of Moscow intellectual friends where the subject of philosophy of history was much discussed. Two problems often debated were the relation of individual freedom to historical necessity and the factor of causality in history. It is very likely that Proudhon's works, which Tolstoy knew, especially *La guerre et la paix*, were also talked about at these meetings. In any event, by March 1867 the final plan and title, *War and Peace*, had been decided, but the expanded design prevented Tolstoy from finishing the novel until 1869, almost seven years after he began it.

The common complaint that *War and Peace* is devoid of form recalls eighteenth-century criticism of the shapelessness of the Alps. In the first place such a complaint overlooks the unique totality of life indigenous, so to speak, to the novel. Given this fact, one naturally asks: What other form, or what changes in the present one, would have resulted in greater aesthetic unity of design in so huge a work? Of course, the logical answer is that Tolstoy surrendered the possibility of satisfactory form by attempting to do too much in a single novel. However, if he had radically reduced its scope, the work would not be the *War and Peace* which so many modern writers of stature have acclaimed as the greatest novel in the world.

A close examination of the structure reveals that a unifying design was worked out once Tolstoy had settled upon the scope and purpose of the novel, although this may be form in the sense that Percy Lubbock defines it: "The best form is that which makes the most of its subject. . . ." Interestingly enough, Tolstoy was convinced that in a work of art form will be determined by the subject, and he believed that this was true of *War and Peace*.

But what is the subject of Tolstoy's great novel? Many have remarked that it has no subject other than life itself and no single hero. The work has such an immediacy for us that we tend to forget what Tolstoy never forgot, that he was writing a historical novel. He makes this abundantly clear from the beginning in his notes, early drafts of chapters, and in abandoned prefaces. In one projected introduction to the novel in 1864, he declares: "I shall write a history of people more free than statesmen . . . ," people, he pointedly asserts, whose faults go unmentioned in the chronicles of history. A little later he repeats in one of the draft versions: "I have been trying to write a history of the people." Then, in replying to criticism of his friend, the poet A. A. Fet, of early published chapters of the novel, he explains that, apart from his conception of the conflict of characters, "I have another conception, a historical one, which complicates my work in an extraordinary way. . . ." This special concern he also mentioned to the historian M. P. Pogodin in 1868: "My thoughts about the limits of freedom and independence, and my views on history are not a mere paradox that has occupied me in passing. These thoughts are the fruits of all the intellectual efforts of my life, and they are an inseparable part of that philosophy which I have achieved, God alone knows with what striving and suffering, and it has given me complete calm and happiness." In short, to write a history of the people, understanding history both as a theory of knowledge and the principal integrating factor in a vast wealth of material, is the real subject of *War and Peace*.

The difficulty is that Tolstoy had his own ideas, which had begun to spawn as early as his student days in Kazan University, on the so-called truth of history and of historians and on the relations of people and their leaders to the historical process. Aware of the significance of his views for the whole course of the novel, he tried to anticipate both objections and misunderstanding on this score by publishing an article almost a year before *War and Peace* finally appeared. There he defends the artist's treatment of history as contrasted with that of the historian. There are two kinds of actions, he explains, those that depend on the individual will and those that do not. In the historical process, he asserts, there is a minimum of freedom of action. That is, the so-called makers of history are fundamentally dependent upon the actions of countless other people and hence to that extent their actions are predetermined.

Among these countless people are the scores of character types of *War and Peace,* often simple individuals like Tushin or Karataev, and all of them are connected in one way or another with the famous historical events described. The sum total of their individual actions, so often fortuitous or independent of their own will, contributes more to the determination of these events than the actions of celebrated makers of history. It is important to realize that Tolstoy's theory of history applies to the activities of these numerous fictional characters as well as to the purely historical ones. To paraphrase his lengthy and rather involved statement in the novel, he contends that in order to understand the process of history, one must begin not with a consideration of the deeds of supposed great men, but with the integration of an infinitely large number of infinitesimally small actions, what Tolstoy calls "the differential of history."

If Tolstoy tends to deflate the historical reputations of those who are credited with shaping great events by insisting that the events themselves are beyond their active control, the actions of his fictional characters are conditioned by the same lack of freedom. But these tremendously vital, well-rounded, and intensely real men and women enjoy the illusion of freedom, the full consciousness that they are directing their own destinies. Yet fate, chance, accident, lady-luck, or decisions thrust upon them by others often determine crucial events in the lives of Natasha, Nicholas, Sonya, Pierre, Princess Mary, Prince Andrew, and others. Tolstoy wisely avoids arguing his thesis on the limitations of man's conscious will in connection with his fictional characters, which may be one reason why its pervasiveness in the total design is often overlooked.

However, the integration of the Napoleonic campaign into the expansive design of the novel, whose subject is the history of the people, is accompanied by lengthy sections of theorizing about war, its leaders, and the historical implications of their actions. Though opinions differ sharply on the necessity of this extensive theorizing, and on its intellectual quality and connection with major and minor fictional characters, Tolstoy obviously regarded it as of the utmost consequence in the definitive plan of *War and Peace*. In this sense these sections are not extraneous and may be considered as necessary and extremely informative. To convey knowledge was for Tolstoy an essential concomitant of the novel.

If it is possible to accept all this theorizing as a vital part of the novel's structure, it is something else again to regard it as a convincing philosophy of history. Tolstoy knew war at first hand and no one would deny that the battle scenes are magnificently described and the characterizations of active figures from plain soldiers to marshals and emperors are unforgettable. Who does not recall the boyish, irrepressible Petya Rostov, full of life and desire for glory in the fury of the cavalry charge, and the next moment lying dead on the field. As the gruff Denisov tenderly turns over the bloodstained body, he remembers Petya's words while generously giving away raisins to his comrades a short time before the charge: "I am used to something sweet. Raisins, fine ones . . . take them all!"

Can such a deed be satisfactorily explained in terms of Tolstoy's conviction that man lives consciously for himself but is an unconscious instrument in the attainment of the historical, universal aims of humanity? A deed done, Tolstoy argues, is irrevocable, and its results, coinciding in time with the actions of millions of other men, assumes a historic importance. In history, he maintains, the so-called great men are merely labels, giving names to events, and like labels, they have only the smallest connection with the events themselves. In the novel Prince Andrew remarks that the best generals he had known were either stupid or absentminded. If Tolstoy can be said to have made a hero of any of the famous generals he treats in the novel, it is the Russian commander-in-chief Kutuzov. In his simplicity, intuitive wisdom, lack of hypocrisy and affectation, and in his conviction of the impossibility of controlling events, Kutuzov takes his place with the innumerable simple and patriotic members of the gentry and peasantry as a representative of the unconscious spirit of the nation which Tolstoy identifies as the true historical force at a time of national crisis. Kutuzov admirably illustrated Tolstoy's theory of war, for his strategy, in so far as he can be said to have had any, is based on the assumption that everything comes to him who waits in war. "Patience and time," declares Kutuzov, are the things that win wars. When in doubt, do not act—that is his great military axiom. And in effect Tolstoy defends this position when he writes toward the end of the novel: "If we admit that human life can be ruled by reason, the possibility of life is destroyed."

What particularly troubled Tolstoy was the prevailing practice of historians to fix responsibility for what occurs in life upon individuals whom they call great men and endow with heroic virtues. He insists that history is not a science, that no acceptable laws of history have ever been discovered, and that attempts to explain people and events in terms of causes, genius, or chance are simply the result of ignorance. On the contrary, he says, there is a natural law which determines the lives of human beings no less than all the processes of nature itself; all is ruled by an inexorable historical determinism.

Lapses in factual information and substantial distortions in characterizations of great figures of the past, which in some cases can possibly be excused as artistic license, reflect badly on Tolstoy's philosophy of history in *War and Peace*. But a more significant flaw in his theorizing may be discerned by relating his views to the ambivalence that dominated his whole emotional, intellectual, and aesthetic life. As Sir Isaiah Berlin has pointed out, the contrast between the universal but nevertheless delusive experiences of free will and historical determinism corresponds to an inner conflict in Tolstoy between two systems of value—a public system and a private one. At times his irrational depreciation of greatness in *War and Peace* seems psychologically to have been motivated by his private set of values—a feeling of personal envy of the historical fame of Napoleon—just as his later depreciation of revealed Christianity may have been inspired by a feeling of envy of the historical perfection of Christ.

Though Tolstoy regarded his theorizing as essential to the development of the main subject of the novel, he was too great a literary artist not to anticipate the difficulties it would present to the average reader. He rather humorously pictures such readers in a draft version of the Second Epilogue as exclaiming, after repeated doses of historical and philosophical argumentation: "What again! How dull." And he whimsically adds that this sort of reader is most precious to him, the kind whose criticism he most admires. A second type of reader, he says, primarily interested in the historical sections, will blame him for impugning reputations of great men. But he defends himself by pointing out that he is writing a history of the people involved in a past that has been misrepresented. For Tolstoy there could be no compromise between art and truth or what he believed to be the truth. The vaunted higher truth of art he would not accept if he found it to be at variance with what he considered the truth of life.

Once the main theme of the novel is grasped, a history of the people and the manner in which all the elements involved in it are integrated by Tolstoy's theory of history, the basic structure becomes apparent and stands as a refutation to the notion that the work is formless. A history of the people is told in terms of the two broad areas of human experience identified in the title—war, symbolizing the vast world of public affairs, and peace, the private manifold activities of the family. A careful examination of the amazingly rich thematic multiplicity of the novel reveals a deliberate and meaningful series of juxtapositions and alternating contrasts, first between war and peace, and then, within this framework, series of alternating contrasts of scenes, situations, events, and characters under each of these two divisions. In war we have the contrasts between Alexander I and Napoleon; good and bad generals; those who think they can direct the course of events and those who make no pretense at doing so; cowardly braggarts among the officers and selfless, unconsciously brave fellows like Tushin. In the division of peace there are the contrasts between the bureaucracy, cultural snobbery, and cynicism of city life and the simple pleasures of country existence; the cold aristocratism of the Bolkonskys and the gay, simple, indulgent Rostovs; or between these two families with their true patriotism and tradition of unselfish service and the Kuragins and Drubetskoys who place their own advancement, financial or career-wise, above everything. So attached is Tolstoy to this device of antithesis, which he regards as a touchstone of the reality of things, that he creates a series of contrasting characters, and in a few individual characters, such as Pierre and Natasha, he stresses their contrasting moods and thoughts as important traits in their natures. This elaborate pattern of juxtapositions and alternating contrasts serves to create an illusion of ceaseless movement involving an endless variety of action, people, moods, and thought.

5

It is this incredibly rich variety of life rather than the historical forces integrating it in the grand design of *War and Peace* that primarily interests the reader, and one suspects that this was also true of Tolstoy. The aim of an artist, he once said, is not to resolve a question irrefutably, but to compel one to love life in all its manifestations. With his belief in the timelessness of human experience, he did not hesitate to project his own into the historical past of the novel. When he read several early chapters in manuscript to a circle of in-laws—the Bers family—and their mutual friends, some in the audience looked furtively at each other as they recognized, among those present, models of a few of the characters. When Natasha Rostova was introduced, a friend winked at the blushing Tanya Bers, Tolstoy's young sister-in-law, known in the family as the Imp. And Tanya was delighted to hear the description of her doll Mimi and the true story of how she asked a young lover to kiss the doll and made him kiss her instead. The exquisitely wrought scene of Natasha's first ball must also have recalled to Tanya her own first ball at which Tolstoy had been her escort. Although his wife jealously insisted that she had served as the model of the unforgettable heroine, and perhaps she did in certain traits, one has only to read the published diary of Tanya Bers to observe the striking correspondences between her image and youthful experiences and those of Natasha Rostova. But the perceptive reader will wonder at how completely the model is transposed, for the realism, vitality, and pure beauty and poetry Tolstoy imparts to his heroine belong only to the witchery of art.

In general, Tolstoy drew upon the Bers family and their friends, as well as upon his own parents and forebears, for a number of the characters in the Rostov and Bolkonsky families. In early drafts the name Tolstoy is for a time used in place of Rostov. In several characters it was a matter of borrowing prominent features, in others, of forming composite portraits from such sources. Though research in the 1812 period provided most of the historical background and local color he used, which was not extensive, he also depended on family archives, the existence of his own family on their estate at Yasnaya Polyana, and on the Moscow life of the Bers family for city scenes and situations of the Rostovs and Bolkonskys. On the whole, he distrusted writers who invented "reality" by seeking material outside their own range of experience. When necessity compelled him, he used his imagination, and there is much of this in *War and Peace*, but he always contended that it was more difficult to portray real life artistically than to invent it.

In Prince Andrew may be found some of the characteristics of Tolstoy—family pride, deep loyalty, and a profound sense of honor belong to both. Andrew's sister says of him: "You are good in every way, but you have a kind of intellectual pride," an observation that could be made of Tolstoy. In fact, the moral conflict between Prince Andrew and his intellectual foil and unwitting *deus ex machina* of the novel, the easygoing, generous, and noble Pierre Bezukhov, reflects an important phase of the inner struggle that had been going on in Tolstoy since his youth and would in a few years plunge him into a profound spiritual crisis. The debate between them reaches its climax in that impressive scene on the ferry which is steeped in the soft counterpoint of nature's twilight beauties. Andrew, embittered by disappointments in his pursuit of fame and glory and conscience-stricken over the death of his young wife in childbirth, sees no further purpose in life. Pierre opposes his despondency: "If there is a God and future life, there is truth and good, and man's highest happiness consists in striving to attain them. We must live, we must love, and we must believe that we live not only today on this scrap of earth, but have lived and shall live forever. . . ." Tolstoy, after his religious revelation, attempted to resolve the dualism of his nature—to cease living for himself as Prince Andrew had done, and accept the moral credo of Pierre.

A Western critic once said that if life could write it would write just as Tolstoy did. Surely some such impression is conveyed by innumerable scenes, especially in *War and Peace*, where the reader's awareness of the author vanishes and life itself seems to take the pen in hand. One thinks of such scenes as that of the impish sixteen-year-old Natasha stealing into her mother's bed at night and smothering her with kisses while she charmingly argues her right to encourage Boris's visits even though she is not going to marry him; the inexpressible joy of the whole Rostov household upon Nicholas' first return from the front, with Natasha shrieking piercingly as she prances up and down in one place like a goat, and his little brother Petya clinging to his leg, shouting for his kiss: "And me too"; Prince Andrew's involuntary eavesdropping on Natasha's ecstasy at the open window of the bedroom above his over the enchantment of a lovely moonlit spring night: "I feel like sitting down on my heels," she exclaims to Sonya, "putting my arms around my knees like this, straining tight, as tight as possible, and flying away!"; or the captivating episode of the young Rostovs, as Christmas maskers, on an evening sleigh ride to their neighbors where the joyous festivities lead the hesitating Nicholas into the arms of Sonya.

Such scenes are not designed for bravura effects. They advance the action in important ways and add something to the characterizations of major participants. Natasha's talk that night with her mother results in the rejection of Boris as a suitor; Nicholas on his return home brings Denisov with him which

sets the stage for his falling in love with Natasha; Prince Andrew's eavesdropping puts in motion the long train of events
that will lead to his proposal to Natasha; and the maskers'
Christmas party initiates a series of significant complications in
the lives of Nicholas and Sonya.

Tolstoy's techniques in characterization are part of the secret
of his extraordinary realism, for one of the most difficult things
for a novelist is to reveal the total personality of a character as a
person in real life reveals himself. The revelation of personality
in real life comes about over a period of time by slow accre-
tions, by the accumulation of much detailed information and
understanding through innumerable small actions and intima-
cies. This is the logical, the natural way, and a close approxima-
tion of it is pursued in Tolstoy's novels. We become acquainted
with his men and women as we would become acquainted with
real people whom we meet for the first time and about whom
our knowledge and understanding increase as our intimacy in-
creases over time and space.

Tolstoy does not confront us at the outset with the familiar
lengthy description of a character, nor does he take refuge in
the awkward flashback of a character's past. We are introduced
to Prince Andrew, Pierre, Natasha, or Nicholas in a customary
setting, as we might in the case of a future friend in real life.
Our first impression of the external appearance of the character
is only that which we would see ourselves, conveyed by the
author's few brief descriptive sentences. We learn next to
nothing of his past or personality at this point. But from the
reactions and remarks of others—this indirect method is a favorite of Tolstoy—and eventually through the conversation, self-
examination, behavior, and actions of the character, spread out
over many pages and years, our knowledge of him grows until
finally we obtain a complete image. There are no startling or
abrupt revelations. Each thought or emotion develops out of

another. And in the case of characters with a pronounced moral and spiritual bent, like Prince Andrew and Pierre, their dissatisfaction with life is resolved, if ever, not by the author's philosophizing, but by a combination of prolonged self-examination, reflection, and extensive experiences on the part of the characters. As Percy Lubbock affirms, these men and women never inhabit a world of their own, they seem to inhabit our world. That is, their world never strikes us as an abstract one. They stand forth fully defined with all their limitations of time, place, and circumstance. Tolstoy does not hover over the destinies of his men and women; they appear to exercise free choice in working out their fate so that what they do seems to be psychologically necessary, even though their consciousness of freedom, in the Tolstoyan sense, is illusory. His psychological insights, like his style, create in the reader a sense of intimacy with the characters, for in his analysis of thoughts, feelings, and actions Tolstoy's points of reference are nearly always the reality of life and not abstractions. "You can invent anything you please," he once said of Gorky's fiction, "but it is impossible to invent psychology. . . ."

Such an approach goes beyond conventional realism and suggests not only Tolstoy's complete identification with his characters, but a genuine love for them. Even in negative characters he nearly always discovers some good, which was his abiding principle in real life. The reprehensible Dolokhov is tenderly devoted to his mother, and the obnoxious Anatole Kuragin is apparently a brave officer in combat. The artist, Tolstoy believed, is called upon to portray his men and women, not to judge them. It almost seems as though he lived among the characters he created very much as he wanted to live among his friends and neighbors. "The best way to obtain true happiness," he wrote in his diary, "is, without any rules, to throw out from oneself on all sides, like a spider, an adhesive web of love to catch in it all that comes: an old woman, a child, a girl, or a policeman."

It has been noted more than once that characters actually grow and develop in *War and Peace*. The vivacious child Natasha who runs breathlessly into the living room with her doll at the beginning of the novel, and at the formal dinner boldly demands to know what the dessert will be, is the same Natasha who fifteen years later at the end of the book appears as Pierre's wife, noticeably plumpish and sloppy, anxiously scanning the diapers of her newest born. That is, they are really one and the same person at two different ages and not merely two different ages attributed to a single person, a familiar fault with novelists who project development of a character over a long stretch of years. And Tolstoy shows us all the intermediary stages of this growth as he does with other major figures of the novel.

Though one criterion of the realistic novel is truthfulness to individual experience, what writer, when truth is dull, gray, or commonplace, has not garnished it with the illusion of bright exaggeration. There is a suspicion of this in that appealing and unusual peasant, Platon Karataev, who personifies the slow, patient but indomitable will of the people that must triumph because its cause is just and its life entirely one of service. Yet Tolstoy rarely deals in illusion. He deals with life itself, and no matter how ordinary it may be, he makes it interesting without the aid of exaggeration. There are no overtly psychopathic cases in *War and Peace*, no lost weekends, no snakepits, and no undue emphasis upon melodramatic, impressionistic effects to titillate the reader's sensibilities. What could be simpler and more unimpressive than the figures of Nicholas Rostov and Princess Mary. They have no particular brilliance, no special abilities, and they do not stand out among the ordinary level of people of their social class. Yet they are evidently admirable souls, they gain our sympathy, and we identify ourselves with

them. Tolstoy achieves this effect by bringing out in such characters what he calls the common sense of mediocrity which, at
crucial moments in their lives, is manifested as a spiritual power
that enables these ordinary people to act nobly.

In an uncanny way Tolstoy adapts his art to meet every
exigency of the human natures he describes. For example, in the
case of Princess Hélène, he wishes to convey the impression of a
soulless nature, of a woman who dazzles all by her beauty but is
devoid of any inner passion or moral substance. The method he
uses to create this effect is one of brilliant externalization. At
Anna Pavlovna Schérer's soirée at the beginning of the novel,
the vicomte is about to tell one of his stories and the hostess
calls Hélène over:

"The princess smiled. She rose with the same unchanging smile
with which she had first entered the room—the smile of a perfectly
beautiful woman. With a slight rustle of her white dress trimmed
with moss and ivy, with a gleam of white shoulders, glossy hair, and
sparkling diamonds, she passed between the men who made way
for her, not looking at any of them but smiling on all, as if graciously
allowing each the privilege of admiring her beautiful figure and
shapely shoulders, back, and bosom—which in the fashion of those
days were very much exposed—and she seemed to bring the glamor
of a ballroom with her as she moved toward Anna Pavlovna. Hélène
was so lovely that not only did she not show any trace of coquetry,
but on the contrary she even appeared shy of her unquestionable and
all too victorious beauty. She seemed to wish, but to be unable, to
diminish its effect.

" 'How lovely!' said everyone who saw her; and the vicomte lifted
his shoulders and dropped his eyes as if startled by something extraordinary when she took her seat opposite and beamed upon him also
with her unchanging smile.

" 'Madame, I doubt my ability before such an audience,' said he,
similingly inclining his head.

"The princess rested her bare round arm on a little table and considered a reply unnecessary. She smilingly waited. All the time the story was being told she sat upright, glancing now at her beautiful round arm, altered in shape by its pressure on the table, now at her still more beautiful bosom, on which she readjusted a diamond necklace. From time to time she smoothed the folds of her dress, and whenever the story produced an effect she glanced at Anna Pavlovna, at once adopted just the expression she saw on the maid of honor's face, and again relapsed into her radiant smile."

Here, with these few strokes, Princess Hélène's nature is completely revealed. And her beautiful white shoulders continue to gleam throughout most of the novel. When she appears at Natasha's first ball, however, Tolstoy used this feature to draw a significant characterizing comparison. Natasha's "slender bare arms and neck were not beautiful—compared to Hélène's, her shoulders looked thin and her bosom undeveloped. But Hélène seemed, as it were, hardened by a varnish left by thousands of looks that had scanned her person, while Natasha was like a girl exposed for the first time, who would have felt very much ashamed had she not been assured that this was absolutely necessary." Special features, such as Hélène's gleaming white shoulders, Princess Bolkonskaya's pretty upper lip, and Napoleon's white hands, are frequently repeated not only to fix the character's appearance, but sometimes to suggest a moral facet of the individual's nature.

This method of externalization used in the case of Princess Hélène contrasts with the internal psychological analysis employed in the characterization of Princess Mary. Her deep spiritual qualities lend themselves to such an approach, for she never appears on the scene without Tolstoy making us feel the peculiar inwardness, the moral goodness, softness, and pity of this woman, whose soul, like her eyes, seems always to illumine her pale and unattractive face with the light of moral grandeur.

In the novelist's business of creating life as Tolstoy envisaged it in *War and Peace*, to convey the ceaseless ebb and flow was central to his purpose. At the end of the book the old order, represented primarily by mother Rostova in her dotage, has passed or is passing. The present generation, Nicholas and Pierre with their wives Princess Mary and Natasha, gathered at Bald Hills with their children, is set in the ways of married people approaching middle-age. Then, of the new generation, young Nicholas, son of the dead Prince Andrew, after listening to his Uncle Pierre's warm defense of political liberals in the capital, murmurs to himself in bed that night: "Oh, what a wonderful man he is! And my father? Oh, Father, Father! Yes, I will do something with which even *he* would be satisfied. . . ." Tolstoy indicates by dots that this last sentence of the novel is unfinished. And so is life, he implies. It will go on and on just as it had in *War and Peace*.

6

Turgenev once remarked that the hounds of thought hunted Tolstoy's head to exhaustion. He had hardly finished *War and Peace* when he plunged into a study of German philosophy. Hegel's works he dismissed as a "collection of empty phrases" and he preferred Schopenhauer. But his wife informs us that he soon dropped German philosophy for it literally gave him a headache. He next turned to a formal study of classical Greek which he learned in three months, a claim certified by his Moscow professor in the subject, and like an arrogant schoolboy he boasted of his prowess in letters to friends. Then for some time a vast epic novel on Peter the Great claimed his attention, but after months of research he abandoned the project because of an inability to enter fully into the spirit of the people of this remote period. Besides, as he said, he had come to the conclusion that Peter was a "drunken fool" and a "syphilitic," which dampened his original enthusiasm for the subject.

As early as 1870, however, Tolstoy had told his wife that he had a new theme for a novel which would concern a married woman in high society who had lapsed morally. "His problem," he explained, "was to represent this woman as not guilty but merely pathetic." An intense and prolonged reversion to his earlier pedagogical interests prevented him from beginning *Anna Karenina* until 1873. By the next year he had the first of its eight parts ready for print. Then the whole thing suddenly became disgusting to him and he again took up his educational work, declaring to a friend: "I cannot tear myself away from living creatures to bother about imaginary ones." An additional factor that interfered with progress on the novel was his mounting spiritual illness so clearly reflected in the last part of *Anna Karenina* published in 1878.

The working drafts of the novel, as in the case of *War and Peace*, underscore Tolstoy's infinite concern far artistic questions of form, style, and the realistic presentation of characters. The theme that had deeply concerned Prince Andrew and Pierre—the function of moral responsibility—encompasses the whole action of *Anna Karenina*. And the planned thematic juxtapositions and alternating contrasts of the earlier novel recur in the new one. The central alternating contrast, of course, is the love story of Anna and Vronsky and that of Kitty and Levin. Within this framework the action involves alternately contrasting scenes of Petersburg high society and that of Moscow, of city life and rural life.

Unlike *War and Peace*, *Anna Karenina*, despite its considerable length, is limited in scope and subject matter, has a definite beginning and end, and preserves an inner unity. All the action is securely tied to the main theme from the opening, when Anna arrives at the station platform in Moscow and hears of the rail-road worker's death under a train, murmuring that it is a bad omen, to the end when she commits suicide under the wheels of a train, the helpless victim of a fate foretold by the novel's epigraph: "Vengeance is mine, I will repay."

In an interesting letter to a critic who failed to discern the novel's architecture, Tolstoy seemed deliberately to avoid indi-cating the main theme of the work: "Quite the contrary, I'm proud of the architecture—the arches have been built in such a way that it is impossible to discover the keystone. That is what I most of all wished to achieve. The structural connection is not the plot or the relationship of the characters (friendship), but an inner link." This link, which is really the main theme, is not hard to guess against the background of Tolstoy's experi-ences shortly before and during most of the writing of the novel. It is the link that connects the opposing situations of Anna's tragic experience with marriage and the relatively happy one of Kitty and Levin. The whole story of Kitty and Levin—courtship, marriage, the birth of their first child, and their family existence—is in many respects the story of Tolstoy's first years of happy married life. The theme is that the sanctity of the family can be preserved only by the mutuality of pure love of husband and wife which is achieved, as Kitty and Levin demonstrate, by sacrifice, pardon, and the desire to make each other happy. On the other hand, the family is destroyed when either husband or wife indulges in the egotistic love of affinity which leads to complete preoccupation with one's personal happiness and, as in Anna's case, to the ruin of her life as well as that of her lover Vronsky. It is the worst of all tragedies, the tragedy of the bedroom, as Tolstoy remarked to Gorky many years later.

Anna's tragedy unfolds slowly, naturally, remorselessly be-fore a large audience of the social worlds of two capitals, of the countryside, and elsewhere. But nearly all the fully realized characters, including the brilliantly portrayed Oblonsky and Shcherbatsky families, are involved in one way or another with the fate of these two star-crossed lovers. For Tolstoy, himself a bit in love with his heroine's large, generous, radiant nature, endeavors to show that she is as much a victim of the hypocrisy of this high society as of her own passion. If Anna had had an affair with a handsome, socially desirable army officer, high society would not have condemned her provided she was discreet and abided by conventions that were supposed to make such affairs permissible. The only one hurt would have been her husband, but this was the generally accepted order of things. Above all, appearances must be kept up. Vronsky's mother thought it entirely *comme il faut* that her son should have a liaison with a charming woman such as Anna; it added a degree of social polish to a rising young careerist. Anna, however, is no casual adulteress. Her love for Vronsky is a deep and lasting passion for which she is prepared to flout convention, sacrifice her security, leave her husband's home, and compromise him openly. She places herself beyond the pale of her social class, but only because of the manner in which she transgresses its hypocritical moral code. Her real suffering begins not when she deserts her husband, but when she receives the snubs of her friends. It is a measure of the moral balance Tolstoy preserves in his portrayal of Anna that he persuades his readers to judge·her severely but with compassion.

Some critics assert that the one flaw in the characterization of Anna is Tolstoy's failure to motivate her seemingly sudden passion for Vronsky. The charge is that he fails to tell readers anything about her emotional nature before she arrives in Moscow to mediate the family quarrel caused by her brother Stiva's adultery only to be caught in the web of circumstances that leads to her own adultery. Her falling in love, however, is not sudden and a careful reading reveals how what Anna regards as a harmless flirtation slowly develops into an irresistible passion, a process which in no sense contradicts anything we know of her character up to that point. The process, as in *War and Peace*, involves the use of subtle details that advance the action and psychologically suggest the emotional transformation taking place in Anna. The first real sign of attraction is seen at the Moscow ball indirectly through the eyes of Kitty who is infatuated with Vronsky. On the train back to Petersburg Anna firmly rejects Vronsky's expression of devotion. She treats the matter lightly but, significantly, she is vaguely disturbed. Then on arrival she notices for the first time the large ears of her husband waiting for her on the platform, and a strange feeling of dissatisfaction comes over her as she introduces Vronsky. That first day home she contemplates telling her husband of Vronsky's declaration, but recalling her rejection of it she decides she has nothing to tell, again a refined psychological detail. That night, however, as she hears the familiar measured tread of the slippered feet of her stiff and pompous husband approaching their bedroom, annoyed with herself she begins to wonder what right Vronsky had to look at him the way he did at the station. But as she went to bed, Tolstoy pointedly remarks: "there was not a trace of that animation which during her stay in Moscow had sparkled in her eyes and smile, but on the contrary the fire in her now seemed quenched or hidden somewhere very far away."

Though the seed had been sown, the affair might have ended there if it had not been for the fact that from the very beginning Vronsky's love for Anna is represented as profound and entirely sincere, and it is made clear that he has dedicated his whole existence to securing her love. Nurtured by his endless attention the seed slowly grows and eventually flowers. Yet Anna's passionate capitulation comes only after long heart-searching into the lost cause of a conventional marriage to a man whose colossal egoism is matched by his utter unrelatedness to the human factors involved in the daily business of living.

If there is nothing abrupt or illogical in Tolstoy's handling of the early stages of Anna's love for Vronsky, neither is there anything inconsistent with her total personality in the disintegration of their love, so aggravated by her unreasonable but understandable jealousy. In the midst of a reconciliation, another of those small details signals the hopelessness of going on: "She took her cup, sticking out her little finger, and raised it to her mouth. After a few sips she glanced at him, and from the expression of his face clearly realized that her hand, her movement, and the sound made by her lips were repulsive to him." Nor is there much point in arguing that Vronsky is inadequate to his allotted destiny of creating so powerful an impression on a woman as fine as Anna. Love after all is neither rational nor analytical, and besides the story of the novel is Anna's and not Vronsky's.

Although *Anna Karenina* is one of the great love stories of the world, it is a tribute to Tolstoy's infallible instinct for reality that he so successfully keeps overt manifestations of love out of the novel. For profound love between two such mature and refined people as Anna and Vronsky is a secret thing, expansive only in hidden ways. The moral and physical effects of their guilty passion are constantly before the eyes of their world, but verbal expression of it is carefully restrained. Their affection for each other is suggested by some kind of mental telepathy in their chats on indifferent topics, or it is conveyed by hints or implications, but rarely by direct declarations.

Tolstoy's art of individualizing his numerous characters, so evident in *War and Peace*, loses none of its effectiveness in *Anna Karenina*. If anything, he adds to his psychologizing a deeper, more searching moral probing. And even more so than in *War and Peace*, Tolstoy creates in *Anna Karenina* the baffling impression, which is the quintessence of his realism, that somehow the characters are telling their own stories without the author's interposition beyond that of acting as an occasional commentator. At times this effect seems to be something less than illusory. Tolstoy relates how once a visitor remarked that he had been too harsh on Anna in letting her be run over by a train at the end. Tolstoy replied: "Pushkin once said to some friends: 'What do you think has happened to my Tatyana [the heroine of *Eugene Onegin*]? She has gone and got married! I should never have thought it of her!' So it was with my Anna Karenina; in fact, my heroes and heroines are apt to behave quite differently from what I could wish them to do!"

And on another occasion he warned critics of the inadvisability of concentrating on separate thoughts in a work of art without taking into account their essential connection. An obvious proof of this, he pointed out in a letter, was the suicide attempt of Vronsky: "The chapter describing how Vronsky accepted his part after the interview had long since been written. I began to correct it, and quite unexpectedly for me, but beyond any doubt whatever, Vronsky prepared to shoot himself. Then it appeared to me that this was organically indispensable for what followed."

In the novel no deviations are made from human nature's exacting and often cruel demands. Anna has a premonition that she will die in childbirth. By her bedside at this solemn and crucial time her sour, formal husband and her lover are reconciled. Karenin's forgiveness has an air of finality and Vronsky's conscience seems deeply moved by the realization of the sin he had committed. At this point another novelist might have made a concession to the public's fondness for a happy ending. Dostoevsky thought it the greatest scene in the novel, one in which guilt is spiritualized and mortal enemies are transformed into brothers before the spectre of death. Had he been writing the story, this experience would no doubt have profoundly altered the lives of the participants for the rest of the novel.

But Tolstoy knew that life does not resolve intense human passions in this manner. Karenin returns to his office routine and his big ears continue to stick out as before. Vronsky conveniently forgets the still small voice of conscience. As for Anna, who had already sacrificed so much for her illicit love, it was too late to turn back. She had already closed the door to her past life, and besides a woman with her pride could never have permitted herself to knock at that door.

Though each of the contrasting couples, Anna and Vronsky and Kitty and Levin, pursues its separate existence, their stories are closely interwoven and from the contrast emerges the moral repudiation of the society marriage of convenience. This contrast involves still another one, with moral implications already broached in *War and Peace*—the superiority of the natural life of the country over the unnatural life of the city. Levin has in him Nicholas Rostov's passion for the land and agricultural activity plus a large increment of the soul-searching and questing mind of Pierre Bezukhov. Kitty is the patient, tolerating wife who accepts life's blessings and sorrows as something ordained by heaven. Though she generously sympathizes with Anna's cruel situation, she believes that there are conventional limits beyond which a married woman could not go without risking the condemnation of society.

On the land Levin's complex nature flowers, and the urgent language of the description of his activities could have emerged only from Tolstoy's remembered similar experiences. Indeed, one has merely to read his *Confession*, written shortly after *Anna Karenina*, to observe how much of himself and his life at Yasnaya Polyana are reflected in the characterization of Levin

—his dislike of hypocritical high society and government bureaucracy, his love of outdoor work, and his brooding search
for spiritual truth. Levin's strident argument with Koznishev
and Katavasov at the end of the novel, in which he roundly
blames the government for forcing the Russo-Turkish war on
the people who know nothing of the issues, was also Tolstoy's
position in this struggle. However, there is a patent incom-
pleteness about the characterization of Levin, for his persistent
self-examination, guided by a rejection of conventional moral
values, seems at the conclusion of the work to be leading him
along the path of a new way of life. And his premises indicate
quite clearly that his solution was tending in the direction of
Tolstoyan Christianity, the path that Tolstoy himself was struggling to find in the spiritual crisis that overtook him about the
time he finished *Anna Karenina*.

7

Though Tolstoy never regarded himself as a professional
writer, nor art as an end in itself, he did not turn his back on art,
as is sometimes said, after his spiritual revelation in 1880. This
erroneous impression was partly inspired by statements in his
treatise *What is Art?*, a work unfortunately more maligned than
read. It is difficult to take exception to the conviction expressed
there, that art is a human activity and as such must have a clear
purpose and aim which are discernible with the aid of reason
and conscience. What distinguishes art from its counterfeit, he
asserts, is its communication, its infectiousness, and the stronger
the infection the better is the art as art. Although he allows for
various gradations and kinds of feeling transmitted by art,
where he is fundamentally at fault is in supplying a set of arbi-
trary touchstones to differentiate between the highest art—

legends, parables, folktales, or religious art appealing to the masses by invoking love of God and one's neighbor—and low or even bad art which is created solely to satisfy the tastes of sophisticated people. If he excluded from the category of high art plays of Shakespeare and some of the music of Beethoven and Wagner, with that maddening consistency, which is as much the hallmark of pride as of humility, he also relegated *War and Peace* and *Anna Karenina* to the category of bad art because they did not conform to the moral purpose of his new theory.

If a moral purpose is apparent in much of his fiction before his conversion, after it a moral purpose tends to be the reason for writing at all. However, there is no diminution of artistic power and some of the works on which he exercises it are among his best. With very few exceptions, the uninhibited style and narrative manner of the earlier novels are put aside. In their place we have a simpler prose, almost classical in its severity, and a more direct, restricted, and sharper method of narration. Realistic effects are achieved with an economy of effort that recalls the practice of Pushkin in his best tales. But so consummate is Tolstoy's art that his new moral emphasis is rarely allowed to obtrude in such stories as *Master and Man*, the folktales, legends, and fables, for he manages to universalize the moral in an allegorical vision of life.

The new approach is brilliantly exemplified in one of his finest tales, *The Death of Ivan Ilyich*, which is essentially focused on the Christian theme of the challenge of mortality. Here the precise realistic description of the process of physical decay of the stricken judge is designed to strip away layers of self-deception from the life of Ivan Ilyich and expose the horrible nudity of its utter senselessness. Tolstoy's irony reaches a point of cruel but effective revelation when, in answer to the patient's timid request to be told whether or not his illness is dangerous, the doctor jokingly replies: "If you do not restrict yourself to the questions allowed, prisoner, I shall be compelled to have you put out of the court." The reply could hardly fail to remind the dying judge of the callous bureaucratic manner he always employed in his court when he unfeelingly subjected the accused to the exact letter of the law. This kind of unpitying rigidity from family, friends, and doctors awakens in Ivan Ilyich an agonizing desire for any measure of that human understanding he had valued so little in his own climb to success. He eventually finds it in the tender ministrations of his faithful young servant Gerasim, one of those humble characters, like Platon Karataev, whom Tolstoy obviously loved because of their selflessness and simple moral dignity. Gerasim's service during the long hours of dying helps Ivan Ilyich to discover the human beauty of caring for others. "There was light instead of death," Tolstoy comments. " 'So that's it,' Ivan Ilyich suddenly said out loud. 'What happiness!' "

In *The Kreutzer Sonata*, however, a work that aroused more public controversy than any of his writings, Tolstoy tried to preach a moral ideal—absolute chastity—through the medium of artistic narrative. It is saved, though not entirely, from being turned into a didactic tract by the sheer force of his art. Nothing could be more realistically and psychologically convincing than the half-mad hero's account of his moral and spiritual struggle. Though the critically sensitive Chekhov scoffed at Tolstoy's exhibition of ignorance on medical matters in *The Kreutzer Sonata*, he praised its design, beauty of execution, and its provocative thought.

Of two longer works of fiction after his conversion, *Hadji Murad*, the moving tragic story of a renegade Caucasian chieftain, is perhaps Tolstoy's best example of that "good universal" secular art embodying his new prescription for a realism pruned of superfluous detail and a narrative manner devoid of all complexities. On the other hand, his last full-length novel, *Resurrection*, represents a return to the popular fictional manner of *War and Peace* and *Anna Karenina*, and probably because he wrote it to raise money to aid the emigration to Canada of the Dukhobors, a persecuted Russian sect. In this story, based on a real incident, of the seduction of Katyusha Maslova by a nobleman Nekhlyudov, her subsequent exile to Siberia for a crime she did not commit, and the conscience-stricken hero's attempt to repair his transgression, are some of the most memorable characterizations and scenes that Tolstoy ever wrote. The first pure love of Katyusha and Nekhlyudov, certainly the finest section of the novel, is all compounded of the same wonderfully elusive quality that transformed the girlish love of Natasha in *War and Peace* into the incommunicable poetry of youthful dreams. There is much of the old master in the abundant realistic details which convey the appearance of indubitable actuality to imagined situations, as well as a roundness, a completeness, and vitality to characterizations, in his handling of the trial scene, the portrayals of high society in Moscow and Petersburg, and in the remarkable realistic treatment of the brutal march of the convicts to Siberia.

Resurrection, however, is badly marred as a work of art by Tolstoy's insistence on turning it into a frankly didactic novel of purpose in terms of his new faith. Forthright condemnation of the violence of government, the injustice of man-made laws, the hypocrisy of the Church, and his special pleading of the Biblical injunction to judge not that you be not judged obtrude throughout the novel. In fact, *Resurrection* is in many respects an account of Tolstoy's spiritual biography, for much that he thought and suffered before and after his conversion is condensed in these pages. Though this purely subjective matter serves to neutralize the artistic achievements of *Resurrection*, it does provide authoritative material for those who wish to understand the tremendous moral and religious struggle of one of the foremost thinkers of the latter half of the nineteenth century.

Nevertheless, truth, which in fiction had been Tolstoy's hero from the beginning, remained his hero to the end. For even after his conversion he never ceased to be a great realist in all questions related to art. His fiction marks the culmination of that development of Russian realism which began with Pushkin and included such great writers as Gogol, Turgenev, and Goncharov. Though Turgenev was known earlier in Western Europe, his works lacked the impact there of those of Dostoevsky and Tolstoy. By the turn of the second half of the nineteenth century, French realism had begun to drift in the direction of Flaubert's conception of impartiality and the scientific theories of Zola and his followers. In 1850 Flaubert had already begun to complain that French realists lacked a comprehension of the inner life, of the soul of things.

It was just this comprehension that Tolstoy possessed and it enabled him to extend the horizon of the tradition of realism which he had inherited. He perceived clearly that the inner truth of a novel must come from life itself. In the real world where everything for him was part of existence, he saw the danger that realistic fiction would lose its connections with the great problems of life and degenerate into the dehumanization of art, into extremes of arid naturalism or excessive and meaningless formalism and symbolism. Further, as he maintained in his introduction to the Russian translation of Maupassant's works, he felt it the moral duty of the artist to distinguish between right and wrong in his preoccupation with the truth of life. However, in observing the human condition in fiction, he wisely understood that man does not go through the wringer of life and emerge all white. "Every man," he declares in *Resurrection*, "carries in himself the germ of every human quality, but sometimes it is one quality that manifests itself and sometimes another; a man sometimes is quite unlike himself, while still remaining the same man."

It is a measure of Tolstoy's integrity as a literary artist that after his conversion the views of imaginary characters are presented with fidelity to the circumstances of their lives and the psychological truth of their personalities, even though they may contradict or disprove his own views. A remarkable example of this triumph of artistic objectivity is the unfinished play, *The Light Shineth in Darkness*, which he frankly admitted was an autobiographical drama. Tolstoy appears as the hero Saryntsov, and like some Pippa in reverse, he passes through his world and everything he touches he blights. Here, in the sincerity of his art, he depicts himself unmercifully, for with devastating reality he reveals the harmful effects of his spiritual struggle on those who surround him, especially the members of his family to whom he often appears in the play as an aggravating, uncomprehending husband and father.

If a valid test of realistic fiction, which is supposed to give a private view of those individual experiences which are the source of reality and truth, is the authenticity of its report, then Tolstoy's fiction must be regarded as among the most convincing in world literature. And if the timelessness and universality of appeal of imaginary men and women are taken as further tests, then Tolstoy's artistic accomplishment must again be singled out as supremely great, for his characters are as much alive today as ever, and among all classes of society, and in many countries.

To have life and meaning, remarked Galsworthy, art must emanate from one possessed by his subject, and Tolstoy's finest novels seem to convey this utter absorption on the part of their author. Much of our pleasure in reading his stories arises from the feeling that our own sense of reality is enhanced and enriched by the workings of an imagination and perception that probe beneath the ordinary surface of life in an effort to explain the unknowable and clarify the obscure in the infinite complexity of human relations. This is reality immeasurably intensified in which art becomes more real than nature and more living than life.

V · CHEKHOV

"It is Impossible to Deceive in Art"

In 1874 Turgenev wrote a friend: "The reign of mediocrity has started." He was a bit premature. However, in 1881 the assassination of Alexander II, who had freed the serfs, and the accession of his reactionary successor, Alexander III, ushered in a period of extreme social and political stagnation. And it was during the stagnant eighties that a new literary star arose in Russia—Anton Pavlovich Chekhov.

In a literary sense the times were anything but propitious. Dostoevsky died in 1881, Turgenev two years later, and Tolstoy, in the midst of his spiritual upheaval, had turned away from belles lettres. Chekhov, as the grandson of a serf and a wretchedly poor student struggling to put himself through medical school and help support his mother, sister, and brothers, was far removed from the social and cultural world of these great writers, although he had read their masterpieces. In fact, at the outset of his career he was little concerned with the lofty traditions of contemporary Russian literature and lacked personal associations with its finest representatives.

His arrival on the literary scene also coincided with a series of political, social, and economic changes markedly accelerating the deterioration of the dominant gentry way of life which had been the main concern of writers belonging to the Classical School of Russian Realism. Since the Emancipation Act of 1861, the "monarchy of the landed gentry" had begun to be transformed into a "bourgeois monarchy" because of the continued impoverishment of the estates and the rapid advance of capitalist enterprises throughout the country. Urban population doubled with the flight of poorer peasants to cities and towns to fill the constantly growing demand for factory workers. Soon a large new proletariat sprang up, often disgruntled because of harsh labor conditions and a bare subsistence level of living. And intellectuals among many ruined members of the landed gentry, who were now employed in city jobs, became part of the composite intelligentsia which had begun to displace the gentry as an important directive force in the body politic.

Strident demands for reforms growing out of these altered conditions, climaxed by the emperor's assassination, provoked the government to set in motion an energetic campaign of suppression after 1881. The virile revolutionary wave of the sixties and seventies collapsed as its leaders were jailed and its publications silenced. People settled back into an existence of humdrum boredom or frustrated aspirations. Literature, which had been the advance guard of Russian progressivism, soon turned against the tendentiousness and "teaching" aspects of writers of the sixties and seventies and sought escape in aestheticism and hedonism. It began to be interested in "eternal" rather than real problems, and in its timid conservatism, to which of course there were exceptions, it declared in various ways that the purpose of art was not to teach, but to make people happy by providing them with one of life's highest pleasures.

If Chekhov was the unwitting victim of a generation of arrested progress, he was also its greatest literary artist in fiction and drama, a writer who faithfully and movingly portrayed all the inhumanity of these years but never lost sight of their human values and future hopes. Though he belongs to the tradition of realism begun by Pushkin, he understood the necessity of adapting it to conditions of life considerably different from those which had confronted his famous predecessors in fiction. In fact, he appears to have been indebted to them hardly at all in the formative stages of his art. Although he once acclaimed Gogol as the greatest Russian writer and at one time was somewhat influenced by *Dead Souls,* he appears to have learned little from him unless it be some of the typical effects of his humor. Chekhov admired Turgenev's *Fathers and Sons,* but he had little good to say about his other novels. His heroines, nearly always regarded by critics as Turgenev's finest creations, Chekhov dismissed as insufferably artificial, crystal-ball gazers filled with high-flown notions out of harmony with their place in society. "When you recall *Anna Karenina,*" he wrote his friend, the publisher Suvorin, "all these ladies with their seductive shoulders are not worth a damn." Dostoevsky he thought "pretty good but too long-winded and too indelicate. There is much that is pretentious." His shrill morbidity and involved psychological analysis were distasteful to Chekhov, and he poked arch fun at the devious mental and emotional torments of his saints and sinners. Nor could Chekhov tolerate Goncharov's celebrated *Oblomov.* The hero, he wrote, "is a far-fetched character, not nearly big enough to make it worth while writing a whole book about him."

Of Tolstoy, who was more than twice his age, Chekhov said: "I have never loved a man as I do him; I am an unbeliever, but of all the faiths I consider his the closest to my heart and the one most suited to me." It was more Tolstoy's beliefs rather than his literary example that sum up his influence on Chekhov who, in the early years of his career, wrote several tales that reflect Tolstoyan moral doctrines. But just as he suspected the pretentious messianism of Dostoevsky, Chekhov soon turned against the omniscient spirituality of Tolstoy's preaching. Prudence and justice told him, he remarked, that there was more love for man in steam and electricity than in chastity and abstention from meat. Though he never lost his awe of Tolstoy, the famous literary artist, he did not hesitate to criticize what he considered faults in *War and Peace* and *Resurrection*.

On his side, Tolstoy had great admiration for Chekhov the man and writer, and unlike nearly all critics of the eighties and nineties, he was quite aware of Chekhov's originality in adapting traditional realistic methods in fiction to serve the needs of portraying the changing times. "As an artist," he wrote, "Chekhov cannot even be compared with the old Russian writers—Turgenev, Dostoevsky, or myself. Chekhov has his own manner, like the Impressionists. You see a man daubing on whatever paint happens to be near at hand, apparently without selection, and it seems as though these paints bear no relation to one another. But if you step back a certain distance and look again, you will get a complete over-all impression. Before you there is a vivid, unchallengeable picture of nature. And there is another sign—the truest—that Chekhov is a real artist: he can be read over and over again. . . ."*

At the time this was a very acute observation, for it recognized the essence of Chekhov's innovation in traditional Russian realism in fiction. Somewhat like the Impressionist painters, he insisted upon reacting to a changing world in a fresh way; to represent its realities by a particular arrangement of selected scenes, situations, and emotions rather than by an exact, detailed linear drawing, so that the total realistic impression conveyed would have greater depth and meaning. He wanted to get behind the appearances of conventionalized society and reveal its

* Ilya Ehrenburg, *Chekhov, Stendhal, and other Essays,* edited by Harrison E. Salisbury (New York: Knopf, 1963), p. 58.

inner substance, and to this end he developed a form of the short story which he made peculiarly his own. The "teaching" aspect of the fiction of Dostoevsky, Turgenev, and Tolstoy was alien to the artistic metabolism of Chekhov, and so were lengthy introductions and detailed biographies of heroes and heroines. From Chekhov's point of view these features, including also long descriptions and excessive use of metaphor and simile, were impedimenta in the art of fiction. In general, his approach may best be summed up in his terse statement: "To write with talent is to write with brevity, to talk briefly about big things."

In his own day, and even later, many critics, unlike Tolstoy, created a false image of Chekhov as a sad singer of tender melodies, a gloomy and pessimistic writer who never understood the depths of his own soul and peered into those of his characters in order to reveal how flabby, sour, and dull were the times in which they lived. For such critics he was "the writer of sunset," "the poet of twilight," or "the poet of stagnant years." Yet nearly all these critics agreed that he portrayed the world in which he lived with complete faithfulness.

If he is loved today, if some fifty million copies of his works have been published in the Soviet Union and many more millions abroad, it is not because he faithfully depicted an age on which history's verdict has long since been rendered. It is because his characters, as is true of those other great Russian realists, are still vital and alive and speak to us in a way that never ceases to stir our conscience.

2

The beginning of Chekhov's literary career, so different from that of any of the famous writers before him in Russia, was in itself a measure of the changing times. The humor magazines in which he got his start sprang up in response to the needs of a growing urban middle class for whom the literature of the landed gentry, with its old concern for vital questions of the day, had become irrelevant. They wanted a new kind of reading matter which would reflect the values, interests, and way of life of the "little people" of the city.

Chekhov began to contribute to these cheap magazines quite simply because he urgently needed money, and they also offered an obvious market for a vein of fun in him which he had begun to exploit as a schoolboy. While he was still a full-time medical student, between 1880 and 1884, he published, under various pseudonyms, close to three hundred pieces in the humor magazines. Most were miniature stories, two or three pages long, and written often at a single sitting. He called them "trifles," "a chewed rag," "junk," or "literary excrement." Incidents and characters were drawn from nearly every corner of Moscow life—clerks, minor government officials and their wives and daughters, clergy, army officers, writers, actors, doctors, musicians, lawyers, merchants, artisans, coachmen, janitors, apothecaries, schoolboys, and soon he added peasants and landowners. The primary ingredient was the humor demanded by his medium.

Most of this is hack work which he rigorously excluded from the later collected edition of his tales. Yet among these efforts of his apprenticeship, often mere anecdotes, are at least a dozen little masterpieces that display an innovating artistic power—sharp realistic dialogue and a groping for the frustrated human being beneath the stereotyped surface of the drunken merchant or the forlorn old maid anxious for marriage. Life is not always funny, he defended himself to the exacting editor of the leading humor magazine. Misery and sadness, he wrote, are also a real part of life. Chekhov had dimly begun to realize that the short-story form, of which he eventually became one of the world's greatest masters, was capable of compressing the whole life of a man within its tiny compass. In the best of these early tales, a faintly dawning social conscience compelled him to mingle the comic with the ugly side of life where humor becomes accusatory rather than purely farcical. The funny situation in *A Chameleon* exposes abuses of power by people of rank, and there is the wry humor of *The Death of a Government Clerk* where the important general, insensitive to the obsequiousness which his lofty position forces upon subordinates, angrily fails to understand why a minor official feels it necessary to apologize for sneezing in his presence.

The marked change of tone and emphasis between the rollicking, laughing quality of these early stories and Chekhov's later mature tales depicting the cruelty, greed, and stupidity of life is often explained by the existence in him of a kind of creative dualism. This is hardly necessary. For despite his essentially happy temperament, one may discern in the finest of his beginning stories that even then he was an acute observer of life's serious moments and responsive to its tragedies.

Chekhov's first visit to Petersburg, really the literary capital, at the age of twenty-five was an electrifying experience. With his unfailing modesty he was overwhelmed to discover that important literary and publishing figures were actually reading and praising some of his stories in the humor magazines. And the distinguished owner of the powerful newspaper *New Times*, Suvorin, sought him out and invited him to contribute longer tales for considerably more than the wretched rates he was being paid. Chekhov wrote a friend: "Formerly, when I didn't know that they read my tales and passed judgment on them, I wrote serenely, just the way I eat pancakes; now I'm afraid when I write."

Though humor was hardly ever absent from his new efforts, he felt freer to handle serious themes and at greater length. As a consequence in the best tales written between 1885 and 1886

his range of observation, emotion, and satire expanded and
deepened and the quality of his descriptions and dialogue began
to approach the perfection of his later writing. The officious
busybody in *Sergeant Prishebeyev* is not only laughable in
insisting upon his outrageous notion of law and order, but he is
also a dark universal symbol of all the noxious killjoys in life
who demand that there be no more cakes and ale. On the other
hand, a typical aspect of peasant mentality is delightfully revealed in *The Malefactor* where Denis stubbornly argues with
the magistrate his right to remove nuts from the bolts of railroad
tracks because after all there are so many of them and they make
excellent sinkers for fishing lines! Then Chekhov moves to the
wonderful artlessness of *Grief*, the old cabby's story. Since
none of his passengers will listen to the sorrow that weighs
heavily upon him—the death of his son—after he has stabled his
little mare that night he turns to her: "Supposing, now, you had
a foal. . . . And supposing suddenly that little foal were to
die. . . . You'd be sorry, wouldn't you?" The horse chews as its
master feeds it, breathes on his hand, and listens to the story.
The same amazing brevity pinpoints a human frustration of
another kind in *The Hunter*—the hopeless contradiction between a peasant girl's passionate longing for her man and his
love of freedom to wander the woods and the fields with gun
on his shoulder.

But among the hundred or more stories Chekhov wrote
during these two years, few contain the enduring qualities of
those mentioned. He was now a busy practicing physician
who, in his well-known phrase, regarded medicine as his lawful
wife and literature as his mistress. No writer of his future emi-
nence ever undervalued his talent more than Chekhov, and
especially in his early years. The few masterpieces that had
emerged seemed almost like the accidental fruit of undiscovered
genius. Though his visit to Petersburg had given him a fleeting

vision of recognized literary success, he still possessed no sense of dedication to art and lacked the advice and encouragement of older authors of distinction who might have aroused him to adopt a serious attitude toward his writing and to develop what he most needed—a sense of self-criticism.

3

One may attribute Chekhov's artistic awakening, his sudden awareness of a newly discovered destiny, to a long letter of exalted praise and sharp criticism which he received three months after his first visit to Petersburg from the old and nationally known novelist Grigorovich. To be told by so distinguished an author that he had "*real* talent" and powers of originality which placed him in the front rank of writers in the new generation, and that above all he must esteem his talent, caused an emotional explosion in Chekhov. "Your letter, my kind, warmly beloved herald of glad tidings," he replied, "struck me like a thunderbolt. I nearly wept, I was profoundly moved, and even now I feel that it has left a deep imprint on my soul." He would not try to justify the faults Grigorovich had pointed out, he said. "I do not recall a *single* tale of mine over which I have worked more than a day, and *The Hunter*, which pleased you, I wrote in the bathhouse!" And he concluded: "All my hopes lie entirely in the future. I am only twenty-six. Perhaps I shall manage to do something, although time passes quickly." Indeed, time was passing quickly, for he knew then that he was afflicted with tuberculosis.

Chekhov's response to Grigorovich's critical strictures was prompt. At first it took the form of improving his working habits and dwelling seriously on the technique of the short story. In a letter to his brother Alexander, who also aspired to be an author, he warned him against hasty writing and added: "Do not invent sufferings you've never experienced, and do not paint pictures you've never seen, for a lie in a tale is even more boring than in a conversation." Shortly after this, when Alexander informed him that he planned a long, descriptive piece, Chekhov offered him a literary formula of success: avoid emphasizing political, social, and economic factors; strict objectivity, absolute brevity, boldness, and originality; complete sincerity, no triteness, and veracity in descriptions. "In my opinion," he wrote, "a true description of nature must be very brief and have the character of relevance. Commonplaces, such as 'the sinking sun, bathing in the waves of the darkening sea, sheds a light of purple gold,' and so forth, or 'the swallows, flying over the surface of the water, twittered merrily'—such commonplaces must be excluded. In descriptions of nature one ought to seize upon the little particulars, grouping them in such a way that when you close your eyes after reading you see a picture. For example, you will get the effect of a moonlit night if you write that a glow like a light from a star flashed from a broken bottle on the mill dam, and the round black shadow of a dog or a wolf appeared, etc. Nature becomes animated if you are not squeamish about employing comparisons of its phenomena with human activities."

Here Chekhov moves close to Tolstoy's sentient descriptions of nature but without his kind of realistic saturation of detail. He once told Bunin that he found the most beautiful description of the sea in a schoolboy's copybook: "The sea was huge." He would never have agreed with Flaubert's advice to the young Maupassant to single out a tree and then seek words which would adequately distinguish that particular tree from all others. Chekhov would have felt that this kind of realism, emphasizing solely the unique character of the tree, isolates it from nature and its relationship with man, amounting to nothing more than the originality of a still life. Grigorovich, in his letter, had commented on the plasticity of Chekhov's nature description when, in a swift stroke, he projects a complete picture —the clouds above the setting sun are "like ashes over dying coals." Chekhov brought to his admiration of nature a spontaneous quality of enchantment with all of God's wonders. His imagination fully possessed nature, and he came home from a contemplation of its beauties with an exhilaration—as he effectively put it—of a lover returning from a rendezvous. It is little wonder that Levitan, Russia's greatest landscape painter and an intimate friend of Chekhov, remarked that the landscapes in his stories were the height of perfection.

In this same letter to his brother Alexander, Chekhov also stressed the matter of psychology. "Details," he wrote, "are also the thing in the sphere of psychology. God preserve us from generalizations. Best of all, avoid depicting the hero's state of mind; you ought to try to make it clear from the hero's actions. It is not necessary to portray many active figures. The center of gravity should be two persons—he and she."

Problems that went deeper than those of form and technique were thrust upon Chekhov by the time his third collected volume of tales appeared in 1887. Criticism of the book brought home to him that writing fiction was not just a means to a material end but an end in itself and one that involved a debt of duty and conscience to humanity. Critics and readers alike were compelling him to face the central problem of the relation of art to society. As a coming new force in Russian letters, he was expected to provide answers to moral and spiritual questions which now absorbed the most thoughtful members of the intelligentsia. However, to use literature as a medium for expressing his personal views ran counter to Chekhov's conviction that art must remain purely objective. Though he was already sensitive to the moral obtuseness, hypocrisy, and mediocrity of society, his artistic response was to reflect these failings in fiction, sometimes with a profound sense of pity, but not with a crusading anger or disgust. He disliked emotionalism, exaggeration, and lack of restraint both in real life and in his writing. His whole nature as a man and artist made him recoil from self-assertion and preaching in any form.

At this stage of his development Chekhov was not sure that art should have a purpose or that writers, in their works, should try to solve the problems of life. He felt that to formulate them correctly in the spirit of objective realism should be the writer's aim and that the reader should be allowed to make up his own mind about solutions. When one reader at this time protested the frank objective realism of his story, *Mire*, and wondered why he did not concentrate upon the "pearls" of life in his fiction, he answered that realistic writers were very often more moral than archimandrites, and that anyway you could not make a man, who had already gone through a whole barrel, drunk on a glassful. "Indeed," he added, "to think that literature bears the responsibility of digging up 'pearls' from the muck heap would amount to rejecting literature itself. Literature is called artistic because it depicts life as it actually is. Its aim is truth, unconditional and honest. To narrow its function to such a specialty as digging for a 'pearl' would be as fatal to it as if you were to require Levitan to paint a tree and omit the dirty bark and withered leaves. I agree that the 'pearl' idea is a fine thing, but surely a man of letters is not a confectioner, or a dealer in cosmetics, or an entertainer; he is a responsible person bound by the realization of his duty and conscience. . . . A man of letters must be as objective as a chemist; he has to abandon worldly subjectivity and realize that dung heaps play a very respectable role in a landscape and that evil passions are as inherent in life as good ones."

An objective revelation of "truth, unconditional and honest" characterizes the finest short stories Chekhov wrote in 1886-87, such as *Volodya*, *The Enemies*, *Polinka*, *The Kiss*, *On the Road*, *Happiness*, and *Verochka*. Even the group of tales about and for children, such as *The Runaway*, *Vanka*, *Kashtanka*, the famous story of the performing dog, and the later *Sleepy*, reflect this same quality. It is perhaps erroneous to describe any of them as "children's stories," for he condemned the practice of writing specifically for youngsters, maintaining that it was better to select something truly artistic that has been written for adults. The wisps of humor that brighten *Vanka*, the story of the maltreated little shoemaker's apprentice who yearns to return to grandfather and his village, are entirely lacking in the unrelieved misery of the orphan girl in *Sleepy* who strangles her cruel mistress' ailing and crying infant in a last desperate effort to secure the sleep she has been deprived of for nights on end.

The inhumanity described in such stories—and Chekhov wrote many others like them—recalls his statement that "One must not humiliate people—that is the chief thing. It is better to say to man 'My Angel!' than to hurl 'Fool' at his head, although men are more like fools than angels." And he never loses a wistful affection for the fools who are victimized by life's tragic ironies, for he perceived that humor and tragedy, like love and hate, are often only the separate sides of the same coin. This subtle mingling of pathos and humor, an outgrowth of the disharmony between people's hopes and the reality of things, is apparent in *Polinka* where the young girl's tearful efforts in the draper shop to obtain sympathy from the salesman who loves her is muted in the small talk of the prices and descriptions of dress goods which she is purchasing for her mother.

Readers and critics were also beginning to speak of a typical "Chekhovian mood" which had begun to pervade his finest tales, a compound of gentle sorrow and a deep feeling that something of importance has been lost and will never be found again. The mood is poetically fused with the substance of the story and is echoed in the background of nature in these tales, as in *Verochka*, where the young scholar's realization of a love irrevocably lost is poignantly synthesized in the whole atmosphere of the story. And the mood of that exquisite poem in prose, *Happiness*, is saturated with man's nostalgic search for meaning in life in the conviction that there is happiness enough in the world if we only know where to find it. Unlike Tolstoy's characters, whose illusions are eventually dissipated by experience, Chekhov's men and women often retain their illusions, for in the end they still seem to be lost in the jumble of life in which the profound exists along with the trivial, the great with the insignificant, the tragic with the ridiculous. He does not try to explain this away. If asked, he would simply say: that's how life is.

4

By 1888 the pressure on Chekhov to do something "big" in literature mounted. The full-length novel of his famous predecessors was the traditional form for coping with those weighty moral and social problems of which he was still very suspicious. Extensive practice of the short story with its single incident, few characters, and swiftly realized denouement tended to inhibit mastering the long and complicated form of the novel. However, at this time and on several occasions later he seriously attempted to write a novel. In its conception he appears to have had Gogol's *Dead Souls* and its protagonist Chichikov in mind, for Chekhov's hero was to wander over the country and become involved in various adventures. He characteristically wrote a friend about the work in progress: "Although in places I do stray into conventional types, I shall try to avoid faithless wives, suicides, kulaks, virtuous peasants, devoted slaves, moralizing old ladies, kind old nurses, rustic wits, red-nosed captains, and the 'new people.' " And significantly he mentions that the whole will consist of a series of separate but thematically connected short stories, a concession to his favorite form which perhaps boded ill for the novel.

After several beginnings he abandoned the work. The principal reason for his failure may be found in the following statement about one of his attempts: "My purpose is to kill two birds with one stone: to draw life faithfully and at the same time show how far this life diverges from the norm. The norm is unknown to me, as it is to any of us. We all know what a dishonorable act is, but what honor is we do not know." Unable to envisage the norm of life, he could not show how certain of his characters deviated from it. As a dispassionate observer of life as it is, he had yet failed to develop a focus in life, a moral and social symbol of faith which he could apply artistically as the unifying principle in the extensive canvas of the novel. Such a vision of life was to come later, but by then death was lurking around the corner and besides his major creative energies were being expended on plays.

In a way his four-act play *Ivanov*, Chekhov's first full-length drama to be performed on the stage, was a compensation at this time for his failure to write a novel. And so was *The Steppe* which he wrote for the *Northern Herald*, the first of a brilliant series of lengthy tales which Chekhov called his "little novels," an ambitious effort to break into the so-called "thick" or highbrow magazines that published the works of the most distinguished authors. But to avoid the superfluous was as much his concern in these long tales as it had been in the short ones, and in them by exercising an artistic economy of means and applying his favorite touchstones of truthfulness, objectivity, originality, boldness, and simplicity, he eventually achieved a classical refinement of expression and an illusion of reality that seemed quite complete.

Though he worried excessively over his initial bid in the great world of letters for the serious attention of those who read Tolstoy, Leskov, and Saltykov-Shchedrin, *The Steppe* was acclaimed everywhere. In this lyrical hymn to the endless expanse of the steppe, Chekhov contributed something fresh and new to Russian literature, a kind of tone poem of nature in which the sights and sounds and smells of all visible and living things on these boundless grassy plains are caught in their ceaseless ebb and flow. The work contains a series of adventures which break up into several short stories, but some unity is introduced by the sustained account of the boy Yegorushka who travels in his uncle's cart across the steppe to be delivered to a family friend in a distant town for schooling. The tale is packed with color, life, and characters—peasants, traders, drivers, innkeepers—who are portrayed with memorable realism despite their short stay upon the scene. The brief description of the storm over the steppe, which cost Chekhov a week of solid effort, takes on a preternatural foreboding as the threatening forces of nature, thunder and lightning, are observed through the wondering imagination of the child Yegorushka: "To the left someone seemed to strike a match in the sky—a pale, phosphorescent streak gleamed and went out. There was a distant rumble as though someone were walking barefoot over a metal roof which gave off a hollow sound."

The praise heaped upon *The Steppe* did not alter Chekhov's growing conviction of the lack of effective literary criticism in Russia. "If we had any criticism," he wrote Suvorin, "I would know that I provide material—good or bad, it doesn't matter— and that to people who devote themselves to the study of life,

I am as necessary as a star to an astronomer. Then I would work hard and would know for what I worked." What particularly annoyed him was the continued charge, now directed against the long stories that followed *The Steppe* in 1888, that he was indifferent to social problems and a "high priest of objectivity." In these new tales he believed that he was dealing with just such problems, but in his own way which seemed to evade the critics. The sensitive, detailed account of a student's traumatic experiences in his first visit to a brothel, in *An Attack of Nerves*, amounts to a deep study of society's personal guilt for the victims of its social order. When the progressive editor of the *Northern Herald* accused him of indifference or misplaced objectivity in *The Name-Day Party*, whose central character, a rank conservative, rails against the evils of liberalism, Chekhov replied: "But I do not balance conservatism against liberalism, which for me are not the chief things at all, but rather lying against truthfulness in the characters. . . . When I present such types or speak of them, I don't think of conservatism or liberalism, but of the stupidity and pretensions of the characters."

In a country where moral and social problems were almost inevitably defined in terms of political allegiances, Chekhov was determined to remain free of any affiliations in both his personal life and his art. With passionate sincerity he insisted on this in another letter to the editor of the *Northern Herald*: "I fear those who look between the lines for tendencies and want to regard me precisely as a liberal or conservative. I'm not a liberal or a conservative, an evolutionist, a monk, or indifferent to the world. I should like to be a free artist—and that is all. . . . Pharisaism, stupidity, and idle whims reign not only in homes of merchants and in prison; I see them in science, in literature, and among young people. . . . I regard trademarks or labels as prejudices. My holy of holies are the human body, health, intelli-

gence, talent, inspiration, love, and the most absolute freedom
—freedom from violence and falsehood in whatever form they
may be expressed."

In his insistence at this time upon depicting life objectively in
a spirit of noninvolvement, Chekhov failed to realize that if art
has any definitive answers to the eternal disharmony of life,
they must be the purely subjective responses of the artist himself. When Suvorin protested that in *The Lights*, a long story
that concerns the decisive relations between man's philosophy
and his actions, Chekhov had failed to solve the problem of
pessimism, he replied that the writer's task is not to settle such
questions as God or pessimism, "but to depict only who, how,
and in what circumstances people have spoken or thought about
God or pessimism. The artist must not be a judge of his characters or of what they say, but only an objective observer." The
reader must make his own evaluation of what is said, he explained; the author's job was to throw some light on his characters and speak their language.

Another friend objected to the concluding sentence of this
same story which reads: "You cannot make head nor tail of anything in this world." It seemed to the critic an admission of defeat, for the reader is unprepared for such a conclusion in terms
of his knowledge of the leading character. The artist-psychol-
ogist, he wrote, must analyze especially the soul of his hero.
Chekhov replied: "It is not the psychologist's business to pretend that he understands what no one understands. Then we
will not be charlatans and will frankly declare that we can't
make head nor tail of anything in this world. Only fools and
charlatans know and understand everything."

The absolutism of this approach struck a new note in Russian
realistic fiction. In their psychological probing into the human
condition, Dostoevsky and Tolstoy had assumed an attitude
almost of omniscience. The scientific training of a physician,

Chekhov admitted, influenced his literary development and it obviously played a part in his emphasis upon objectivity in art. "Familiarity with natural sciences and scientific method has always kept me on my guard," he declared, "and I have tried, whenever possible, to take scientific data into consideration, and where that was impossible, I've preferred not to write at all." This training also led him to accept a materialistic view of life, for he believed that outside matter there was no experience, no knowledge, no absolute truths. In criticizing the eminent French writer, Paul Bourget, whose novel, *The Disciple*, indicts determinism and the evils of science, Chekhov declared that to compel man to turn his back on the material world meant to forbid him to seek truth. Such authors, with their infinite talk about freedom, love, honor, and morality, contribute to the degeneration of man, as they do in Russia, Chekhov maintained, where they "help the devil to beget the wood lice and mollusks we call the intelligentsia. The drowsy, apathetic, lazy, philosophizing, cold intelligentsia, who cannot even invent for themselves a decent design for paper money; who are patriotic; who, sad and colorless, get drunk on a glass and visit brothels for fifty kopecks; who grumble and blithely negate *everything*, since it is easier for a lazy brain to deny than to assert. . . ."

At this time Chekhov was willing to admit only that if one denies problems and purpose in creative work, then one must recognize that the artist creates without design, under the influence of some aberration. But, he insisted, the artist must remain objective, free from any tendentiousness, and not confuse the solution of a problem with its presentation. An enemy of everything romantic, metaphysical, and sentimental, he preferred to diagnose life as it is, the way a physician might diagnose a disease, but in his tales he refused to offer prescriptions for the moral and social ills of mankind.

Shortly before he turned thirty, however, Chekhov began seriously to wonder whether his insistence upon noninvolvement in questions of the day was not somehow connected with not having developed strong philosophical convictions of his own. The matter deeply disturbed him and is most cogently and effectively reflected in one of his outstanding long tales, *A Dreary Story*, written in 1889. (In typical fashion he said that he did not fear the scamps who would indulge in poor jokes about the title, and if by chance some good ones were invented, he would be happy to have provided the opportunity.) The work represents a new departure for him in conception and treatment, and is more subjective than he had allowed himself to be in any tale up to this point. It is the story of an old professor, a celebrated scientist, who, on the threshold of the grave, reviews the whole course of his life and comes to the terrible conclusion that he is a spiritual bankrupt, that his life has had no meaning, is devoid of any "general idea" which might have served as "the God of a living man." The narrative reaches its climax in a poignant final scene where the professor's beloved ward, Katya, who might have brought him some comfort in his disillusionment, seeks his aid. Though he fully understands the tragedy of her hopeless drifting, he is unable to help her because he lacks any focus in his own life.

In a sense the old professor in his lengthy analysis defends one of Chekhov's main contentions that the democratic intellectuals, lacking a ruling idea, are unable to know themselves and hence are incapable of offering solutions to the "accursed questions" that confront their backward country. Some critics compared *A Dreary Story* to Tolstoy's *The Death of Ivan Ilyich*. Both protagonists perceive the tragic emptiness of their lives, but unlike the old professor who can discover no hope for himself, Ivan Ilyich finds faith and love before his death. Perhaps the most perceptive critical article on the story was that of the well-known populist leader Mikhailovsky, who had not been too kind to Chekhov's previous writings. He concluded his review: "From time to time talent ought to feel with horror the anguish and dullness of 'reality,' it ought to erase such anguish by 'what is called a general idea or the God of a living man.' *A Dreary Story* is the begetter of such anguish. That is why this tale is so fine and lifelike, for the author has put into it his own pain."

Mikhailovsky was right; Chekhov was experiencing mental and spiritual pain in his personal life and in his writing. The problem of the relation of literature to life still greatly troubled him. This and other disappointments, the exact nature of which is unclear became of his extreme reticence about everything connected with his private affairs, brought about an acute spiritual crisis by the end of 1889. "There is a stagnation in my soul," he wrote Suvorin. "I want passionately to hide myself somewhere for five years and engage in serious, painstaking work." A few months later he was on his way to the Island of Sakhalin, a tortuous journey of some six thousand miles to the Pacific Ocean, to conduct a lengthy sociological investigation of the convict colony there.

5

At the end of 1890 Chekhov returned to Moscow after an absence of eight months. Varied and unusual experiences in the penal colony and extensive study of its inmates, from which eventually came his notable but purely scholarly book, *The Island of Sakhalin*, clearly helped to bring about a catharsis of the incessant inner agitation that had driven him to undertake the venture. He recognized the effort as an important salutary experience in a transition period of his life and a significant influence on both his social outlook and his future writing. Upon his arrival he wrote Suvorin: "God's world is good. It is only we who are bad. . . . One must work, and to hell with everything else. The important thing is that we must be just, and all the rest will come as a matter of course. . . . My soul is in an upheaval."

He lived the remainder of his life in this spirit. These years, despite remorseless inroads of tuberculosis, were crammed with an intense kind of civic activity: endless hours of unpaid medical practice among poor workers and peasants, designing and building rural schools, working at village improvements, famine relief, fighting cholera epidemics, aiding libraries, and service on many district committees. Added to this, as his fame spread, was personal aid to numerous petitioners, untold hours spent on manuscripts of struggling authors, and activity in various public cultural endeavors. Meanwhile he led a staggering social life, ceaselessly entertaining hordes of admiring visitors, and he engaged in extensive travel over Russia and Western Europe, remodeled estates, built homes for himself and family, and developed into an expert gardener. On top of all this was his writing; the finest of his stories and the greatest of his plays had yet to come. Yes, he worked, and he was just.

Among the stories that Chekhov wrote in 1891, after his return from Sakhalin, *The Peasant Wives* is something of an exception, an impressive study in the evil-begetting power of evil in two village women who plan to commit a monstrous crime. As in a number of his stories, one is struck by the realistic effectiveness of presenting inhumanity in an entirely human way. However, *The Duel*, of novella length, involves a new and more imaginative treatment of the problems of the intelligentsia. If *A Dreary Story* marked a maturer and psychologically denser period in his writing, *The Duel* may be considered a continuation of this trend. Here he probes deeper into factors of emotional disharmony that contribute to the mutual isolation of characters, a familiar situation in later tales and much emphasized in the great plays. It is now interesting to observe Chekhov introducing what appears to be a subjective note of human conciliation which he would not allow himself in the mutual isolation of leading characters in *A Dreary Story*. For at the end of *The Duel* the parasitic Laevsky does not take the customary defeatist intelligentisia way out in his failure with his mistress. He realizes that his isolation and harsh treatment are responsible for the weakness that led her into temptation, and he is determined to try to begin their life anew. "In the search for truth," he speculates, "men make two steps forward and one step back. Suffering, mistakes, and weariness of life thrust them back, but the thirst for truth and a stubborn will drive them on. And who knows? Perhaps at the end they will arrive at the real truth."

In *The Wife*, which is steeped in Chekhovian poetic atmosphere as lyrical as that of a Chopin nocturne, the mutual isolation of husband and wife is partly resolved by a kind of spiritual experience when he learns the hard lesson that giving should come from the heart. Quite different is the famous story *The Grasshopper* which Chekhov seems to have designed as a satire on one level of the Moscow artistic world. He stresses the tragicomic aspect of the grasshopper, that vulgar lover of the arts, who in her philistine pursuit of beauty is blind to the beauty of her physician-husband's self-sacrificing death on behalf of science. ·

The new country sights and sounds, landscapes and people of the little estate and its surroundings, not far from Moscow, where Chekhov settled in 1892 spurred his imagination and filled his mind with fresh subjects for his pen. Of the twenty-one pieces that he published in 1892-93, the most celebrated is the long story *Ward No. 6* where Chekhov's social awareness, aroused in part by the government's cruelty to convicts on the Island of Sakhalin, is now reflected in his treatment of the shocking conditions that exist in the mental ward of a provincial hospital. The kind and gentle head of the hospital Dr. Ragin, who has long since lost his reforming zeal in the face of local indifference, takes refuge in the conviction that man must seek happiness, not in the world outside him but in his inner self. This comforting philosophy enables him to rationalize away all the filthiness and mismanagement of the hospital as well as the regular beatings which the brutish watchman of the mental ward administers to its patients. Finally, an ambitious assistant, scheming to supplant Dr. Ragin, has him locked up in Ward No. 6. There he is soon convinced, by the watchman's huge fists, of the years of suffering and indignity his quietist philosophy has inflicted on unfortunate patients of the mental ward. The deliberately understated realism of the narrative only serves to magnify the horror of human degradation.

Though liberal-minded critics, sensing a new social emphasis in Chekhov, enthusiastically placed the tale at the top of his fiction, they were frankly puzzled by its symbolic significance. Did the ward and its sadistic watchman symbolize the "mental prison" of Russia and its autocratic tsar? And was the philosophical Dr. Ragin a satire on well-intentioned members of the intelligentsia who offered pious rationalizations of the government's oppressive measures and its violence? The critic A. M. Skabichevsky, who predicted in a review of an early volume of Chekhov's tales that he would "die completely forgotten in a ditch," saw in this symbolic uncertainty a manifestation of ineffable art. For it was supremely difficult, he pointed out, to say who were the healthy and who the spiritually ill people in the stupid society of this provincial town, or where Ward No. 6 ended and the region of sane thinking began.

A letter from Suvorin, complaining that the tale lacked an "alcoholic kick," elicited a significant reply which unquestionably indicates that Chekhov had at last rejected his belief in the complete objectivity of art and its corollaries of portraying only life as it is and eschewing the introduction of any subjective purpose, an altered position which had been encouraged no doubt by his moral and social experiences of the last few years. What contemporary Russian writers, he asks Suvorin, have given the world even one drop of alcohol? They are all lemonade, he asserts, and with his usual modesty he includes himself in this group of failures. "Let me remind you," he continues, "that the writers whom we dub immortal or just simply good and who intoxicate us have one very important trait in common: they are going somewhere and summon you to go with them, and you feel, not with your mind, but with your whole being, that they have a purpose. Looking at some of them in terms of their caliber, they have immediate aims—the abolition of serfdom, the liberation of their country, politics, beauty . . . God, life beyond the grave, the happiness of humanity, and so on. The best of them are realistic and paint life as it is, but since every line is saturated with a consciousness of purpose, as though it were a juice, you feel, in addition to life as it is, life as it should be, and you are captivated."

In the rest of the letter, again because of his almost pathological modesty, Chekhov lists himself with those writers of his generation who lack purpose, a fault which he describes as a disease of the feckless times in which they live, but his tales and plays after his return from Sakhalin contradict this avowal. Further, his real position is plainly revealed in a follow-up to this letter. For Suvorin showed his reply to a friend, Madame Sazonova, a contributor to his newspaper, and sent on her reaction to Chekhov. Madame Sazonova, Chekhov answers, argues that the purpose of life is life itself; that the artist ought to value only what is, and that all his misfortunes come from seeking lofty and remote aims. Here is real insincerity, Chekhov declares: "She believes in 'life,' and that means that she does not believe in anything if she's intelligent. . . . I write that aims are lacking, and you realize that I consider aims necessary, and that I would willingly go in search of them; but Sazonova writes that man must not be lured by delights he can never attain. . . . If this is not a hag's logic, then surely it is a philosophy of despair."

Chekhov's tales from this point on, including many of his greatest, reflect his altered views on the relation of art to life, although the beginning of the change may be observed as early as *A Dreary Story*. Taken altogether, they present an unusually comprehensive analysis of Russian society in which a social purpose is nearly always implicit, although it is never allowed to obtrude on the essential unity of the tales. That is, he never falls into overt preaching. Individual characters are as realistically portrayed as ever, but in general the emphasis is on the social pattern of a group—peasants, workers, merchants, the intelligentsia, the growing bourgeoisie. The gentry, largely absent from these tales, is treated in a similar fashion in the plays. The themes, with some exceptions such as the rare supernatural subject in *The Black Monk*, concern problems of readjustment by members of a group or class to an old order that is changing, but changing into what is never quite certain. Usually the atmosphere is one of mingled doubt and faith in the future.

If by now Chekhov has developed an integral view of life, the fantastically mounting number of characters in his tales are more often than not at variance with it—hundreds of them, grown men and women, youths, children, coming from all walks of life, all classes, representing every conceivable employment, and all with their special claims on the turn of fortune's wheel. Yet nearly every one of them is magically individualized, whether it be a nine-year-old boy or a seventy-year-old man. Thomas Mann marvelled at this faculty and wondered how Chekhov, not yet thirty, could so convincingly think the thoughts and enter into the psychology of the old scientist in *A Dreary Story*. Yet Chekhov, whose empathy for human beings passes all accounting, never stoops to caricaturing them, perhaps because he loved life and people, especially the lonely ones who crowd the vast patchwork quilt of his short stories.

Among the tales written between 1894-95, in *A Woman's Kingdom* the personal story of Anna, who had inherited a factory and considers marrying into the working class from which she has emerged, is subordinated to realistic scenes in the factory, workers' hovels, and in Anna's kitchen on Christmas Eve. It is a tale revealing Chekhov's new interests. *Rothschild's Fiddle*, on the other hand, is a perfect study in the harmony of mood and tone like the best of the early miniature tales which it resembles. And so is *The Student*, a simple narrative of how a poor seminary student encounters two people by a campfire on the eve of Good Friday and moves them to tears by telling in an artless manner the Biblical story of Peter denying Christ thrice when the Savior was bound and taken before the high priest. It is pure universal art, like a limpid lyric of Pushkin, and one likes to think that Tolstoy had in mind the exquisite harmony of all its effects when he described Chekhov as the Russian Pushkin in prose. Chekhov regarded this brief story as his favorite and most finished piece, and he once cited it as a refutation of those critics who considered him a pessimist. As the student parts with the listeners, his soul is filled with joy, for he suddenly realizes that the truth and beauty which guided life there by the campfire and in the yard of the high priest had continued without end to the present. And Chekhov concludes, "the inexpressible sweet expectation of happiness, of an unknown, mysterious happiness, took possession of him little by little, and life seemed to him rapturous, marvelous, and full of lofty meaning."

But in other stories of this period, such as *The Teacher of*

Literature, At a Country House, Ariadne, and *The Helpmate,*
Chekhov is mostly concerned, and often with irony and humor,
in exposing the crass vulgarity and morals of petty provincial
officialdom and bourgeois types. His intention, perhaps, is more
directly expressed by what he condemns in *The Polaniecki
Family,* a novel of the popular Polish writer Henryk Sienkie-
wicz which was much admired by Suvorin. It consists of a dev-
ilish heap of scenes of family happiness, Chekhov wrote his
friend, and the result is sickeningly cloying and clumsy, just as
though one had received a wet, slobbery kiss. "The novel's aim,"
he continued, "is to lull the bourgeoisie by its golden dreams.
Be faithful to your wife, pray beside her at the altar, make
money, love sport—and your affairs are all set, both in this and
the next world. The bourgeoisie admire so-called positive types
as well as novels with happy endings which calm their thoughts
so that they can accumulate capital, maintain their innocence,
behave like beasts, and be happy all at the same time."

Russian variants of such characters with their vulgarity and
false moral values appear in Chekhov's well-known tale, *Anna
on the Neck,* but they are treated with integrity, insight, and
complete sincerity. The whole social machinery which enables
the new pretty young wife to turn the tables on her pompous
bureaucrat of a husband in obtaining for him the Order of Anna
is also used to expose the venality and immorality of all this
petty bourgeois officialdom. But Chekhov does not stop there.
He drives home the real pathos of life in this milieu by letting
us see how the young wife, once she had achieved social success, turns her back on the poverty of her brothers as well as on
her father who has taken to drink.

Yet in this tale as in many others, it is Chekhov's compassionate understanding of the human weaknesses of such characters
rather than his condemnation of them that strikes the reader. It
is a special essence of Chekhov's art. He indirectly reminds a

young disciple of it when he observes that the women in a story are allowed to regard syphilis as something unspeakable. "Syphilis is not a vice," he writes the disciple, "not the result of wicked excesses, but an illness, and those afflicted with it require sympathetic and understanding treatment. It is not a good trait if your wife deserts her sick husband because he has an infection or loathsome disease. She, of course, may take what attitude she likes toward it, but the author must be humane to the tips of his fingers."

The major literary effort of this period, a very long story entitled *Three Years*, can possibly be regarded as Chekhov's last attempt at a novel, for the ending plainly suggests the continuation which he never wrote. For Chekhov it is a leisurely paced tale concentrated on the deterioration of a wealthy Moscow family portrayed against a background of city life which is described with rich realistic detail. There are autobiographical elements and a complexity of plot consistent with the length of the story, features yet unique in his fiction. Further, there are more characters than he allows himself in his tales. Some of them, especially Laptev, the younger son of the old merchant, who has become a captive of the very wealth he detests, are profound psychological studies in the making. *Three Years* has more of the flavor of a novel than anything Chekhov wrote, and the unresolved ending of the dawning love of Laptev's wife and his close friend carries the promise of further intriguing but unfulfilled developments.

6

A detailed analysis of Chekhov's plays would be out of place here, but the extent to which they reflect his theory of art and conception of realism has some relevance. Although he once asserted that writing plays was not in his character, the focus, incident, treatment, and dialogue of many of his tales, especially the early ones, are essentially dramatic. In fact some of the highly successful one-act plays are dramatized versions of these stories. All of Chekhov's youthful dramatic efforts have been lost with the exception of the incredibly long and rather melo-dramatic *Platonov*, written at the age of twenty-one and never performed in his lifetime. It contains a gallery of realistically portrayed characters taken from different strata of Russian society which is represented in the throes of transition from the decaying old order to the rapacious greed of the new. Such lines of dialogue as Osip's "The common people have no guts now-adays," and Platonov's observation on his father: "To be a blackguard and at the same time refuse to recognize it—that's the fearful characteristic of the Russian scoundrel," are surpris-ing as coming from the youthful Chekhov, but it must be re-membered that this play was never passed on by the censorship commission.

Ivanov, his first staged play, is a more or less conventional drama. The hero, whom Chekhov satirizes, is an entirely be-lievable image of the disillusioned intellectual of the eighties obsessed by the emptiness of his life. But in the unsuccessful *Wood Demon* in 1889, which he later transformed into *Uncle Vanya*, Chekhov consciously moved in the direction of the "inner action" plays of his great period of dramatic writing. However, its theme of the struggle between good and evil is lost in the welter of melodramatic effects, and instead of cre-ating life as it is, he failed to create life at all.

By 1895, when he began work on *The Sea Gull*, observations in his notebooks indicate that Chekhov intended to approach this play in the spirit of his recently revised thinking about art. Without losing sight of artistic objectivity, he was then willing to believe that the literary artist must also have a purpose and be prepared to pass moral judgment on the endless disharmony between life as it is and life as it should be. The poetic power to evoke man's vision of life, even his idealizing flights into the realm of the irrational, and to convey all this, as he had done in his tales, by creating an emotional mood with which the theater audience will identify itself—this was the new direction he wished to impart to *The Sea Gull.* He now realized, as he had not in the case of *The Wood Demon,* that in order to reveal people as they really are and not as they appear to be, he must concentrate on their inner substance. In short, what he sought was a realism that stressed not the events of life, but a character's inner reaction to them, a process which in turn must be articulated by dialogue that reflected inner rather than outer action.

The resounding failure of the first performance of *The Sea Gull* was a crushing blow to Chekhov. Though various adventitious factors contributed to the debacle, all evidence indicates that directors, actors, and audience failed to appreciate or interpret correctly the play's innovations: the significance of its symbolism, the indirect appeal of the emotionally evocative dialogue, the eloquent implication of the silences, the effective mood of fused lyricism and wit, or the unanticipated truth that emerges from a group of characters disappointed by life. Some critics even assumed that the two writers in the play, Trigorin and Treplev, were mouthpieces for Chekhov's ideas on art, although in real life he would have condemned the personalities and artistic achievements of both. If any character reflects Chekhov's ideas on art, it is Dr. Dorn in his brief statements that there is no beauty without seriousness; that an author must always have a sincere purpose; and that every work of art should express a great idea.

Though Chekhov never ceased to be grateful for the superb success of the new Moscow Art Theater's performance of *The Sea Gull* two years later, the event also marks the beginning of his prolonged disagreement with that theater's famous director

Stanislavsky who insisted upon tragic interpretations of what Chekhov had intended as comedy in his plays and substituted naturalistic effects for his realism. He accused Stanislavsky of turning his characters into crybabies. "I desired something other," he informed a young writer. "I wished only to tell people honestly: 'Look at yourselves, see how badly and boringly you live!' The principal thing is that people should understand this, and when they do, they will surely create for themselves another and better life."

When Chekhov was attending a rehearsal of *The Sea Gull*, one of the actors told him that Stanislavsky intended to have frogs croaking, the sound of dragonflies, and dogs barking on the stage.

"Why?" Chekhov asked.

"It is realistic," the actor replied.

"Realistic," Chekhov repeated laughingly. "The stage is art. There is a canvas of Kramskoi* in which he wonderfully depicts human faces. Suppose he eliminated the nose of one of these faces and substituted a real one. The nose will be 'realistic,' but the picture will be spoiled."

When another actor informed him that Stanislavsky would introduce a woman with a weeping baby at the end of the third act, Chekhov objected: "It is just like playing a *pianissimo* at the very moment the lid of the piano drops." In life it often happens that a *forte*, entirely unexpectedly, becomes a *pianissimo*, a third actor commented. Chekhov answered: "True, but the stage is subject to known conventions. You have no fourth wall. Apart from this, the stage is art, the stage reflects in itself the quintessence of life, so one must not introduce on it anything that is superfluous."

Characters in the plays, like those in his tales, are not copies of real people, but an amalgam of real people plus Chekhov's

* A celebrated Russian painter.

imagination and personal experience of life. No matter how spiritually healthy they may seem to be, in his own conception he stressed their social loneliness and requested that it be brought out in the acting which, he said, should avoid any naturalistic emphasis, stage conventions, or nonessential effects that might destroy the typicality of a portrayal. If it was an innovation to have his characters make puzzlingly swift transitions from the comic to the sad, so also was their seemingly disconnected dialogue. But the dialogue does not really bear the central burden of the plays; their striking fullness is concentrated rather on the silences and on the sense of life.

These and other innovations in *The Sea Gull, Uncle Vanya, The Three Sisters,* and *The Cherry Orchard* somewhat bewildered their first audiences, but once fully comprehended and expertly interpreted, they contributed to Chekhov's international fame as a dramatist. When he told his brother that morals do not purify plays any more than flies purify the air, he had in mind the stereotype love-and-duty situations of conventional drama of the times. Chekhov's moral values in his plays are something else again. The lovely idealistic Nina in *The Sea Gull* rises above the anguish of her seduction by Trigorin, her dead baby, and her bitter experiences in provincial theaters in her consuming ambition to become a great actress. "I now know, I understand, Kostya," she tells the young author Treplev who is in love with her, "that in our work, whether it is acting or writing, what matters is not fame, not glory, which I used to dream about, but the power to endure. Know how to bear your cross and have faith."

Uncle Vanya, Sonya, and Astrov, in a play where the realism is raised to heights of inspired symbolism, are not overwhelmed when they finally discover the cruel truth that they have been working for years to sustain the false fame of the old professor. Astrov speaks for the others when he declares: "In man everything should be beautiful: his face and his clothes, his soul and his thoughts." And courage born of defeat in a group of human beings dedicated to work and service to others rings out in Sonya's wonderful declaration to Uncle Vanya at the end of the play.

In *The Three Sisters*, where the subtle interaction of symbol and reality creates an atmosphere of unusual psychological depth, Chekhov once again distills from frustration positive values that amount to a renewed faith in life and its purpose. The passionate hope of the sisters to get to Moscow fades. Irina had placed hope in her lover Tuzenbach who identifies himself with her doctrine of work and eagerly looks forward to the time when labor will be cheerfully accepted by all. The practical Masha, who believes that life is all right if you don't waste it, had some hope in Vershinin who loves her and dreams of the glorious future when the world, led by cultured people, will be a better place. But Tuzenbach is killed in a duel, and Vershinin has to leave this dull provincial town on a new military assignment. As the band plays and the troops march off, Masha refuses to surrender the illusion of happiness. They must begin life anew, she tells her sisters. Irina agrees and rededicates herself to work and service to others. Olga embraces them both and gallantly declares: "Oh, my dear sisters, our life is not yet at an end. Let us live! The music plays so gaily and joyfully, and it seems that in a little while we shall know why we live and why we suffer. If only we knew! If only we knew!"

The values of *The Cherry Orchard* were considerably distorted in the production of Stanislavsky who regarded it as a social tragedy of the passing of the old gentry order, symbolized by the sale of the orchard, and the arrival of a new order of commercialism represented by Lopakhin. Though there are serious sequences, Chekhov characteristically mingles them with humorous incidents, action, and dialogue, for he definitely designed the play as a comedy. There is no contradiction here: the comic effects are as life-affirming as they are accusatory. That is, Chekhov compels these characters, who pose as idealists, liberals, lovers of beauty, and victims of fate, to ridicule themselves by word and action while at the same time arousing the sympathy of the audience because of their inability to see themselves as others see them. In short, by dwelling on their inner substance, he shows them as they actually exist and not as they appear to be in real life.

The values inherent in *The Cherry Orchard* resemble those of the other plays. Hard work, Trofimov declares, is the only solution for Russia's ills. Indeed, he and Anya, who answer for the hope of the young generation, rejoice over the cutting down of the cherry orchard, for it creates for them exciting possibilities of a new life elsewhere. "All Russia is our orchard," Trofimov tells Anya. "Our land is vast, and beautiful; there are many wonderful places in it." These words convey the real symbolism of the loss of the cherry orchard—Chekhov's favorite theme of the destruction of beauty by those who are blind to it.

7

Chekhov, however, always felt much more at home in fiction than in drama, and during the last few years of his life he continued happily to write stories as well as plays. When admirers appealed to him as a celebrated author to pass judgment on the merits of his own tales or those of others, in his shy way he would usually fob them off with a joking reply. Like most creative writers he tended to dislike critics, who, he said, were like horseflies that plague a horse while it is ploughing. When he was queried about the art, tendencies, or realism of this or that literary work, he confessed that he would become lost and hesitantly endorse anything. "I divide all works into two kinds," he once remarked, "those I like and those I don't. I have no other criterion. . . ."

Nevertheless, when he was asked by a younger writer for advice, Chekhov usually gave it with critical penetration and candor. This was particularly true of Gorky who worshiped Chekhov and said that in his presence everyone involuntarily felt in himself a desire to be simpler and more truthful. No one could write so simply about simple things as Chekhov could, Gorky declared, and on one occasion he told him: "Your tales are exquisite phials filled with all the smells of life. . . ." The main burden of Chekhov's strictures was Gorky's typical visceral abandonment so alien to his own artistic restraint. In his writing, Chekhov told him, Gorky was like a spectator in a theater who expresses his rapture so unreservedly that he prevents himself and others from hearing. Gorky lacked what Chekhov called "grace" in fiction, that is, the ability to expend the least possible movement in coping with scenes and the actions of characters. In commenting on the proofs of Gorky's novel *Foma Gordeyev*, Chekhov urged him to delete as many superfluous words as possible because the reader finds it hard to concentrate on them. "You understand it at once," he instructed Gorky, "when I write: 'The man sat on the grass.' You understand because it is clear and makes no demand on the attention. On the other hand, it is not easily understood and it is difficult for the mind if I write: 'A tall, narrow-chested, middle-sized man, with a red beard, sat on the green grass, trampled by passersby, sat silently, looking around him timidly and fearfully.' This is not immediately grasped by the mind, whereas good writing should be grasped at once, in a second"—an artistic principle, incidentally, that seems to have lost its force in a good deal of literature written over the last forty years.

Yet there was much about contemporary writing, including

that of Gorky and Leonid Andreyev, which Chekhov casti-
gated because of its political tendentiousness, and the popular
Decadents he described as knaves dealing in spoiled goods. He
detected a lack of sincerity and truthfulness in such writers. One
must not lie, he told a young author: "In this respect art is
especially precious, for it is impossible to lie in it. One may lie in
love, and in politics, and in medicine one may deceive people
and the good Lord Himself—there have been such cases—but it
is impossible to deceive in art."

Chekhov has sometimes been charged with adopting an attitude of restraint and coldness toward his characters, but this
impression derives more from deliberate artistry rather than
personal temperament. "One may weep and groan over one's
own tale," he wrote a correspondent, "one may suffer with one's
heroes, but I believe this should be done in such a way that the
reader does not notice it." He answered more whimsically to
the complaint that his heroes were gloomy: "Alas, I'm not at
fault in this! It happens involuntarily, and when I write, it
doesn't seem to me that I'm being gloomy; at any rate, I'm always in a good mood when I work." He was harsher on those
who accused him of avoiding positive heroes in his tales: "But
where am I to get them? I would be happy to have them!
Our life is provincial, cities are unpaved, villages poor, the
masses abused. In our youth we all chirp, rapturously like spar-
rows on a dung heap, but when we are forty, we are already old
and begin to think of death. Fine heroes we are!"

On several occasions Chekhov insisted that he never wrote
his stories directly from nature but rather from memory. He
had to let the subject first filter through his memory, he explained, until only what was important and typical in it remained in the filter. The process is concretely illustrated in the
short story *On the Cart*, a crushing indictment of country
schools. In his notebook are observations drawn from real life

about a particular rural school and its teacher, his heroine, whom he knew well. One may study the important and typical features that remained in the artistic filter and appear in the story enhanced in their artistic presentation.

Among these tales of Chekhov's last period, *The House With the Attic* is one of his most poetically conceived and executed. The rather anarchistic views of the artist in his arguments with the harsh, reformist older sister may well be a satire on sweeping verbal panaceas for social improvement among certain elements of the intelligentsia. But these ideological debates are really a device for working out the destinies of two of Chekhov's most charming lovers. The moonlit, fairy-tale atmosphere that presides over the secret meetings of the artist and the younger sister, a wraith of feminine loveliness, loses nothing of its enduring enchantment because of the realistic note of intervention which the stern older sister injects into the romance.

There is not a drop of poetry in the long tale *My Life*, a searing, realistic indictment of the social pattern of provincial towns, with all their bribery, vulgarity, and cruel inequality. Of the two central characters, a son and daughter who revolt against their father whose meanness is typical of leading inhabitants of the town, the son takes a Tolstoyan way out. He becomes a common worker and argues that the strong and the weak, the rich and the poor should share equally in the struggle for existence. At the end, however, one gathers that the main characters, enlightened by their sorrows, are moving toward the Chekhovian conviction that progress and happiness are not to be found in the Tolstoyan doctrine of the golden rule, but in truth.

No work in this last period created such a public furor as the long story *Peasants*. There were violent polemics in the press and a flood of laudatory letters from enraptured liberal readers and critics. Chekhov and his publisher lost a battle with the censor before permission was granted to print the tale. There is no plot and no truly central characters; the story concentrates on a particular family in the village. It is a picture, drawn with unsparing realism, of peasants—living ten or twelve in a family, in a one-room hovel, dirty, stinking, swarming with flies, their food consisting largely of black bread soaked in water, with a herring added on feast days. They are depicted as Chekhov had come to know them as a country doctor and a rural district official. Drunkenness and immorality are endemic, and so are cruelty and bribery among themselves and their overseers. The presentation seems like a truthful, realistic answer to idealized pictures of peasantry found in some of the writings of Turgenev and Tolstoy. In the bestiality of their savage existence, however, Chekhov searches out the humanity of those few who attempt to lead more Christian and helpful lives. Genre pictures are drawn with impeccable detail, and several of the characters, especially Olga and her little girl who are forced by relatives to beg on the highway, are portrayed with beautifully restrained pathos. In keeping with Chekhov's artistic principles, there are no denunciations or preaching. He simply seems to be suggesting that light be brought into the darkness of peasant life and that some relief be accorded them in their hopeless poverty.

Chekhov is a bit more forthright in social protest, at least through the medium of his characters, in the brilliant series of tales *The Man in a Shell*, *Gooseberries*, and *About Love*, unique for him in that they are connected by a common framework involving two characters who appear in all three stories. Belikov, the wonderfully realized image of the petty man made arrogantly servile by the impossible bureaucracy that enslaves him, is a symbol of countless men in shells, the monochrome end-products of the Russian social system of the time. The veterinary Ivan Ivanych was no doubt intended to be the spokesman of thinking people when he says of the system that produces the Belikovs: "To see and hear how they lie. . . . and they call you a fool for putting up with these lies; to endure insult, humiliation, not dare to declare openly that you are on the side of honest, free people, and to lie and smile yourself, and all for a crust of bread, for the sake of a warm corner, for some lowly rank in the service that is not worth a kopeck—no, one cannot go on living like this."

In *Gooseberries* Ivan Ivanych tells the story of a man who half starves himself to buy a bit of property in the country where he can at last be his own master and eat his own gooseberries. In this monasticism without self-denial Ivan Ivanych sees a corollary to Tolstoy's gloomy parable that a man needs only the six feet of earth that his corpse will require. On the contrary, he declares, undoubtedly echoing Chekhov's own thirst for life: "Man needs not six feet of earth, not a farm, but the whole of the globe, all of nature, where he will have room for the full play of all the capacities and peculiarities of his free spirit."

Love is a great mystery, Chekhov remarks in the last tale of the trilogy, and everything written or said about it is not a solution, but only a statement of questions that have remained unanswered. Here he is concerned with another variant of personal freedom. Month after month the hesitant lovers allow life's uncertainties to erode their passion, and at last, when it is too late, the anguished man declares "that when you love, you must, in your reasoning about love, start from what is higher and more important than happiness or unhappiness, sin or virtue, in their usual meaning, or you must not reason at all."

In truth love rarely succeeds in an ideal sense in Chekhov's stories. *The Darling* is an exception, and perhaps this is the reason why Tolstoy made it his favorite and included it in his compilation *Readings for Every Day in the Year*. With delicate insistence Chekhov emphasizes Olenka's need to love somebody and we are not disillusioned when circumstances rather humorously compel her to transfer her affections often until finally they are bestowed on a little boy—a last measure of love for one who can offer least in return.

Chekhov comes back to his more familiar emphasis upon unhappy love in the beautiful tale, *The Lady with the Dog*, the first to make use of the captivating scenery of the resort town of Yalta where Chekhov, because of illness, was compelled to spend the last years of his life. In this tale, as in others with the same general theme, his sympathy is obviously on the side of the illicit lovers whose unhappy separation is ordained by factors beyond their control.

Of the last three tales that Chekhov wrote, *The Bishop* and *The Betrothed* are relatively short pieces. Chekhov, who was himself a nonbeliever, treats the life and death of the bishop, the monastery and its priests and visitors with more religious feeling than the believer Dostoevsky in handling somewhat similar subject matter in *The Brothers Karamazov*. There is no frenetic fussiness about saints and sinners in *The Bishop*. Chekhov's quiet, objective realism, manifested in a series of exquisitely narrated homely impressions, movingly evokes the faith of the old bishop and at the same time creates the hallowed atmosphere of the Church that gives meaning to his faith. *The Betrothed* does not have quite this memorable quality. But its leading character is the first Chekhovian heroine to have the courage to break away from her bourgeois environment. Unlike the three sisters, we know that this emancipated woman will participate in the realization of the dream that haunted Chekhov in a number of his tales and plays. For she declares at the end: "Oh, if that new, brighter life would only come quickly, then one would be able to look one's fate boldly in the face, to know that one was right, and to be happy and free! And sooner or later such a life will come!"

Much more formidable than either of these two stories is the long tale *In the Ravine* which created almost as much public stir as *Peasants*. At the time of its publication Chekhov wrote Suvorin that Russian society "is weary, hatred is making it as rank and sour as grain in a bog, and it has a longing for something fresh, free, and light—a desperate longing." All the ugly intrigues and uncontrolled passions of a typical merchant family are starkly revealed but without direct criticism. Chekhov invented nothing, most of the reviews pointed out, but neither did they miss the fact that he treated these sinning men and women with a compassion born of a love of life. The arresting peasant girl Lipa, sacrificed in marriage to the merchant's noisome son, embodies that desperate longing for something fresh, free, and light about which Chekhov had written his friend. As she wanders home from the hospital, cradling in her arms her dead infant horribly scalded by a jealous rival, crazed with grief she carries on a dialogue with the strange voices of the night. The old carter, who gives her a lift, provides the peasant's simple, fatalistic answer to her plaintive query why her innocent child should have been so painfully tormented before its death: "Yours is not the worst of sorrows. Life is long, there will be more good and there will be more bad, there is everything yet to come. Great is Mother Russia!"

In a sense realism as a word explains nothing, but we all understand what is meant when we say that a writer imitates or mirrors life. And though one may insist on the fictiveness of fiction or the oblique relation of the writer's world to the real world, of all Russian realists Chekhov's own world seems to be most closely identified with his world of fiction. He portrayed the world in which he lived with fastidious accuracy, and the extraordinary thematic scope and unexampled richness in situations and characters in the many volumes of his tales testify to an imaginative power rarely equalled by other writers.

Although Chekhov finally realized that no writer whose subject is human life can be purely objective, that all is inevitably colored by what he has enjoyed and suffered, the special quality of his realism and its unique contribution to the Russian realistic trend he inherited lies precisely in the degree of objectivity he achieved. Unlike Scott Fitzgerald, he never had to wonder whether he was real or a character in his fiction. If the artist declares the intensity of his rejection of certain phases of reality by the kind of treatment he imposes upon it, Chekhov hardly ever betrays overtly his approval or disapproval of life's condition. He knew that moral values are aspects of time, culture, and adjustment, and though he hated hypocrisy, self-interest, and the power of money, in these respects he let his art speak for him; his message never lies in any teaching but in his art. If his tales ever echo him directly, it is only in that quality of his nature that stirred him most—his pronounced affirmation of life. This is perhaps one reason why his realism seems so vital and modern, whereas the realism of Hemingway, let us say, which seemed so poignantly intense in 1927, is beginning to be considered somewhat romantic and even a bit sentimental today. That is, though the Russian world of the 1880's and 1890's has lost relevance for both natives and foreigners, all still feel close to the emotional world of Chekhov's characters who help us to understand ourselves and our contemporaries.

If the profound depth of conscience in Russian fiction is what appeals most to foreign readers, then it must be said that no Russian writer was ever more truthful or more guided by conscience than Chekhov. Conscience was his highest arbiter. At a party once a guest asked him to write in his album which was arranged in the form of a calendar, with printed epigraphs at the head of each page. Under an epigraph taken from a poem of Lermontov,

> Believe me,—happiness is there only
> Where we are loved, where we are believed. . . .

Chekhov wrote: "*Where we are loved, where we are believed,* there it is dull for us; but we are happy there where we ourselves love and where we ourselves believe." And he signed his name.

VI · SHOLOKHOV

□◆□◆□◆□◆□◆□◆□◆□

Literary Artist and Socialist Realist

THE MORNING AFTER the 1917 Revolution was a tragically difficult yet excitingly challenging time for Russian writers. Two
centuries of struggle for freedom had been climaxed by a tremendous explosion that rocked the whole vast country from
one end to the other. And for a few short years, before the intellectual and artistic *rigor mortis* of Stalinism set in, writers
enjoyed the freedom and creative *élan* of the only revolutionary
period of Soviet literature. Numerous contending movements
sprang up and the radical artistic aims of their strident manifes-
toes belabored the dead past and called for fresh beginnings.
Innovation was the watchword, and particularly in poetry, traditional muse of revolution, the degree of blatant experimentation trumpeted the determination of poets to preserve their individual values in a world in revolt.

In fiction as well there was also widespread demand for
change. New forms of prose narrative were sought in which to
cast the different content of revolutionary life. Some innovators
even argued for the total abolition of the novel. After all, they
declared, the novel was obviously the creation of bourgeois

capitalism and its favorite literary form for propagandizing middle-class individualism and false liberal ideas.

Even if new forms of literary expressions had been possible, this revolutionary fervor for experimentation in the arts was not allowed to exist long enough to develop them. From Lenin down the early Bolshevik leaders were often men of considerable culture and, of course, radicals in political, social, and economic matters, but they were largely conservatives in the arts. They vaguely hoped that writers would embody the new life in old literary forms but in a context of values inspired by devotion to Marxian socialism. Moderate critics, such as the able Alexander Voronsky, saw the problem in terms of the "living man," actually a variant of Russian classical realism, which would require the writer to treat everything objectively—the Communist with all his faults and the class enemy with all his virtues. And the brilliant Trotsky, who knew more about literature than any of his colleagues on the Politburo, declared as late as 1924 in his book, *Literature and Revolution:* "Art must make its own way and by its own means. Marxian methods are not the same as artistic methods. The Party leads the proletariat but not the historic processes of history. . . . The domain of art is not one in which the Party is called upon to command. It can and must protect and help it, but it can only lead it indirectly." Heaping scorn on young radicals who demanded a repudiation of the great artistic achievements of the Russian past in an effort to build an entirely new proletarian culture, Trotsky called for creative repossession of the artistic heritage, envisaging the future development of Soviet literature as one in which collective interests and passions and individual competition would have the widest scope, and the human personality, "with its invaluable basic trait of continual discontent," would grow and become polished at all points.

In this early climate of relative tolerance, it was only natural that Soviet novelists should have sought their models in nineteenth-century Russian realism. That is, the supreme literary form of the middle class was taken over and became the favorite one in the Soviet Union which in the meantime was struggling to achieve a classless society. In the complex pattern of change and continuity between old and new, in literature the aspect of continuity has dominated the Soviet scene. This was true not only of the early period but has persisted right up to the present time. In fiction, Tolstoy and Dostoevsky have been major influences, but Gogol, Turgenev, Chekhov, and at one point the prose ornamentalists among Symbolists at the end of the century have also played a part. At times, especially during and immediately after the Second World War, critics made a virtue of this continuity for nationalistic reasons, professing to see Russian literature of the past and Soviet literature of the present as a single, unified stream of development moving majestically upwards across the decades from the classical realism of Pushkin to its transformation into the highest art in the Soviet Union— the art of socialist realism.

Without commenting on whether a movement upward or downward has taken place, it may be said that this so-called transformation is really a fusion, at least among the best Soviet novelists of the middle and later period. In the fusion another aspect of continuity has been involved. For the doctrine of socialist realism, initially formulated at the First Congress of the Union of Soviet Writers in 1934, has its roots in critical controversies between radical democrats and liberals of the 1860's. The "new Soviet man," the politically oriented positive hero of socialist realism, is an infinite extension in Communist Party terms of the finite "new man" whom the radical democrats of the sixties called for in fiction and for which Rakhme-

tov, in Chernyshevsky's novel, *What Is to Be Done?*, was an
early model.*

Socialist realism insists on the complete identification of literature and politics. The primary justification of its literary
products is to offer ideological and practical instruction to readers and to subscribe to the moral that the Communist Party
knows best. Its positive heroes have taken on lineaments of the
all-conquering knights of medieval romance, with the difference that the Soviet hero commits no mortal sin because his
heart is socialistically pure. Though Marx and Engels, with
their rather humanistic views on literature, would hardly have
sanctioned this Soviet debasement of it, their authority has frequently been invoked and distorted to support the Soviet version of socialist realism. In practice socialist realism seems to
result in the union of revolutionary romanticism and revolutionary realism, in which the author appears to see tomorrow as
the basis of today. That is, he writes as if ideals were already
facts. Or put another way, he starts with a version of idealized
life as he thinks it will be in the Communist future and then
adapts it to Soviet reality today. In these circumstances, there is
perhaps much point in the excellent article on socialist realism,
published abroad by the Soviet pseudonymous Abram Tertz,
who suggests in one place that the irreality of Soviet life, especially in the days of Stalin, could be more effectively rendered
by a phantasmagoric art than by socialist realism. However that
may be, the mechanical fusion of Russian classical realism with
Soviet socialist realism does violence to the honesty and sincerity of the former and serves to expose the shallow artistic
pretensions of the latter. Nineteenth-century realism also en-

---

* For a convincing and perceptive study of this thesis, as well as of
much related matter, see Rufus W. Mathewson, Jr., *The Positive Hero in
Russian Literature* (New York: Columbia University Press, 1958).

countered governmental repression, though never in the manner of Soviet total literary manipulation, but its posture always remained a libertarian one. The difference is that Soviet leaders have come to regard literature as a tremendously important ideological weapon, whereas the tsars took little notice of it provided writers refrained from attacking any fundamental feature of the autocracy. To this extent artistic individualism, so necessary to the free functioning of genuine realism, found elaborate expression in great Russian novels of the nineteenth century whose enduring and vast popularity today in the Soviet Union reflects unfavorably on the fiction of socialist realism.

Some earlier Soviet fiction, before the curtain of socialist realism came down, was written in the full tradition of nineteenth-century realism, and often with originality and on a high artistic level. One thinks of the early short stories and novels of Zamyatin, Fedin, Leonov, Olesha, Pilnyak, and Babel. A prevalent theme in much of this fiction is the tragic struggle of allegiances between old and new which revolution always thrusts upon a population. The complex tensions of this cruel dilemma are psychologically analyzed in terms of the desperate choices that confront men and women compelled to reject or furtively compromise with a past life, which they sometimes loved, and adjust to a new existence which often seemed incomprehensible. Perhaps the realism of novels concerned with this problem, such as Fedin's *Cities and Years* and *The Brothers* and Leonov's *The Badgers* and *The Thief*, gained in convincingness and emotional impact because their authors were undergoing the same agony of adjustment or alienation as their characters.

Individual values, however, were still more violently wrenched in the physical aspect of the struggle between old and new—the bloody fratricidal strife of civil war. The ter-

rible urgency of shattering social change was enforced by gun, dagger, and sabre over hundreds of battlefields by millions of kith and kin, who maimed, killed, despoiled, and ravaged one another. Here was the richest material for fiction, not only horror-haunted situations of mortal strife between master and man, father and son, brother and brother, but also the love and hate, tenderness and cruelty which the violence of civil war mysteriously spawns in a world of sudden change where the hard choices between old and new may often be choices between life and death.

On this theme the one Soviet novel that can take its place beside all but the greatest of nineteenth-century fiction, and which has long since won for itself the reputation of a classic, is Mikhail Sholokhov's *The Quiet Don*. To be sure, as an exemplar of the best in this respect one may prefer *Doctor Zhivago*, which is also concerned with the struggle between old and new in war and civil war and is likewise written in the tradition of nineteenth-century Russian realism, although Pasternak has brought to it his own increment of originality. Pasternak's masterpiece, however, though steeped in the tragedy of Soviet life, is really devoid of the typicalness of Soviet literature, for it rises above the battle into the clear air of universal art.

The Quiet Don, on the other hand, represents with near perfection that fusion of traditional Russian realism with Soviet socialist realism, and was written by a Communist who, because of his artistic integrity, all but refused to sacrifice either the logic of his design or—in the Tolstoyan sense—the truth of his hero to extraneous demands of Party doctrine. If there is any point in the old cliché that all literature is propaganda, but not all propaganda is literature, then it may be said that propaganda is brilliantly sublimated in *The Quiet Don*.

2

In a society determined to encourage the collectivist spirit of man, nature seems to have endowed Sholokhov with the temperament of a pronounced individualist. Perhaps the fabled independence of the Cossack may account somewhat for his aloofness. His fame in the Soviet Union is legendary, his books have sold in millions of copies, and he has received every honor a grateful country can bestow on him, nevertheless, he prefers to shun writers and the literary turmoil of Moscow for his simple Cossack neighbors on the Don and his quiet homestead there. He loves this river and the rolling steppes expanding from its banks, and he intensely enjoys living through the changing seasons of his picturesque region, observing its animate and inanimate life. It is the throbbing heart of his fiction and he draws from it his strength and tenderness as a literary artist.

Unlike a number of immediate contemporaries who achieved fame as writers, Sholokhov appears never to have had any fellow-traveler inclinations. After a little formal education and some experience in fighting on the side of the Reds in the Don region, he joined the Communist Party at the age of twenty-five. He has always been an indubitable Soviet writer, untroubled by memories of Russia's cultural past. If he has learned from its great fiction in a literary way, and he has learned much, he has been impervious to its libertarian ethos. As for the culture of the West, he regards it as rather effeminate, scorns it, and also any Soviet art that is influenced by it.

When he came up to Moscow for a short time in 1923, at the age of eighteen, to obtain more education, the loner instinct insulated him from contending writers' groups and exciting lit-

erary controversies. He went his own way, made very few friends, and has persisted in this practice ever since.

In 1925 *Don Tales*, later augmented in a second volume, unobtrusively began Sholokhov's long literary career. In the mass of Soviet civil-war literature, these short stories fall somewhere between the notable documentary novel, *Chapayev*, of Furmanov and Babel's collection of tales, *Red Cavalry*, but they avoid the sententious political harangues of the first and the incredibly cruel yet meaningful detachment of the second. Sholokhov sets out to counter mistaken romantic notions of Don Cossack fighting in the civil war, but he does not labor the point. Some of these stories tell of bitter political enmities in families whose members are torn between loyalty to the Reds or the Whites, but their grimness is nearly always relieved by passages of tenderness and warm human sympathy. In others humor dominates, as in *The Impudent Brat* where the boy's idealized notion of an heroic-sized Lenin is amusingly debunked, or in the tale about the fire-eating chairman of a village revolutionary war council with his comic use of hard words and malapropisms. Every so often manifestations of little acts of commonplace kindness, like spring flowers pushing through the blood-drenched soil of a battlefield, reveal Sholokhov's larger humanity: the sentimental Cossack who sacrifices his life in combat to save a beloved horse, or the old father in another tale who, heartbroken over his son's death in the cause of the Whites, transfers his affections to a badly wounded Red Army youth whom he nurses back to health. Left-wing Soviet critics stigmatized such deviations from the fictional pattern of civil-war harshness as the lubricating humanism of middle-class consciousness. However, this concern for the gentler attributes of man in the midst of cruel fratricidal strife, an understanding that man's need to love and be loved will often rise above doctrinal hate, is part of Sholokhov's wisdom of life.

One thinks of the youthful Tolstoy's early Caucasian army tales with their refined reasoning about such problems as bravery, why men fight, and the uselessness of war. There is none of this in Sholokhov's short stories, only a curious combination of psychological realism and his own ideological empathy with the moral rightness of the Red cause. Yet he has some glimmering of the impartiality of art, for if his sympathies are with the Reds, he does not spare their failings.

Clearly Sholokhov is not entirely at home with the short story and he rarely turned to it later. Its confining form inhibits the revelation of his heroes, for he is primarily a writer of expansive action which he employs in subtle ways to illuminate the conscious and unconscious world of his characters. Then, too, he favors extensive descriptions for which he has positive gifts. Nevertheless, these first tales, despite occasional faults of immaturity, convincingly announce the emergence of a highly talented artist. He obviously understands realism in the meaning of the Russian classical tradition, that is, a lifelike representation of character, and fidelity, through style, to details of objects, manners, and speech which he carefully orchestrates in scenes and dialogue. His use of language is already impressive, especially in nature descriptions which are suffused with striking poetic qualities. And bold dramatic situations are most effectively handled with a narrative skill that combines the sharpest realistic detail with qualities of humor and feeling. Only characterization in these early stories, which is in no sense unskillful, fails to suggest fully the brilliance which he later achieved in this respect.

3

The Quiet Don appeared serially, and then separately in four volumes, over a period of twelve years (1928-40). Though

reasons for the long delay of seven years between publication of the third and last volumes are not definitely known, the terrible purges of the thirties no doubt played a part, as well as objections of officials in the Union of Soviet Writers and of Stalin himself to certain political aspects of the novel.

Cossacks had been portrayed, somewhat idealistically, by previous writers, notably by Gogol and Tolstoy, but never before had they been treated so fully and so realistically as in this work of some fifteen hundred pages. *The Quiet Don*, essentially a historical novel of a tragic decade (1912-20) in the life of the Cossacks, tells the story of how world war, revolution, and civil war cruelly uprooted this proud, liberty-loving people and finally brought them under the power of the Soviets.

Like Tolstoy's *War and Peace*, with which it has so frequently been compared, *The Quiet Don* concentrates on the histories of five families, of which the principal one is the Melekhovs, belonging to the social category of middle Cossacks and consisting of the irascible father Pantaleimon, the wonderful old mother Ilinichna, and three children—the attractive daughter Dunya, the older brother Pyotr and his wayward wife Darya, and the younger son and hero of the novel, the nineteen-year-old Gregor. In addition to these families, scores of other characters are introduced, types drawn from lower and upper classes of Cossacks, and also a number of historical figures of the period.

No greater contrast can be imagined than that between the social milieux of *War and Peace* and *The Quiet Don*. Tolstoy's cultured families and their sophisticated city life and idyllic existence on country estates have nothing in common with the three hundred peasant households of the Cossack village of Tatarsk. There, existence was often unbelievably harsh. Manners and customs, guided by age-old superstitions, were almost primitive. In the winter months animals of the barnyard vied

with humans for space in the tiny thatched huts with their earthen floors; hands, greasy from being dipped into the common family stew bowl for meat, were wiped on the hair. War, which was waged with some of the civilized amenities of nobility and honor in Tolstoy's classic, was fought with incredible ferocity and horrifying cruelty in Sholokhov's novel. Troubled over the impact such a rude order of life would have on foreigners, Sholokhov wrote a foreword, which was never published, for the English translation, in which he explained that readers should take into account the dislocation of existence and human psychology among Don Cossacks caused by revolution and civil war. For he passionately loves his Cossacks, and if he faithfully reveals their uncultured manners, primitive customs, and moments of savagery, he also brings out their sterling virtues and spiritual strength under human stress, their humor and kindness, their love of nature, and their deep sense of honor.

A novelist of action, Sholokhov is not a particularly reflective writer, a limitation often adversely commented on by Western critics. The varied substance of his masterpiece is not illuminated by the intellectual brilliance and profound philosophical and moral probing of a Tolstoy. Such qualities, without begging the question of Sholokhov's artistic limitations, would be singularly irrelevant in coping with the simple life and behavior patterns of artless Cossacks of *The Quiet Don*. Sholokhov's characters live in the chaos of action and what they do and not why is the focus of their being.

Gregor's nature, for example, is devoid of any sophistication of thought and he is incapable of resolving in his own interests the bitter conflicts of political and human values that confront him in the course of revolution and civil war. Pride, injustice, love, or hatred trigger his impetuous actions. Like the elemental and headstrong Dmitri Karamazov, Gregor's actions and feelings are the best measure of his nature. The tragedy that breaks

over his head, however, is no less compelling and moving than that which has engulfed the great tragic heroes of literature.

As the novel opens, the happy young Gregor, an accomplished Cossack in riding, hunting, and fishing, and also a hard worker in the fields, has not a care in the world except his passionate love for the beautiful Aksinya, his neighbor's wife. Gregor's first disturbing experiences in bloody combat at the front in 1914, war scenes which Sholokhov describes with unsurpassed vigor and verisimilitude, are neutralized by Cossack conformity to martial glory and he soon learns to fight and kill with exceptional bravery. However, a sensitivity to acts of cruelty, to any form of violence visited upon the weak and defenseless, and, as the war wears on, a feeling of rebellion against its horror and stupidity tend to differentiate him from his comrades in arms. Then the revolutionary propagandizing of Garanzha in the hospital, where Gregor is recovering from a wound, forces him to question his devotion to tsar, country, and military duty.

When the 1917 Revolution comes, Gregor's confused, tormented groping for certainty symbolizes the divided loyalties of the Don Cossacks at this time of turmoil. "It is hard for me to make head or tail of it," he mumbles. "I'm all over the place, like drifting snow in the steppe."* His search for political truth in a world of swiftly shifting values is guided by appearances rather than substance. He fights for the Reds at first, but an incident of their slaughter of unarmed captives sickens him, and when the Bolsheviks invade his beloved Don region, looting and raping in the villages, he turns against them in cold fury.

In Gregor's anguished struggle for a way out of his uncer-

* Quotations are from *The Silent Don*, translated by Stephen Garry (2 vols. in one; New York: Knopf, 1943): *And Quiet Flows the Don*, pp. 123, 409; *The Don Flows Home to the Sea*, pp. 113, 142, 653, 662-63, 763, 772, 774, 777. In a few cases the translation has been slightly altered on the basis of comparison with the original Russian.

tainties, which are endlessly complicated for him by contradictions between political truth and the truth of nature, it is part of Sholokhov's scheme of things to represent him as a man opposed to history. On the level of socialist realism Gregor's tragedy is that he defies historical necessity and hence becomes its victim. In Communist terms the individual cannot rebel against the immanence of political and social change and hope to survive. Historical necessity, as it were, takes the place of the Greek Nemesis in the resolution of a hero's fate. One is dealing with a new moral order in which sympathy for man's doubts and vacillations in the face of life's major decisions and his eternal right to change allegiances on the basis of principles must be surrendered to the imperatives of history's assumed laws. The individual's right to rebel, the celebrated virtue of so many great figures of literature, now becomes his tragic flaw if the rebellion is against forces of history preordained to establish the dictatorship of the proletariat. And Sholokhov leaves no doubt about his view that history is the matrix enveloping Gregor's destiny, for the events which ultimately bring about the hero's downfall are carefully documented with footnotes and quotations from official reports.

Throughout most of the novel, however, the cards do not appear to be stacked against Gregor. Sholokhov turns his search for truth into a tremendous human drama of a man perplexed in the extreme by agonizing choices. Gregor's deepest instincts urge him to reject both Whites and Reds. They are all alike, he protests to Communistically inclined boyhood friends, for they are a yoke on the necks of the Cossacks. And when he hears that revolt is spreading among Cossacks in the Upper Don province against the occupying Red Army, he gladly joins the insurgents and leads several thousand troops in the struggle. For now he can fight for something he holds dear, and his thoughts on this occasion provide the clearest image of his nature: "It

was as though those days of search for the truth had been lifted from his shoulders, those stumblings, transitions, and painful inner struggles. Those days had passed like the shadow of a cloud and now his searchings seemed aimless and empty. What had there been to think about? Why had his spirit twisted and turned, like a hunted wolf seeking to escape, in search of a resolution of his contradiction? Life seemed absurdly, wisely simple. Now he believed that there never had been any such truth beneath whose wings all might shelter; now he believed each had his own truth, his own furrow. For a piece of bread, for a strip of earth, for the right to live, men had always fought and would fight so long as the sun shone on them, so long as their blood flowed warmly through their veins. Those who wanted to deprive him of his life, of his right to live, must be fought resolutely and with no wavering, but steeled in hatred."

4

The disharmony of political loyalties in Gregor finds one kind of resolution in his faith in Aksinya. It is the greatest love story in Soviet literature, and the deep sympathy its tragic course arouses is some measure of Sholokhov's acute understanding of the simplicity of passion in simple people. Aksinya is a natural woman, beautiful, free, and proud in her movements, contemptuous of local gossip, and capable of any sacrifice for the sake of her love and her lover. Her life has been harsh: raped at sixteen by her father and then married off to the dour, sadistic Stepan Astakhov who regularly beats her, compels her to slave in the fields, and locks her up at night while he plays around with other women. Yet it is not just escape from the futility of existence that brings her to Gregor, but a kind of destined affinity written in the very stars that shine down on their nightly

trysts in the comforting emptiness of the steppe. Their illicit love survives Gregor's marriage, thrust upon him by his worried parents, to the shy, attractive Natalya Korshunova, and also Aksinya's understandable lapse with the well-born Cossack officer Listnitsky. Unlike Gregor's wife, Aksinya offers no protest over his debauchery on a campaign when he seeks to forget in drink and loose women the political doubts that torment him and his revulsion to the endless slaughter of war.

Aksinya, however, really fears the devoted, religious, and highly moral Natalya, who possesses strength of will and inner beauty and has also borne Gregor twins whom he adores. Two confrontation scenes between wife and mistress are executed with consummate art. One's sympathy goes out to the crushed, abandoned wife, but in the second meeting Aksinya's simple dignity contrasts strikingly with Natalya's bitter moral rectitude. Aksinya quietly declares that if the Queen of Heaven saves Gregor from death and he comes back, then he'll choose for himself. She is diseased with love, Gregor laughingly tells the passionate Aksinya. And when he asks her if she will go away with him, she instantly replies: "I'll sleep with the cattle to be with you, Grisha. Anything to be with you." And Gregor, during long periods of separation, sees Aksinya in his dreams, and he realizes in moments of deep dissatisfaction with his married life and the whole senseless business of fighting that he still loves her "with all his old exhausting love; he felt that he loved her with all his body, with every beat of his heart."

There can be little doubt that Misha Koshevoi, Gregor's boyhood friend, was designed as his ideological foil, but on these terms or any others one may well question the successful realization of the portrayal. Won over to the Communist cause by the shadowy and unconvincing agitator Stockman, Misha's gentle and genial personality is completely changed into that of a stern and uncompromising Bolshevik, a fantastic transforma-

tion that can be neither explained nor vindicated by his lowly class origin or the indignities and perils he is subjected to by the enemy. As a Red fanatic he has his prisoners shot down and personally executes his old friend Pyotr, Gregor's brother, murders in cold blood the ancient Bible-reading Grishatka Korshunov, orders the houses of well-to-do Cossacks in the village to be burned, and in the course of informing Gregor's mother that he intends to marry her daughter, he warns the old lady that his first business as chief Soviet official in Tatarsk will be to catch and hang her son. In a judgment that must be regarded as somewhat official, although one hesitates to conjecture that Sholokhov would have entirely concurred, a prominent Soviet critic declared: "The behavior of Koshevoi is justified on the whole both politically and psychologically. The very image of Koshevoi is conceived with great sensitivity and in places achieves beauty and the perfection of poetry."*

This monster of Party loyalty, who justifies his actions by Communist doctrine and the terrible exigencies of civil war, falls infinitely below Gregor in any scale of human values. On one occasion, when Gregor hears that Misha Koshevoi, as a Red, is in danger of being beaten to death by infuriated Cossacks, at some personal risk to himself he immediately gallops off to save him, murmuring: "There's bad blood between us, but after all there's our old friendship." If Gregor everlastingly vacillates in the political struggle and is unable to achieve the doctrinal forthrightness of Misha Koshevoi, it is because he is loyal to himself, to human dignity, decency, and justice, and because he values his individual freedom higher than submission to any cause.

Whatever may have been Sholokhov's intention in the characterization of Misha Koshevoi, he hardly emerges as a sym-

* I. G. Lezhnev, *Mikhail Sholokhov* (Moscow: Soviet Writer, 1948), p. 222.

pathetic, shining image of the new Soviet man. No Western reader would prefer his company to that of Gregor, and it is hard to imagine that many Soviet readers would. He is less believable, psychologically speaking, than the patently idealized Party member Bunchuk whose love for Anna Pogoodka—one Communist in the novel who seems to have been born with a conscience and retained it—is beautifully and movingly told.

It may be that in the image of Misha Koshevoi we have an example of artistic "intentional fallacy" in the sense that what Sholokhov intended in the characterization was never realized in the novel. Of course, the same reasoning in reverse could be applied to the image of Gregor—he has probably turned out to be much more attractive to readers than Sholokhov had ever intended. Or one could explain the unpalatableness of Koshevoi and his Bolshevik cause in a novel written by a Communist the way Soviet critics, following the lead of Engels, explain the artistic achievement of Balzac. That is, Balzac, despite his royalist aspirations, was compelled by the integrity of his art to reflect in fiction the truth of what he did not want to believe—the successful bourgeois development of progressive social change in France.

5

Long before the ending of *The Quiet Don* had been written, there was widespread expectation that Sholokhov would bring his hero into the Communist fold or have him die in a last glorious act of bravery in the ranks of the Red Army in expiation for his sins in siding with the Cossack insurgents and the Whites. Such a resolution of Gregor's fate would have been false to the whole psychological meaning of the portrayal up to that point. Whatever one may think of the actual conclusion Sholokhov fashioned, its realistic and artistic relevance is unassailable.

The likelihood that the officer class will lord it over the Cossacks as of old if the White Guard is victorious is as distasteful to the liberty-loving Gregor as the possibility of the imposition of Red rule on the Don. In the last volume of the novel demotion because of insubordination to a White General, the death of his wife Natalya, who had come to hate him, from an abortion attempt on herself, and the final dispersal of the White Army bring Gregor to a point of utter despair. He eventually joins Budyonny's Red cavalry and fights the Poles bravely, imagining this service as a purging of his offenses against the Bolsheviks. Nevertheless, when he returns to his village after demobilization the unrelenting Misha Koshevoi, who has married Gregor's sister and become chairman of the Revolutionary Committee of Tatarsk, makes it clear that he will still have to stand trial before a military tribunal. "I've served my time," Gregor frankly tells him. "I don't want to serve anybody any more. I've fought more than enough for my age. I'm fed up with everything, with the Revolution and the counter-revolution. Let all that—let it all go to hell! I want to live the rest of my life with my children, to return to the farm, that's all."

But there was no escape for Gregor in a Soviet world where even neutrality was regarded as heresy. Wryly, Gregor remarks to his old orderly that he has always been envious of the Red, Koshevoi, and the White, Listnitsky. "Everything was clear to them from the very beginning, but nothing is clear to me even now. Both saw straight roads before them; but since 1917 I've been going round and round in a circle, reeling like a drunken man."

One night at Aksinya's hut (her husband had disappeared in the fighting), Gregor's sister runs in to warn him that Koshevoi and his men are on their way to arrest him. Aware that this probably means execution, he flees. After months of hiding out, he yearns for his children and Aksinya, who is taking care of

them, and secretly returns. She clasps him around the legs, presses her face to his wet greatcoat, and sobs through her tears: "Kill me, but don't leave me again." After persuading his sister to take the children, he and Aksinya steal away in the night, hoping to reach the Kuban and begin a new life.

Riding by his side a rapturous joy fills the soul of this passionate woman as she exults over the thought that she is with her Gregor once again. But at one point they are confronted by guards, and as Gregor lashes her horse and they gallop off shots ring out in the night. Later, in the safety of a ravine, he discovers that Aksinya is fatally wounded and realizes that the most terrible thing that could happen to him has come to pass. Gregor buries his Aksinya in the early morning light. The author writes: "With his palms he diligently pressed down the damp yellow clay over the mound and remained long on his knees beside the grave, his head bowed, his body swaying a little.

"Now he had nothing to hurry for. Everything was finished.

"The sun rose above the ravine through the smoky haze of the burning wind from the east. Its rays silvered the mass of gray hair on Gregor's head and slipped over his pale and terribly immobile face. As though awakening from an oppressive sleep, he raised his head and saw above him the black sky and the blindingly glittering, black disc of the sun."

Weeks of refuge in a deep forest only intensify Gregor's longing to see, as he puts it, "the old spots once more, to feast my eyes on the children; and then I can die." He returns to Tatarsk, and Sholokhov, after touchingly narrating Gregor's meeting with his young son, concludes his long novel: "And now that little thing of which Gregor had dreamed during so many sleepless nights had come to pass. He stood at the gate of his own home, holding his son by the hand. This was all life had left to him, all that for a little longer gave him kinship with

the earth and with the spacious world which lay glittering under the chilly sun."

In Sholokhov's words Gregor is to enjoy these pleasures only "for a little longer." Obviously he had come home to die. The Nemesis of Communist historical necessity, personified by Misha Koshevoi, is waiting for Gregor. In a novel filled with violence and executions, Sholokhov wisely drew the curtain on this last one. Perhaps for him, as for many of his readers, the account of it would have been unbearable.

Though *The Quiet Don* is not free of tendentiousness, at least in the first edition of it Sholokhov does not overtly abuse the license accorded the historical novelist, for he does not appear to manipulate events to conform to a political ideology. The behavior of both Whites and Reds, with all their cruelty, ugliness, deception, and occasional nobility, is described with artistic honesty. If one cares to, in fact, one may read the novel as the unvarnished narrative of the bloody conquest of the majority of Don Cossacks by the Red Army. For unlike Tolstoy, who in *War and Peace* argues a philosophy of history to justify his approach to events and people, Sholokhov can hardly be accused of offering an exposition of Marxian historical materialism in *The Quiet Don*, although this dogma is implicit throughout the whole novel.

Soviet critics, unhappy over Sholokhov's failure to subordinate life to political ideology, have supplied a Marxian rationalization of the novel and its hero's fate. As an individualist in an epoch of socialism, Gregor's fate was predetermined by the class struggle. Caught in the web of contradictions of his own social class of middle Cossacks, so the explanation runs, he was unable to perceive that the future lay with the masses of poorer Cossacks who were supported by the Soviet Revolution. His destruction follows as a logical consequence of his failure to understand the workings of history's laws at a time of violent

social change. In the kind of reading of the novel mentioned above, however, one can easily conclude that the vast majority of Don Cossacks over these years made their choices, not on the basis of political conviction or class consciousness, but because of fear of the naked force of the Red Army, or for calculated reasons of gain and security.

6

Sholokhov was too fine a literary artist to sacrifice the reality of living life in *The Quiet Don* to doctrinal expediency. If he pays his kopeck's worth of tribute to socialist realism at the end by allowing the rigidly righteous, baleful Bolshevik Misha Koshevoi to triumph over Gregor, Sholokhov, in the best traditions of nineteenth-century Russian realism, preserves the integrity of the personality of his proud, sensitive hero in terms of its total development throughout the novel.

It is a remarkable fact that in an epic story of war, in which so many hundreds of pages are devoted to the dying and the dead, the dominant flavor of the work is one of unquenchable, omnipresent life. This quality reflects Sholokhov's own optimistic zest for life in which he so much resembles Tolstoy. There are many memorable scenes spanning the whole range of Cossack domestic and public existence, vivid with vital activity, humor, and Cossack incongruities. This lively sense of humanity is garnished by a constant outpouring of Cossack lore—ancient traditions and customs, colorful sayings, proverbs, and charming folksongs. And the earthiness of these people, their passionate love of the land, is wonderfully caught by Sholokhov in his concentration on nature's lyric moods which he describes in abundant detail and often in a poetically symbolic antiphonal manner as they respond to the joys and sorrows of his characters. His language pattern, subtly assimilating the special flavor

of Don Cossack speech, is extremely varied and most effectively adapted to the individualized speech of his characters.

Although Sholokhov once remarked that he was indebted to all the great Russian writers of the past, as already indicated he owes most to Tolstoy, for *The Quiet Don* demonstrably contains many stylistic and structural resemblances to *War and Peace*. But the differences are more apparent than the similarities. Sholokhov, of course, lacks Tolstoy's supreme talent, and then, as has been pointed out, he is concerned in *The Quiet Don* with a totally different order of life and with simple, unreflective characters. If certain qualities of his realism may be attributed to Tolstoy's influence, others are peculiarly his own and bear analysis from this point of view. Sholokhov's descriptions, whether they concern nature, things, the external appearance of his characters, or the varied action covered in the novel, derive from the "saturation method" first employed by Gogol and continued by others in Russian fiction, especially Tolstoy. Sholokhov accumulates detail, but it is precise, perceptive and sensuous, and like Tolstoy, in his nature descriptions he often relates the thoughts and emotions of characters to their environment. At times an offensive naturalism results from Sholokhov's piling up of horrifying, sadistic details in his descriptions of blood-curdling scenes, such as the execution of Podtielkov and his band and the harrowing death march of the twenty-five Red-infected Cossacks through the villages. He tends to dwell suspiciously long on these scenes and with an almost inhuman detachment that recalls Babel rather than Tolstoy.

Where Sholokhov's realism differs most from Tolstoy's is in the treatment of characterization. His approach is similar to that of Chekhov in his early literary period—one of complete objectivity—a most unusual practice for a Soviet writer. But Sholokhov goes beyond Chekhov whose determination to let his characters speak for themselves did not exclude the omnis-

cient author's prerogative of commenting on them. Sholokhov, as it were, *reports* on his characters, never appearing to identify himself with them, and he avoids associating himself with their actions or philosophizing about their thoughts and feelings. To expect the half-literate Gregor and Misha Koshevoi to engage in an intellectual debate on their political and moral differences in the manner of the highly cultured Prince Andrew and Pierre on their return to Bald Hills, would be both absurd and unrealistic. But there is less excuse for the almost complete absence in *The Quiet Don* of what is one of the glories of Tolstoy's art —the self-communing of either author or character, that expressive dialogue of the mind constantly illuminating the darkness of thought and feeling. If Sholokhov has a higher Communist vision of life, it seems to be beyond debate and therefore no cause of tension within the consciousness of himself or his characters. The divided soul of Gregor is revealed, and quite realistically, in his actions rather than in his thinking. Sholokhov is simply a profoundly interested observer of men and events, and he sets down his record of them objectively but without any deep concern for the inner turmoil of human beings forced by circumstances to make agonizing choices. In this avoidance of analysis of feelings and thought, he retreats behind Russian classical realism to that of the eighteenth century.

If we fail to learn much about the inner world of Sholokhov's men and women, his brilliant descriptions of them and of their outer world of activities, and his sensitive handling of the manifold experiences that form their characters bring them thoroughly to life. Gregor, for example, is perhaps the most fully realized and sympathetically portrayed tragic figure in Soviet literature, and it is a striking commentary on the impartiality of Sholokhov's art that his hero remains in the end a complete individualist, essentially hostile to the political cause that destroys him.

7

Sholokhov interrupted work on *The Quiet Don* in 1930 to start another long novel, *Virgin Soil Upturned*, the first volume of which appeared two years later. If he had begun his great masterpiece with an unfettered mind, he undertook this second novel in the spirit of the Party directive encouraging literature to propagandize a huge national endeavor—the First Five-Year Plan. His response to this "social command" may also have been connected with the fact that he joined the Communist Party in 1930 and, for the first time, met Stalin with whom he talked about agricultural problems. Further, he had acquired some experience in the Don region as a worker in the drive for agricultural collectivization.

Although this new novel, which is the story of how a collective farm was started in the Cossack village Gremyachy Log, anticipates the credo of socialist realism in its optimism and political correctness, editors of the magazine *New World* refused to publish the first volume of *Virgin Soil Upturned* unless Sholokhov removed certain passages regarded as ideologically suspect. He remained adamant, appealed to the Central Committee of the Party, and, according to one account, only Stalin's intervention brought about the publication of the novel.

Once again, Sholokhov's insistence on truth as he sees it is in the best tradition of the great nineteenth-century Russian novelists. Truth required that there be no prettifying of the often ugly means employed to achieve what he himself thought was a justifiable Party goal. The heartless dispossession of kulak families at Gremyachy Log, scenes which editors of *New World* particularly objected to, is told with unsparing detail. Some of the kulaks had reached positions of relative well-being only after years of hard labor and sacrifice on their farms which

were now to be turned over to the collective. The cruelty of the action arouses the sympathy of some of the poorest peasants who stand to gain most by the dispossession: "He's saved and saved," mutters one of them as she watches the eviction of a kulak family, "and now it is out into the steppe with him."* Before it is over the Communist chairman of the village Soviet, Razmyotnov, comes dangerously close to rebelling against this form of official tyranny.

In fact, Sholokhov's special emphasis on the element of opposition to the Party effort to introduce collectivization in the village intensifies the reality of the struggle and adds immeasurably to the excitement of the narrative in this first volume of *Virgin Soil Upturned*. When the hero, Davydov, the stocky, gap-toothed ex-sailor and locksmith, arrives from Leningrad as one of the many "shock workers" sent out by the Party in 1930 to push the lagging collectivization drive, he simply cannot understand, because of his proletarian prejudices, why all these Cossack peasants, whose forebears had lived on the soil for generations and knew only individual farming, hesitate to merge their land and livestock in one large collective farm. Davydov soon discovers the staggering extent of the opposition and its main cause—the peasant's "cancerous yearning for his own property"—at the village meetings he calls, scenes which Sholokhov handles with consummate realism, bringing out the characteristic virtues and foibles and the rough humor and colorful speech of these Cossack peasants.

The struggle is on and it is mercilessly waged by both sides in the course of a series of dynamic events filled with tension and surprise. Davydov emerges from the contest a rather successful precursor of the Soviet positive hero, but more human-

* Mikhail Sholokhov, *Virgin Soil Upturned*, translated by Robert Daglish (Moscow: Foreign Languages Publishing House, n.d.). All quotations are from this translation, but they have been checked with the original Russian and in a few cases slightly altered.

ized than the grim, two-dimensional Party organization men and ideological puppets among the numerous positive heroes in later fiction. As a proletarian and non-Cossack, he presented Sholokhov with obvious difficulties in characterization which are not always effectively overcome. Instead of the racy Cossack speech, of which Sholokhov is a master, Davydov speaks a rather unnatural, contrived language. His personality is brought out more by his actions and by what other people say about him. He lives by Party dogma and when absorbed in reading its dull preachments he forgets to eat. There is no doubt a touch of sly and amusing caricature in this and other foibles of Davydov. So exacting is he in following the Party line that at times he overreaches himself as in his illegal exiling of kulaks and his insistence on socializing the village fowls in the collective. In fact, he feels self-conscious and guilty, after Stalin's well-known March 1930 speech, "Dizziness from Success," because he has used force instead of persuasion in compelling peasants to join the collective farm.

One element of Sholokhov's conception of this Party votary is his fallibility, a human dimension not frequently encountered in positive heroes of Soviet fiction. Through harsh experiences he grows in self-knowledge in the course of the first volume of *Virgin Soil Upturned*, although his acquired wisdom rarely leads him beyond an understanding of his duties as a good Communist. His fortitude in overcoming every discouragement and his capacity to learn from his mistakes eventually recommend him to the good graces of the hostile villagers.

Davydov's most serious deviation perhaps is love, an emotion sternly frowned upon in Soviet positive heroes whose whole-souled devotion to the collective good is supposed to leave no room for personal indulgences of any sort. If weakness for the alluringly raffish Lukeriya, the estranged wife of his close comrade Nagulnov, lowers his Communist stature by a cubit, it is

the most human thing about this positive hero whose only ambition in life is that when he dies the inhabitants of Gremyachy Log will name their collective farm after him. Sholokhov, with sure realistic instinct, sees all the comic incongruities of a love affair pursued in terms of Davydov's established character. As might be expected, it is Lukeriya who does the seducing. At an appropriate moment during a moonlit walk, she sweetly coos to her practical-minded, expository companion: "Enough of the grain and the collective farm! This isn't the time to talk about them. Can you smell the scent of the young leaves on the poplars?"

Of Davydov's two chief aides in the collectivization drive, Razmyotnov, head of the village Soviet, is an uncomplicated and even kindly disposed Party worker, memory-haunted by the loss of his young wife who killed herself during the civil war after being raped by Whites. But Nagulnov, secretary of the tiny village's Communist cell, is a complex individual driven by the Furies of world revolution to the edge of doctrinal madness. As a humorless, left-wing deviationist who has the temerity to criticize Stalin's "Dizziness from Success" speech, Nagulnov becomes an object of satire while at the same time remaining a symbol of utter selfless loyalty to the Party. Though in his strange way he deeply loves his anti-Soviet wanton of a wife Lukeriya, whom he has driven from his house, he has come to the conclusion that marriage should be forbidden Communists. If Sholokhov is driving home a patent propaganda lesson in the characterization of Nagulnov, he is also at pains to indicate that his political errors can be corrected, for such passionate zeal for the cause of Communism is unexpendable.

There is an unintentional comic-opera flavor to the organized opposition to collectivization in the village which is centered in a White Guard conspiracy headed by an improbable former Cossack officer, Captain Polovtsev, who for months hides unde-

tected in Ostrovnov's farmhouse, receives mysterious visitors, and at night rides out over the countryside on his great black charger to persuade kulaks and middle peasants to join an imminent rebellion against Soviet power which, he promises, will receive aid from abroad.

The unwilling conspirator Ostrovnov, however, is one of the most interesting characters in the novel. Originally a poor peasant, he has worked his way up to the comfortable position of a middle peasant by herculean labors and tireless self-education in scientific agriculture. Faced with the loss of his land and all his stock whether or not he enters the new collective farm, he finally joins it with instructions to sabotage from within. Davydov, impressed by his skill, makes him director of the collective, and henceforth Ostrovnov is torn between the challenge to exercise his farming abilities on a much larger scale and his conviction that the hated Soviet government has deprived him of the opportunity to live his own life and accumulate wealth.

As in the case of Gregor Melekhov, the honesty of Sholokhov's realism and perhaps his natural affinity for a human personality in conflict with itself tend to transform the villain Ostrovnov into a sympathetic portrayal, at least, in this first volume of the novel. In his driving individualism and fervent desire to get ahead by his own self-sacrificing efforts, Ostrovnov represents the incarnation of the peasant instinct for property and acquisitiveness which still continues to bedevil the whole Soviet structure of agricultural collectivization.

There is nothing of the tragic grandeur of *The Quiet Don* in this first volume of *Virgin Soil Upturned*, which is essentially the story of how Party-directed agricultural collectivization wins out over greedy individualism. Though the poetry of nature reappears in the lyrically described landscapes and in the fine ploughing scene, man's unity with nature and the sense of its biological and historic importance in the lives of these Cos-

sacks, effects so all-pervasive in *The Quiet Don*, are not stressed in the second novel. But there is the compensation of abundant humor, involving often language, incident, and caricature in comic combinations that convey the flavor of picaresque exaggeration. A good deal of this humor is concentrated in the character and adventures of the garrulous, boasting, lying Daddy Shchukar, a much-derided and much-loved inhabitant of Gremyachy Log and a creation of pure fun.

The major artistic achievement of the first volume of *Virgin Soil Upturned* rests on Sholokhov's brilliant realism which brings so vividly to life the whole social pattern of Gremyachy Log and its striking personalities. It is little wonder that this work soon became a fixture on the reading lists of Soviet schools, for some critics pretended to value it higher than *The Quiet Don* because of its propaganda effectiveness, ideological correctness, and its positive hero Davydov. Quite apart from these dubious qualifications, there can be no doubt that the artistic worth of the novel places it far ahead of the abundant Five-Year Plan fiction devoted to the theme of agricultural collectivization.

8

There is substantial evidence that Sholokhov originally designed *Virgin Soil Upturned* to be a kind of epic of agricultural collectivization in which he would carry his story well beyond 1930, the year of action of the first volume. However, the publication of the completed second volume (1959-60) was delayed almost thirty years after the appearance of the first. The reasons vary, but basically they seem to turn on political obstacles. Stalin's violent reprisals against peasant opposition to collectivization, which brought about the devastating famine of 1932-33, made it impossible for Sholokhov to cover this period in the

novel's sequel in the spirit of the relatively objective realism of the first volume. The misery inflicted on his own Don region by these harsh events profoundly depressed Sholokhov and drove him into literary silence which continued through the terrible purges of the later years of the thirties. During the Soviet Union's struggle with Nazi Germany he was largely preoccupied with his still unfinished war novel, *They Fought for Their Country*. And in the period of severe literary regimentation that followed the war, it would have been unthinkable to attempt to publish a work that involved an outspoken treatment of enforced collectivization. Although he may have worked on the continuation earlier, it was not until after Stalin's death that Sholokhov resumed writing the second volume of *Virgin Soil Upturned* with the certain hope of publication.

Khrushchev, in his speech at the meeting of writers and artists on March 7, 1963, in which he excoriated those who failed to follow the Party line in the arts, revealed an interesting fact connected with Sholokhov's difficulties in continuing *Virgin Soil Upturned*. By way of heaping scorn on Ehrenburg's admission in his recent memoirs that he had been aware of Stalin's iniquities but remained silent, Khrushchev declared that in April 1933 Sholokhov wrote Stalin to protest the Party's repression of peasants in the Don region, and he praised the author for his denunciation of "scandalous injustice" and for rebelling against "the illegality going on at that time." Then, with a bewildering illogicality that defies the dialectic, Khrushchev pointed out for the benefit of defiant angry young men of Soviet literature, that the Party orientation and Communist spirit of Sholokhov, their greatest writer, did not prevent him from expressing his artistic individuality.

There is both truth and falsehood in this assertion. The Party line was largely responsible for delaying the sequel to *Virgin Soil Upturned*, and it also held up the publication of parts of

The Quiet Don—according to one Soviet account, the last part was held up for two years because of Stalin's insistence that the hero be transformed into a loyal Red Cossack at the end. And it was the Party line again before Stalin's death that forced many artistically unfortunate changes, some of them deliberate historical falsifications, in the 1953 edition of *The Quiet Don* and the first volume of *Virgin Soil Upturned*. These changes could hardly be regarded as free expressions of Sholokhov's artistic individuality, especially since the original readings in most cases were restored in the 1957 edition after Stalin's death. However, there can be no question of Sholokhov's courage over the years in insisting that his works be published as he wrote them, despite frequent ideological objections, although some of his success in this respect must be attributed to his immense fame and widespread popularity.

On the other hand, the Party line is followed so rigidly in the continuation of *Virgin Soil Upturned* that a kind of deterministic inevitability takes the place of the excitement and tense expectancy in events that characterized the first volume. It is hardly a sequel in an epic of collectivization, for Sholokhov restricts the action to two summer months of 1930, the year in which the first volume was centered, thus avoiding any consideration of the important and bitter events in agricultural planning in the years immediately following. The sense of history is further lost in its updating to the present, for the continuation portrays the goals of the Party in 1930 as identical with those of peasants who find their interests cheerfully merged with Communists in a triumph of socialism. In short, in ideological terms at least, socialist realism seems to have taken over entirely in Sholokhov's writing.

The continuation is loosely constructed and excessively episodic, with a disproportionately large part of it devoted to inserted stories, often of an anecdotal nature. Sholokhov's gift for

humor is reflected more fully than in any of his previous writings. Sometimes these tales advance the action or the characterization of the narrator, at others they are told simply as comic interludes such as those of old Daddy Shchukar, whose inimitable language is a marvelous invention of Sholokhov.

The political conspiracy lumbers on to its inevitable debacle as the leaders, in anticipated cowardly fashion, shamefully vie with each other in betraying their comrades. One thinks of the distance Sholokhov has come since *The Quiet Don* when in the cause of truthful realism he recognized virtues and even qualities of nobility in the enemy. In particular the image of the peasant conspirator Ostrovnov is morally debased in a horrifying sequence where he starves his old mother to death because he feels she might unwittingly reveal his part in the conspiracy.

The three main characters of the first volume, Davydov, Nagulnov, and Razmyotnov, still hold the center of the stage in the continuation. Their Party bickerings are over. They work in complete harmony for the good of Gremyachy Log collective farm, and for the most part they have by now won the hearts of the formerly recalcitrant peasants.

The earlier interesting love affair of Davydov and Nagulnov's debauched wife Lukeriya turns out to be simply an object lesson on how not to be a good Communist. Davydov's passion leads him into neglecting the business of the collective farm and arouses the ire of some of its members. While seeking to forget Lukeriya in hard physical labor on the farm, his emotional disturbance is conveniently sublimated in a developing affection for a seventeen-year-old girl who worships him. The early stages of this new feeling are sensitively and, in places, charmingly handled, but once Davydov's love turns serious and he thinks of marrying the girl, it becomes stiff and unnatural, caught up in a variant of socialist realism's stuffy moralism and the faithfulness of the Soviet worker in love.

Nagulnov, who still believes—as he tells Razmyotnov—that "Wenches for us revolutionists, brother, are pure opium for the people!" has lost his left-wing deviationism in the continuation of the novel but not his deep love for his erring wife. After shooting her kulak lover Timofei, he orders her to leave Gremyachy Log forever, but this totally unsatisfactory conclusion of their relations offers no resolution of Nagulnov's psychological difficulties which had been so effectively posed in the first volume. In general, Sholokhov, who had depicted love so powerfully and movingly in *The Quiet Don*, seems to have been content in *Virgin Soil Upturned* to channel all its manifestations into the rut of the politics and morality of socialist realism.

In the last chapter of the continuation, after Davydov and Nagulnov have been killed by conspirators whom they seek to apprehend, Sholokhov reverts to the theme of love with all the exquisite sensitivity and human feeling of his earlier writing. But like the scene of the death of Aksinya which it echoes, it is in the cause of a tragic lost love, the dead wife whose memory the kindly Razmyotnov cannot efface. Sholokhov evokes the memory with that expressive lyricism in which the dead and the living are fused with nature in the irrevocability of a love never to be forgotten. Razmyotnov, after the death of his two comrades, visits his wife's grave and softly says:

"I don't look after your last home at all well, Yevdokia. . . ." He bent down, picked up a dry clod of clay, rubbed it into dust between his hands, and added in a thick undertone: "And yet I love you even now, my unforgettable one, the only one in my life. . . . You see, I've never any time. . . . We rarely see each other. . . . If you're able to forgive me for all the evil I did you. . . . For all the ways in which I have done you wrong, you . . . the dead. . . ."

He stood there a long time with bared head, as though listening and waiting for an answer. He stood without stirring, his back bowed

like an old man's. A warm wind blew in his face, a warm rain
drizzled. Beyond the Don, sheet lightning flashed white over the
sky; and now Razmyotnov's stern, joyless eyes gazed not downward,
not at the sunken edge of his wife's grave, but beyond the invisible
line of the horizon where half the sky lit up suddenly with a lurid
light. Awakening all sleeping nature, majestic and vehement as in the
heat of mid-summer, the last thunder of the year rolled overhead.*

9

Method and not madness has dictated the selection of Sholokhov as the subject of the concluding essay of this introductory
study of developments in Russian realism over the last hundred
years or more. For his total artistic achievement in fiction demonstrates better than that of any other Soviet novelist both a
continuation of Russian classical realism of the nineteenth century and the change to socialist realism in the twentieth. Russian literature, past and present, has been the product of an
endless struggle between authors who strove to remain autono-
mous in their art and the state which has insisted on manipulat-
ing them, in one way or another, for its own purposes. If the
Soviet state is far more rigid in its controls than that of the
tsars, it has also tried to justify them by a political system that
provides both a faith and a way of life. In the nineteenth century, creative writers and critics, with the possible exception of
the radical democrats, would have agreed with Tolstoy that the
political excludes the artistic because, in order to prove, it must
be one-sided. Not a few Soviet writers, including some of the
finest, have come to accept the identification of Communist
politics and literature. In such cases subscribing to socialist real-

* Mikhail Sholokhov, *Harvest on the Don*, translated from the Russian
by H. C. Stevens (New York: Knopf, 1961), pp. 366-67. Some slight
alterations have been made on the basis of a comparison with the original.

ism, the aesthetic credo of Soviet Communism, has usually followed as a matter of course.

For example, Sholokhov's position today on the Party's relation to art is not essentially different from that of the more talented writers of his own generation, such as Fedin and Leonov, although they have all reached their conclusions through a variety of disparate experiences and express them in terms of conflicting artistic personalities. The Soviet Union's incredible struggle to survive and then grow strong, a struggle that involved members of this older generation of writers in its bitter hardships, cruelties, and wrenched allegiances, has finally claimed from them a devotion that transcends ordinary patriotism. It is a kind of Soviet *mystique* deeply rooted in a community of suffering.

Out of devotion to the Soviet Union has come devotion to the Communist Party that leads it. It would be a mistake to question the reality of this loyalty of the older writers, among whom must be included the late Boris Pasternak. However much they may differ on the extent to which the Party ought to interfere in literature, they do not question its right to be deeply concerned with it. Few of them perhaps would go quite so far as Sholokhov who declared at the Second Congress of the Union of Soviet Writers: "Malicious enemies abroad say of us Soviet writers that we write according to the dictates of the Party. Matters are somewhat different. Each of us writes according to the dictates of his own heart, but our hearts belong to the Party and to our people whom we serve with our art."

Loyalty rather than rational conviction may prompt such views, but both tend to merge when older writers are confronted by a barrage of criticism from the West on the propaganda nature, regimentation, and dull uniformity of content and style in Soviet literature. Such attacks provoke rejoinders such as Sholokhov's who said in an interview in 1934: "Capitalism

domesticates writers and makes them mercenary; it destroys honest literature. The bourgeois writer is placed in such financial circumstances that attributes of individualism are nurtured in him, forcing into the background the significance of literary art." These writers would also point out that readers in democratic countries are as much protected from some issues as are those in the Soviet Union. They look askance at the literature of violence and sex in the West and at writers who, convinced that existence is meaningless and absurd, concern themselves with the anxieties and conflicts of a character's inner life which are more important to them than either the individual's actual behavior or the community's well-being.

Through necessity, habit, and a shared devotion to their country, the older writers, with some few exceptions, make a virtue of the Party's vigorous interest in the arts and in all who practice them, an official interest so different from that of political parties of the West. And they have come to believe that there is nothing incompatible between the development of a thriving literature and the authoritarianism of a Communist state. They tolerate the official doctrine of socialist realism, but they would prefer not to have their loyalty to the regime tested by any artistic credo. Actually their roots are still deep in nineteenth-century Russian realism which gives an old-fashioned flavor to their fiction. For example, the recent fine trilogy of Fedin, except for those parts concerned with Soviet subject matter, could well have been written before the 1917 Revolution.

The new generation of writers, not excluding the so-called "angry young men," express the same devotion to their country and Party. Indeed, they are often fiercely patriotic and scorn Western charges that they are being regimented in practicing their art. There is an element of truth in this despite official attacks on them during the last three years, for the naked compul-

sion of the Stalin period seems to have been supplanted by the persuasion of the Khrushchev regime. Not long ago the well-known young fiction writer Yuri Nagibin declared in the *Nation:* "Nobody in our country can boss a writer either from above or below." And he went on to add, by way of informing Americans that young Soviet authors prefer their own approach to art: "Faith in the future has delivered us from dejection, let alone hopelessness, which many in the West consider an indication of good literary taste."

These are brave words and top Party leaders would probably approve of them without in any way relinquishing their determination to insist that it is the duty of all writers to adhere to the Party line in literature. But progressive writers among the young are impatient with Party paternalism and doctrinal shibboleths of socialist realism. They desire to express their loyalty to the regime in creative spontaneity rather than be guided by Party nostrums. They look back with envy to the early Soviet pre-Stalinist period when experimentation in the arts was possible, and they make heroes of its victims who were later persecuted under Stalin. Their movement, both in prose and poetry, should not be dismissed simply as a current manifestation of the de-Stalinization process, for it has deeper implications which the Party clearly and anxiously perceives. The movement's conscious or unconscious aim is to reestablish an independent humanist tradition, to make Soviet literature the conscience of the nation as Russian literature was in the nineteenth century.

Certainly it is man's conscience in the struggle between good and evil in Soviet life that now primarily interests progressive fiction writers such as Nekrasov, Tendryakov, Antonov, Aksenov, Kazakov, and Nagibin, to mention some of the better-known names. Contemporary Western writers with their highly individualistic perception of reality have made an impression on them, but they appear to seek inspiration in the

fiction of Turgenev, Chekhov, and Bunin in their revolt against the systematic cant of socialist realism with its undiscriminating emphasis upon Soviet achievements and virtues. In numerous short stories, their favorite genre, these emotionally literate writers strive for a deeper realism which will faithfully reflect moral crises in the lives of simple, "little" people who in these tales always seem to be untouched by the mythical joys of Soviet collective existence. The certainties of human behavior do not impress them as much as the incommunicable monologues of the minds of people who live, love, and suffer to no purpose. In underground literature in the Soviet Union, and in some published anonymously abroad, there is evidence of experimentation in nonrealistic form and content in an effort to reveal more adequately the submerged substance of Soviet reality.

One may detect in all this a continuation of the libertarian spirit of nineteenth-century Russian writers in their struggle for some measure of autonomy in the practice of literature. Quite clearly some of the experimentally minded new generation of writers regard art as a means of defining and sharing their responses to a Soviet reality that has little in common with the make-believe work of socialist realism. But it is unlikely that these efforts, under present Party controls in the arts, however much they may have been lessened since Stalin's death, can be considered harbingers of a full-fledged return to Russian classical realism of the past or some Soviet variant of it.

The Party leaders, of course, are aware that a subservient literary bureaucracy produces lifeless books, but they have never discovered any way to compel people to read them. And they also realize that thought control must leave a margin of freedom of expression if it is to be even partly effective. Further, because of the shattering of the monolithic nature of the Communist world, Soviet leaders now evince a new sensitivity

to opinion beyond their borders, especially among allied foreign Communist parties, as was plainly indicated in the recent unsuccessful attempt of Soviet Party officials to whip young progressive artists and writers back into the happiness of socialist realism.

In this situation, however, it would amount to wishful thinking to imagine that the Soviet hierarchy is slowly moving in the direction of allowing writers freedom of expression as long as they do not indulge in overt criticism of the Party, its leaders, and the government, somewhat as in the autocratic days of the old regime writers were permitted freedom of expression provided they refrained from attacking the tsar, the government, and the Church. The Soviet leaders are hardly prepared to grant even this limited freedom which, in the nineteenth century, did not prevent the creation of a magnificent body of literature.

However, the present fluid and promising situation in the arts in the Soviet Union does suggest a rethinking of our unvarying criticism of its literature from the point of view of our own artistic values as though there were no room left in the world for other values. This may be regarded as an argument for ideological coexistence which the Communist Party of the Soviet Union adamantly rejects. But should we reject it? The official Soviet position is that peaceful coexistence between states is desirable, but coexistence of different ideologies, that is, the free interchange of different approaches to life, art, and politics, is impermissible. This unnatural relationship has understandably compelled Western critics to regard all Soviet literature and art in a somewhat distorted light. Our critical standards tend to alter and become infected with a stereotyped contempt which is political in origin.

Though it is true that official Soviet literary criticism is also political, recent steady pressure among some writers and critics, if not among Party pundits, for a more open policy toward

"bourgeois" literature and art should not be cynically disregarded. Unless physical coercion is once again employed, writers are unlikely to lose permanently the small measure of freedom they have achieved. Such a development demands greater openness on our part, a willingness to appraise Soviet literary works with the tolerance and detachment which have always been hallmarks of the best criticism in the West. This does not mean that differences and tensions between two political systems must be ignored, but they should not be allowed to dominate evaluations of artistic differences between, let us say, the fiction of Soviet socialist realism and the more or less abstract realism of the Western anti-novel today. That is, an effort to respond objectively to Soviet artistic values may, hopefully, inspire a similar response there to Western values and eventually encourage free literary discussion across the frontiers.

INDEX